Slowing Down to Catch Up With God

Slowing Down to Catch Up With God

By Jim Pool

Copyright © 2025 Jim Pool
All rights reserved.
ISBN-13: 979-8-9927538-0-6

Unless otherwise indicated, scripture quotations are taken from the Holy Bible, New International Version®, NIV®, Copyright © 1973, 1978, 1984, 2011 by Biblica, Inc.™ Used by permission of Zondervan. All rights reserved worldwide. www.zondervan.com The "NIV" and "New International Version" are trademarks registered in the United States Patent and Trademark Office by Biblica, Inc.™

Scripture quotations taken from the (NASB®) New American Standard Bible®, Copyright © 1960, 1971, 1977, 1995, 2020 by The Lockman Foundation. Used by permission. All rights reserved. www.lockman.org

Dedication

This book is dedicated to The Pool Party:
Elijah, Esther, Eden, Olive

You fill my days with joy.
My heart is full.
I am so proud of you.

May my ceiling be your floor.

And remember, the wise man or woman may fall down seven times
but gets up eight.

Appreciations

One of the most common questions around our home is "What are you thankful for?" What is bringing you gratitude since we last were together? My wife and I are learning, from readings in brain-based research bolstered by the classroom of experience, that expressing gratitude fosters strengthened relational connection. So I'll begin by expressing appreciation since it's my hope we'll be sitting together for a while to have a long, friendly conversation as I share my story.

The first idea for this book came when I bumped into my friend, Julie, at our local coffee shop. Julie stopped me as I walked by and introduced me to her friend, sharing about her experience of me. I was moved by the unexpectedly meaningful impact of our brief time together at the church I pastored, even more so because Julie is a dynamic leader, compelling speaker, and insightful coach. She looked me in the eye and said, "Jim, when are you going to write a book? You need to tell your story. I think it'll be a blessing to other leaders like me." Honestly, it wasn't the first time someone had encouraged me to write, but I never felt like I was experienced enough in any topic to merit adding to the noise. Julie helped me see that the one thing I did know enough about was my own story.

This landed because of a conversation I had with a respected classmate a few months earlier. We knew each other well at West Point but hadn't spoken much in the three decades since. After three hours of catching up in the hotel lobby at our mutual friends' promotion to Brigadier General, she said, "Jim, you have a unique voice and perspective. Book, podcast, something. You need to tell your story."

A month or so after talking with Julie, I was with a dear friend, whom I regard highly, who has humbly and graciously suffered for his faith. As I would share some of the questions or insights, I was thinking about our mutual endeavors, he would reply, "Jim, have you written this down anywhere? When will you write it?" Only a few weeks later, Meg and I were having dinner with Bruce and Allison, whom you'll meet later in these pages. As I shared about these invitations over the previous months, they both agreed, "You should write that book. We would buy it. We would read it." Over a dining room table of traditional Spanish charcuterie and a bottle of red wine, I committed to writing this book.

I appreciate each of these friends who have encouraged me to share my story. Many others followed, encouraging me, asking about the progress, supporting the effort. I'm mindful particularly of my friend, Lynn, who has cheered me on every step of the way. I appreciate everyone who sat with me during those early days and patiently waited while I noted a story on my phone ("Oh, that's a good one, that's got to be included!") after we'd reminisce and laugh or lament, as the case may be. I appreciate Ramon, himself an author twice over, who dispensed this timeless wisdom: "write 500 words a day, no matter what, even if no one sees it, and 1000 if you can."

Most of this book was written in a quiet corner in the basement of Bamboo, a wonderful co-working space in Detroit. I appreciate the team for cultivating a space conducive to creativity and keeping the coffee flowing. I listened to endless hours of William Augusto's *Soaking in His Presence* while writing. I appreciate the thoughtful artistry of their instrumental worship. They opened up a space for focus and beauty.

I appreciate the editorial team of Jill Hurst and Phil Cook (contact Phil at PCediting@proton.me to ask about his services). I believe it was Brené Brown who first introduced me to the concept of "vulnerability hangover." That morning after feeling you get when you've bared your heart. I wasn't unfamiliar with this, sometimes experiencing it after preaching a particularly personal sermon or sharing a more than typically transparent post on social media. Yet there's nothing quite like submitting your life story for editorial review. I'm grateful they were kind and thoughtful surgeons, the sharp cuts of their feedback designed only for my growth. They refined all that's good in what follows. Any errors that remain are my own.

I appreciate my friend, Corey, who had the kindness and courage to share with me about Jesus and invite me to follow him.

I appreciate the four spiritual companions who walked with me throughout my transition. You are each a "Barnabas" to me.

I appreciate each of the women and men, young and old alike, who are taking the risk to journey with me in (re)discovering a new, ancient, authentic way of being the church and practicing the way of Jesus.

I appreciate my wife, Megan, who has come alongside me to help me live and tell my story more truly. In the immortal words of Donne, she "keeps my circle just." Though it's not often been easy, our union is a treasured prize. I cherish our adventures together and anticipate the ones to come. I am grateful for the home we've established: a simple, cozy, haven for souls. I admire the family we're raising and releasing together: exuberant, life-giving and mature. I'm in wonder at the missional spirituality we've forged and live out together, practiced in relationship, honoring health, formation, simplicity and multiplication.

Acknowledgement

Lives are lived in relationship. To tell my story necessarily involves the stories of others.

It's taken me a long time to know my own story. I'm obviously limited in my understanding of the story of others. I know there is more to their lives than what I have access to. I try always to be aware of this, particularly their longings, dreams, desires and hurts. I've tried always to talk with folks about their story, whenever and wherever possible. So I understand that my sharing is necessarily limited to my perspective, my opinions.

In some cases, important details of the persons identified herein have been changed to protect their privacy. In telling my story as truly as I know how, I have always tried to speak with humility, honor and honesty about everyone you'll meet on these pages.

Table of Contents

Of Mountains High and Valleys Low 1
How I Started Walking 8
Bottom Line Up Front 11
A Church that was God's idea 15
Truly Alive 19
Adventurous Overcomer 22
G-Movie 32
From Parachutist to Pastor 44
Doin' The Stuff 56
Where's Waldo? 86
Midwife or Mother? 111
… It Didn't Work 125
The Journey Inward 151
From Pastor to Pioneer 160
I Would Walk 500 Miles 183
A New Way 196
Discoveries 213
Postscript 236
Epilogue 242
Leaders are Learners 246
About the Author 248

Of Mountains High and Valleys Low

Meg and I sat patiently as Councilmember Dan Martin approached the podium to speak. The evening was wearing on and we wondered about our kids. Aged 13 to 7, it was getting to be a long time to leave them alone at home unsupervised.

Councilmember Martin had invited us to this special evening, though we weren't sure yet why. It was an awards celebration sponsored by one of the many charitable civic groups in our city. It was more formal than the venue would perhaps suggest: the community room above the bar at the local chapter of the Elks Club. The leadership of all our city departments were present, plus several members of the Council, and leaders from numerous local organizations. We were invited as pastors of the Renaissance Vineyard Church in Ferndale, Michigan, an inner-ring suburb of Detroit.

It wasn't that unusual for us to be invited to such affairs. Almost all of these people were known to us and many were our friends. We sat with the new director of the Parks Department and her assistant, with whom our church had recently co-launched a new City-wide Easter Egg Hunt in four major parks across our community, blessing hundreds of neighborhood kids. It took the egg hunts that had begun on our block years ago to the next level.

I was thinking about all this when I was startled back to the present. I had heard my name. *What?!?* My friend Dan was announcing that Megan and I were being awarded "Citizens of the Year" for 2016. As we made our way to the front of the room, Dan emphasized how he was recognizing both of us since he knew it was a team effort. Even though I was more the face of the operation, Dan knew what I knew: that it couldn't happen without Meg.

I was humbled and honored by the award, of course, and I think we came up with some appropriately thoughtful spur of the moment remarks. To be honest, the recognition was equal parts surprising and satisfying.

Surprising because we were pastors being recognized for this award in our city. It was 2016 and our city wasn't interested in Making America Great Again. Ferndale was spiritual but not religious if you know what I mean. Based on an educated guess of the attendance figures of the main churches in town, I'd estimate less than 5% of the city attended church on any given Sunday. As I sometimes joked, on Sunday Fundays in Ferndale more people lined up for bottomless bloody marys at the local bars than they did for the blood of Mary's son. And what's more, while I didn't take myself very seriously, we really did take Jesus, his cause and the scriptures as seriously as we knew how.

Satisfying because we had been working really hard. We had merged our church with another church in town almost five years earlier. We operated at 100 mph for 9 months straight to make that work, then navigated non-stop headaches for nine months more. Then we'd been working really hard with lots of long hours for the past few years to take advantage of the moment and be as faithful as we knew how to be.

My friend Derek, who worked in City Hall, sat me down for coffee one day. "Jim, you and your church have crashed onto the scene in town in some really exciting ways. It's wonderful. My question is, will you be able to sustain it?" I suppose this award felt like a recognition that we had been able to effectively maintain a high level of service to our city.

I wrote this poem that the Chamber of Commerce used in one of their annual "Welcome to the City" booklets.

Ferndale.
What more could be said
About this fashionable,
Fabulous, friendly
City of Eagles?
Truly a treasure at the end of this
Rainbow city.
A pot of gold and sparkling gems
Of all shapes and sizes and colors.
Ferndale's riches are its people:
Passionate for all things crafted locally;
Committed to community, justice, service
And giving all an equal chance.
Truly a city of
Good neighbors.

I know Jesus says to *"take care not to practice your righteousness in the sight of people, to be noticed by them; otherwise you have no reward with your Father who is in heaven."*[1] Facebook posts about what our church was doing aside, I think I can honestly say it hadn't been my intention to be noticed by whatever had justified the award. I didn't do the service to be noticed, but it did feel good to be seen. I wonder if that's something we all desire, to be seen and heard and known. I hung that plaque on the wall outside my office as a reminder of gratitude and God's blessings.

That year of 2016 was filled with mountaintop moments like this. On the personal side, that was the year I completed my bucket list item of visiting every state in the US (Arkansas, Louisiana, and Mississippi, though I've still never slept the night in the latter). It was also the year that my son and I began our quest to hike America's 10 Hardest Day

---

[1] Matthew 6:1

Hikes as identified by Backpacker magazine.[2] In the end, we succeeded in five, got turned back on four, and never tried one. Just the year before, I had finished a summer project of walking the 100 miles of every street in my city and was surprised by how much this seemed to inspire people. Plus, not only were Meg and I honored with the Citizen of the Year award, I was also recognized by our local Chamber of Commerce with a Special Service Award for our contributions to the community.

Locally it felt like our church's service towards our city was having an impact. In a community where the Church's reputation was banged up, it seemed like we were helping make Jesus famous.

We had successfully navigated our church merger. Though many said we wouldn't be able to do it, especially as we had shared power at the board level with the other church, it was now our fifth year and we had truly become the Renaissance Vineyard Church. We were embodying our vision to be a Jesus-centered community that is a great friend to the city.

Two years earlier I had co-founded a Facebook group to seek the success of our city, by bringing together residents and leaders from diverse sectors of society. We now had several thousand members and realtors would routinely tell new homeowners to join the Ferndale Forum as the best way to find out what was going on in the community. In 2015, we were blessed to have the National Director of our denomination host a weekend conference at our church building.

That fall of 2016 I was invited by the planning team for our denomination's annual missional leaders' meeting to be one of the plenary speakers. I spoke about God's invitation to compassionately serve our cities and shared our church's story. In 2016 I took three international ministry trips in the same year. One was a learning excursion with my missions mentor to countries in East Africa. On another I led an amazing team from our church to Ethiopia, with several first-timers including my daughter, Eden.

---

[2] https://www.backpacker.com/trips/america-s-hardest-dayhikes

The third trip was one of my most memorable trips ever, to Malawi. We hosted a gathering of 30 leaders from around Africa, Europe and the US in the shade of an enormous mango tree along the shores of Lake Malawi in Monkey Bay. We took some free time one afternoon to enjoy a boat ride and swimming excursion. Never mind the risk of bacteria present in the area that were known to swim upstream into any of the holes in your nether region, this was a chance to snorkel in what was, essentially, a giant real world fish tank. Lake Malawi is home to the world's highest concentration of cichlid fish. It was beautiful.

When the gathering was over I joined my friend Akim and a few of his leaders for an arduous daylong trip to his hometown in Blantyre. We changed taxi vans multiple times. For most of these packed rides I was honored to sit immediately next to the driver, with the gear shift between my legs. I was glad when we arrived at his home and humbled to see that his family had rearranged their sleeping arrangements to accommodate me having my own room. The giant spider in the corner didn't seem to get the memo at first, but I was a mix of grateful and nervous to see that it wasn't in the corner when I went to sleep that night. Akim had stayed in my home the year previously. He and his wife were such gracious and sacrificial hosts. Akim's church was in the process of constructing a new building to house their services. The members of the church worked tirelessly over the next several days to complete the project so that I could be the first person to preach in the new building on Sunday! That's next level hospitality! I've stayed in regular contact with Akim and he is such an encouragement to me.

The year 2016 was filled with plenty of mountaintop experiences, yet there were even deeper valleys.

Early in the year we discovered that four years earlier, in the closing days before our church merger, the board of the other church voted to sell the parsonage next door to their pastor. The price was never disclosed, but I can only assume it was deeply discounted. Neither the board members, nor the pastor (who stayed on staff with us for a year) told us about this sale. Legally that was their right, yet it certainly eroded feelings of trust at a time when loving relationship was too often in short supply.

All throughout 2016 we had a decaying relationship with one of our key ministry leaders, culminating in them leaving the church, attempting to steal their ministry away, and a cutoff of relationship.

Despite all the high points, it was a very hard year for me. I had four kids at home, all in elementary school. Meg was busy riding that chaos.

After eight years of having someone on at least some form of paid part-time staff to be with me, I was alone. Both of the staff hires we had made three years earlier had quit by that summer. Also by that same season we lost the most emotionally healthy and spiritually mature core of the church. They also happened to be the most financially generous. This included: five large families, plus a few singles and empty nesters, including several former board members and key ministry leaders. A number of other committed, though less involved, people moved on too.

Some folks came around as volunteers to help, so I was never truly isolated, but I experienced a sense of being in it by myself. For several years my office had been on the first floor, near the main entrance. I was in a separate room behind the administrator's desk, with plenty of windows through which I could see people coming and going and they could see me. What had been a gift soon became a burden. With no gatekeeper, people would see me alone, sitting at my computer, and assume that was a great time to talk to me because I wasn't with anyone. I couldn't get anything done. I felt exposed.

One day I made a spontaneous executive decision to move my office upstairs, out of the way. I'm a little embarrassed to admit it, but I needed some separation.

I felt pained, though I had no language for it. It wasn't until much later, like the year before writing this book, that I finally gained clarity on how this year, 2016, was the most difficult year of my ministry.

There was trouble in the building and trouble on the streets. After several years of fruitful work in our city, I was being publicly criticized by other residents who often misunderstood my motives.

I was definitely being very stretched in my leadership capacity and competencies.

Yet, it wasn't really that anything was wrong. We had high levels of buy-in around our vision to be a Jesus-centered community that was a great friend to the city. A team of over a dozen influencers in the church had spent more than a dozen hours over several sessions crafting that vision together. As I've mentioned, we were obviously thriving in our service to the community. And all of these mature folks left well and for normal reasons. It just all hit the fan at the same time. The system simply couldn't replace these mature disciples and influential leaders fast enough.

All the pressure culminated in 2016. It's as if all the mountaintops were swallowed by all these sinkholes of loneliness and breaking relationships. Despite our best efforts, the stuff we did didn't seem to work. It didn't produce multiplying maturing disciples who winsomely lived the way of Jesus, nor did it produce a deep fellowship of joyful loving attunement. Too often, actually, our work had the effect of enabling spiritual infancy.

When I think back on that year, my main response is wonder. I'm amazed that we managed to make it. Truly, it is only because of God.

How I Started Walking

It was the small hours after midnight. I had been up since about 4 a.m. and likely had a few more hours to go before I slept. The day was busy with what soldiers affectionately called "Hurry Up and Wait." Anyone who's been in the military knows what I'm talking about. In my experience, "hurry up and wait" was the Army's default speed. Like someone late for work stuck in a traffic jam on the freeway, speeding up to slam on the brakes, you're hurrying and going nowhere. So much of life can feel like that, right? Always in a hurry, yet seemingly standing still.

This day had been like that for me: early morning PT at the break of dawn, taking care of necessities, getting to the hangar to prepare for our first jump of the day (involving gearing up, safety briefings, plus an hour or more of fully loaded uncomfortable waiting), then cleaning up gear, back to post, a light meal and repeat the process. It had been a long day of hurry, and I had plenty about which to worry before graduating from Airborne School in a day and a half. Yet none of that mattered for these 45 seconds. After two and a half weeks of hurry, here I was on my fifth jump of five, the famous "night jump," and I was floating through space. The night was bright with a crystalline sea of stars, radiating over the South Georgia-Bama border. I suppose it might've felt like I could reach out and touch them, but I didn't want to. In those brief moments, all I could do was float in awe and wonder.

After weeks of running, the force of the parachute opening after one-one thousand, two-one thousand, three-one thousand, fooouuurrrr, I was brought to a standstill, slowed to what seemed like the pace of an inflatable on a lazy river. All was silent around me as I surrendered to the wind and the simplicity of embracing the moment and floating to earth. I've rarely ever felt closer to God than in that brief window of time. As I hung suspended in the heavens above those grassy fields of red clay, I felt what it was like to slow down to experience joy and encounter God.

I'd like to invite you on a long, slow walk.

They say a typical person tends to walk three miles in an hour. That makes three miles an hour the pace of walking. For many years now that's the pace at which I've been trying (not always successfully) to live my life, vocation, spirituality and more.

Most people walk at least a little. Even from a young age I always enjoyed a good hike through the woods. Despite being in the Army, I've never been much of a camper. Maybe it was the weeklong mudfest at Lake Frederick, culminating our summer Cadet Basic Training (aka "Beast Barracks") as a plebe at West Point. Think Woodstock minus the bands and partying. The 100 year rainfall we experienced that week overwhelmed all the trenches we dug around our tents and washed over our woolen sleeping bags. And still we camped. I don't camp much anymore. Yet I love hiking.

Early in the 2010's I started walking more intentionally. Mostly by taking an afternoon walk around the block instead of snacking or walking while talking on the phone instead of sitting at my desk. After a while I made the commitment that walking would be my primary mode of transportation. "I didn't know you drove!" a friend once exclaimed, "Do you even have a license?" Yes, I do drive. Getting the kids to school, out of town meetings for work, long road trips for family vacation, even a quick trip across town for an appointment. My friend's incredulous question was tongue in cheek, but only mostly so.

I started walking more and more. All around our city. And it didn't take long before I sold our family's second car because we just didn't use it enough. Along the way I started using #ThreeMileAnHourPastor as a hashtag, because I was walking everywhere, as much as I could. And now it's something even greater.

More than a way to get around town, more than a way to save money, more than a means to exercise. It's bigger than a hashtag.

It's become a way of life.

I hope that doesn't sound too grandiose, but it is really how I think about it. I am trying to take a three mile an hour approach to life. Walking slows me down, literally. By nature I'm a fast-paced person, a doer, an adventurer, so I'm learning to let slowness saturate my soul. I want to learn to pay attention to people I interact with: my friends, my wife, my kids, strangers I share the street corner with, the members of my spiritual family. I want to learn to really see them. And then love and lead and serve from that place.

I want to be interruptible. No one interrupts a car, not without getting flipped off by the driver or run over. But I'm learning to create margins in my life, white space at the edge of my awareness, my calendar, my budget, so that I can approach interruptions as opportunities. Opportunities to connect. Opportunities to learn. Opportunities to serve. Opportunities for wonder. I guess it's like that cliché to stop and smell the roses, yet for me it's more about the opportunity to pause long enough to pay enough attention that we discern God's presence and recognize God's work.

That's a little of why I walk. I hope you're able to make the space to walk with me through my story. It's my joy to be with you on the journey.

Bottom Line Up Front

A few months shy of fifty years old, I quit my job of twenty one years to start a new ministry venture of intentionally cultivating maturing, multiplying disciples and embodying a simpler, healthier expression of the church in movement.

I did it voluntarily. No one forced me out. There was no scandal. I didn't have to "retire." All was well. The church I had been serving was the same one my wife and I had planted with a few friends two decades earlier. We were blessed with great favor (as well as some pushback) in our church and city. Our finances were fine and we had navigated Covid with surprisingly little heartache. I had a good relationship with the board. I could've kept going for twenty more years and everyone would've patted me on the back and told me how faithful I had been, what a great job I had done. And I would've been dead inside.

Why am I telling you all this now? Well, somewhere along the line, I think it was in the Army, I learned this maxim about public speaking:
1. Tell them what you'll tell them
2. Tell them
3. Tell them what you told them.

Another way to say it is another Army principle this time about the written word: Bottom Line Up Front. And though you're reading this in a book, every time I put fingers to the keyboard, I always imagine that

11

we're sitting down in my living room, or at my dining room table, or somewhere else cozy enjoying the beverage of our choice.

I never intended to be a pastor. I didn't up grow up in church, and went only to a handful of holiday masses before I was in high school. As you'll discover in the pages that follow, I'm a perfectly capable sinner, pretty good at it in fact.

Despite that, or perhaps because of it, God has seemed very happy to work through me to serve his cause of love and be a blessing to others, all the while working to transform me.

I'm a regular guy through whom and with whom God is working.

After saying Yes to Jesus the summer before 10th Grade, I started going to church. I sat in the second-row pew and sleepily nodded on and off through most of the sermons. The only sermon I have a strong memory of is when the pastor used the pulpit as a public counseling session for his problems.

A decade later, as a young seminary student, I visited that church again with my parents (who were now active members). I had recently discovered the power of God to heal, and as the pastor complained repeatedly during his message about his back pain, I had this uncomfortable conviction that perhaps I should pray for him. In between the service and Sunday school was a brief time for coffee (I guess to caffeinate everyone for "Round Two" of church?), and I arrived at the courageous decision to stand near to him, sipping my percolator coffee in the porcelain cup, and take it as a sign that if the pastor turned to talk to me God was telling me I should pray for him. (This experience was the beginning of my reevaluation of how the Church honors Gideon and his fleeces by the way). Sure enough, he asked me how I was doing, I asked if I could pray for him, and he hastily whisked me away to his office, away from prying eyes.

Once there, I described what I would do (put my hand on his lower back, ask for God to heal, he didn't need to imagine angels or anything, just receive God's love, nothing weird), and he replied, "You know I don't believe in this, right?" I nodded, he assented, I prayed, and a few moments later he was getting his suit coat back on to gather everyone for Sunday school.

Nothing had happened.

The Sunday School lesson that week incorporated a video reenacting the scene in Lystra from Acts 14:8-20. Spoiler alert: it's about a man being miraculously healed. After the class, the pastor made a bee-line for me. My mom elbowed me and wondered what I had done. "Nothing, mom, I promise. I just prayed for him!" The pastor pulled me aside, saying, "I don't know what you did or what happened, but when Paul told that man to get up, I felt like I should stand up in the back of the room, and when he said to walk, I felt like I should bend down and touch my toes. Until today I haven't been able to do that in months. I don't know what happened!" Even when faced with the power of God in response to prayer, just like happened in the Bible passage we read, this Bible-believing pastor couldn't believe it.

I didn't have a strong role model for what it looked like to be a pastor.

When I got to seminary, my closest friends kept telling me that I should be a pastor. That I would make a great pastor. I kept telling them that pastors were like the teachers in the Charlie Brown show, *Peanuts*: "*wah wah wah wah.*" They keep talking, but you can't understand them.

Nonetheless, somewhere along the way, I did become a pastor. I did almost everything you could do in that world:

I was a pastoral intern.
I served as a lead pastor.
I was an interim pastor.
I'm now a pastor emeritus.
I've planted a church.
I've closed a church.
I've merged a church.
I've transitioned a church.
I was offered to apply for the senior pastorate of a larger church
I've ordained other pastors.

I've pastored other pastors.
I've assessed, trained and coached church planters.
I've served on the leadership team for church planting in the US.
I've served on the leadership team for church planting outside the US.

The only thing I haven't done is serve as an assistant pastor.
Seems like I've done just about everything else.

Then one day I left it behind.

I slowed down enough to catch up with God.

Through slowing, surrender, and simplicity, plus a fair share of suffering, I serendipitously stumbled upon a deeper discovery of myself, God and my vocation, along with a whole new definition of success.

This is that story of how I got there, a little of what's happening now and the lessons I'm learning along the way.

The Church That Was God's Idea

Most church planters I know believe that their mission is God's idea. They hope that's the case. It certainly was my experience that this was God's idea.

The pastor that became my mentor really wanted me to stay in Chicagoland. A friend pastoring a church in Hyde Park had a small group in the Bridgeport neighborhood that he wanted me to join and turn into a new church. I knew that wouldn't work because I like my hot dogs ketchup only, and if I ordered that on Maxwell Street I'd be run out of town. My mentor, Steve, recommended I plant in the northwest suburbs of Chicago. He thought growing a midsized church in the cool shade of the much larger megachurches that sprang from that soil would be very doable, plus we could stay close to one another. Appealing, but driving the streets, it just didn't feel like home.

Megan and I visited Las Vegas, Nevada. Yes, by the way, we had gotten married in this period. We had met at the Evanston Vineyard Church. She was an active member of the large homegroup my roommate co-led. Almost every Sunday we'd host folks from the group at our apartment for an evening of storytelling and laughter. I strategically located myself at our church's missions board, where she'd have to walk by me, to ask her out for our second date. I found out later she gets cold very easily, so mercifully it was too warm for my original plan of outdoor ice skating. We were married almost exactly a year later.

Slowing Down To Catch Up With God

Meg had been planning to be a missionary to Mexico before she met me. She loved the culture, food, people and language, though her fear of flying was a big barrier. She was a marvelously skilled hospice nurse. She has taught me the value of slowing down, attending to people holistically, and the value of embracing pain. Decades later, she used similar skills in a more focused way as she began to practice the art and vocation of spiritual direction. When she turned forty, she committed to regain Spanish fluency and to learn to play guitar and piano by 50, so she could lead worship. She's still working on Spanish, but she accomplished the worship leading by 45. She inspires me with her commitment to lifelong learning.

Las Vegas had been the fastest growing city in the US for the entire decade of the 1990's. New people meant the need for new social infrastructure, including new churches. We also visited the Research Triangle region of Raleigh-Durham in North Carolina since I had grown to love that area while stationed at Fort Bragg. But one time while taking the back roads between Durham and Raleigh, we realized ten minutes outside of town it still had that Dukes of Hazzard vibe. We decided maybe that wasn't our thing as northerners.

In the end, we settled on Metro Detroit. Maybe saying I had vowed never to return to Detroit is too strong a word, but it certainly wasn't on my list of desired places to live. Yet one summer day, I found myself IM'ing with a good friend (who happened to be the best man at our wedding) and every time he would mention he was going to **Royal Oak** to visit family, that's exactly how the word looked to me: *italicized* in **bold**. I talked with Meg and planned a quick recon trip early the following week. Having made that decision, unknown to anyone else, a friend and fellow prayer team member came up to me and shared how she had had a dream about me a few weeks ago but hadn't felt released to share it with me until that morning. It was clearly about me planting a church in Detroit.

Two days later I walked the streets of Royal Oak and felt a sense of home we hadn't experienced anywhere else. Later that week I was on a ministry trip with Steve, helping him train members of a church to hear God's voice and minister in the presence and power of the Holy Spirit.

In the final session he asked the folks he had been training to pray for me and the other intern since both of us were soon stepping into our next roles. One of the young guys in the room, who had never had this happen before, had this extended vision for me: I was walking on a path through a dark forest, leading a growing throng on a journey, and as we walked we sang, inviting people to join us from out of the shadows, lifting them up on the trail and giving them robes of white. It went on from there.

In eight days I had received four confirmations of various kinds. Whenever I would visualize the map of Detroit in my mind, I could see this sea of shining stars at intersections all across town. A few weeks later Meg and I took a weekend visit. She loved it too. We both sensed God in it.

We talked to thirty different people about joining our church planting team. Most replied with something equivalent to, "Wow, Detroit, um, yeah ... cool. Let me know how that goes?" As we talked to Jesus about this, he seemed to be saying, "Jim, did I call you or not?" I knew the answer to that question. I developed my own little mantra in response, "Nothing ventured, nothing gained." It seemed to fit me well. I took one guy out for Thai food, heard his story (which included nothing about a church plant in Detroit) and then asked him to join our team. He said yes.

So Halloween weekend of the year 2000, we packed our Chicago apartment into a U-Haul with some friends. We moved to the inner ring suburbs of Detroit on a new adventure. To start what would be the Royal Oak Vineyard Church and later become the Renaissance Vineyard Church.

One helpful piece of advice we received was to plant a church that we would want to be a part of. I think this is an idea that is sometimes missed. And if it is overlooked, it can have long lasting impact on the health and well-being of both the pastor and the church.

We discerned that God's invitation for us as a church was to be a Jesus-centered community that was a great friend to the city, as we were rooted in God, growing in community and reaching out in love.

This meant we really worked at keeping Jesus at the center of our church: not politics, not ideological ideals, not our denominational distinctives, not those we were trying to serve, and certainly not me as the pastor. Simply Jesus. It was his church.

This meant that we were less concerned with who was "in" and who was "out." Most gatherings of humans default to this, especially (though not only) churches, worrying about people's relationship to the community boundaries. Rather, we were concerned with the orientation and momentum of our lives: was it towards or away from Jesus?

We wanted to help people—beginning with ourselves—(re)orient their lives towards Jesus and gain momentum in drawing closer to him, perhaps falteringly at first and growing in confidence and consistency over time.

We also didn't want to be a private membership club. We were a church that existed for the sake of others. We wanted to be intentional in living out God's admonition to the exiles in Jeremiah 29: "*Also, seek the peace [the shalom, the well-being] and prosperity of the city to which I have carried you into exile. Pray to the Lord for it, because if it prospers, you too will prosper.*"[3]

We envisioned ourselves like a tree. Our roots were deep in God. Our trunk grew up in strong circles of community. We spread our branches, bearing fruit, in blessing to our neighbors near and far. This would be a church I wanted to be a part of.

---

[3] Jeremiah 29:4-7

Truly Alive

How did I end up pastoring if I never intended on being a pastor? How did I get there?

Remember the marketing line for the Mel Gibson blockbuster, Braveheart? "Every man dies, but not every man truly lives."[4] This quote is attributed to William Wallace, though historians are divided on if he ever said it.

Life. A significant dimension of this book is the story of my quest to truly live.

Jesus of Nazareth once said, *"I have come that they might have life, life to the full!"*[5]

Life can be an overused word, like love. The Greeks have four words for love. The Inuit have many words for snow. Yet English has only one word for life.

"When do you feel truly alive?"

This is a question I try to ask people that I'm getting to know. I'll ask them, "If you can put yourself in a place or situation that makes you feel truly alive, what would that be?" Then I'll share several things that I appreciate about them. If I'm in a group, then I like to invite everyone to participate as we go around the circle. It's amazing how powerful this can be. I've seen grown men moved by this experience, sharing, perhaps

---

[4] https://www.imdb.com/title/tt0112573/quotes/
[5] John 10:10

for the first time, when they feel truly alive, then hearing, perhaps for the first time, what others appreciate about them as they look them in the eye.

"When do you feel truly alive?" Maybe take a few moments right now and journal your thoughts in response to that question, even if it's simply to type it into the notes on your phone. And if you've got a friend or family member nearby, try out the exercise together.

I've discerned that there are four times when I feel most fully alive:
1. Walking along mountain paths in the dappled light of forest halls
2. The fellowship of laughter and stories with good friends over good food and drink
3. The eureka of a new idea
4. Being alongside someone when they take that next step in their personal development

I'm discovering that life is a mix of love and joy and peace, with both purpose and playfulness, best lived in community.

This peace is understood not so much as the absence of conflict. The absence of conflict is nice, of course, yet probably we all know people who endure hardship yet experience thriving. Or at least we've watched movies or read books about them. Rather, this peace is more about the presence of well-being. Shalom, as the Hebrew prophets put it. We experience life when we experience this well-being.

Love is when we experience delight. Delight in what we do. Delight in who we're with. We experience being loved when we're seen and heard and known. When we have a strong, safe and secure attachment to those in our circle of relationships, who attune to how we're doing in our current circumstances. We express our love for others when we offer them this gift. To do so is to experience life.

Joy is connected to desire. We might have ordered and disordered desires. Our desires are ordered when they're in alignment with our deepest convictions, values and priorities. For me, my desires are ordered when they're in proper relationship to God and the purpose for which God made me. My desires get disordered when they fall out of alignment and/or when the priorities get skewed. When my desires are aligned, we are on the path of life.

My journey has been one of learning to attend to my desires so that I might find lasting joy, encounter deeper love, and in doing so experience authentic peace and well-being.

Becoming a pastor was, for me, an attempt to be responsive to the invitation of Jesus and live into my unfolding understanding of my desires.

Adventurous Overcomer

I survived the mean streets of Livonia. That's where I grew up: Livonia, Michigan. A 1950s growth bedroom community in Detroit's western suburbs that happened to be the whitest city in America over 100,000 people the entire decade of the 1990s. That's the year I left for college.

This isn't really a story about my family, yet I've read and lived enough to know that the fruit is in the seed, and the soil shapes the plant. This isn't determinism, of course. Our stories are a complex mosaic of nature, nurture, circumstance and choice, and one dimension of the glory of God is the transformation of our stories so that we become even more fully and deeply who we could always be.

So here's a little bit about the soil of my life.

For those key formative years from 18 months to 15 years, it was just me, my mom and my grandma, growing up in the western suburbs of Detroit.

My father divorced my mom shortly after returning home from his second tour as an Air Force pilot in the Vietnam War. He was an entrepreneurial free spirit who loved people and their stories, never met a stranger, savored all his appetites, relished in the risk of a venture, didn't put much stock in typical societal expectations and was always running just a little late. Both he and my step-dad were small business owners who were incorrigible story tellers. I come by it honestly.

Seriously, though, I barely knew him. My father and I lived together less than a year total my entire life, yet he really did try to love me in his own way.

When I graduated from West Point, he flew from Hawaii and took a Greyhound bus from San Francisco to NYC, so that he could be with me for a few days that Graduation Week. He grew up in West Africa, among the Yoruba people of Nigeria, where his parents were Southern Baptist missionaries running a Bible college. By all accounts they were an amalgam of faith, devotion, courage, joviality and sternness. They never really wanted to leave Africa.

My mom's parents met during the Great Depression. They met on a double date, and when my grandpa dropped his date off, he immediately went and called upon my grandma. He died young, hit by a car as he stopped to help someone broken down on the side of the road. My mom was just nineteen.

I spent a lot of time with my grandma: Sunday afternoons and many, many summer days. She taught me a love of words as I helped her with crossword puzzles, a hatred of baseball as she grumbled about "Those damn Tigers!" while watching them lose again, how to be "curious" about your neighbors as she watched their comings and goings, and how to cook. Specifically, she taught me how to make a mean Sloppy Joe, which I later tweaked and renamed Sloppy Jim because no one wants to eat a sandwich called a Sloppy Granny. She also taught me about being tough. My grandma contracted polio when she was five and thrived her whole life, carrying two children to full term. Despite having a back severely curved by Post-Polio Syndrome, she eventually retired from being the principal of the largest primary school in the state.

As for my mom, what can I say? She was very sick while she was pregnant with me. For three days she lay on the floor, bleeding internally, with no one to help her, while she visualized her body fighting for me, willing me to survive. I grew up hearing of how she was held up at knifepoint in the middle of the street on the east side of Detroit as she tried to help a family as their social worker. I watched how she battled glass ceilings in the corporate health care industry. She managed my Pee Wee hockey team and later drove me all over the Midwest when I reached the travel leagues. She always tried to make birthdays and Christmas special.

There's a picture of me being held by my paternal grandpa when I was about twelve months old. My mom is sitting next to him, looking at me with a smile. That's the sense I have of her. She's been looking at me like that my whole life long. Even when I've made her mad, even when I've hurt her and brought tears, I've always experienced her love like sunshine on my journey.

There's much more that could be said of course. The good stuff, the hard stuff, and all the gray moments in between. Some of that will come out as my story unfolds, but beyond that, as I mentioned, this isn't really a story about my family.

I suppose for the purposes of my story, let's set the scene at twelve or thirteen. I'm chunky in that way young boys are when they haven't yet lost their baby fat. I've got gray corduroy pants and a gray Member's Only© jacket. My feathered sandy blond hair is center parted. It's Easter morning and I've just been given my first "Boombox" as a gift. For some reason I decide to take this new treasure with me to Easter Mass that morning, and as I'm getting in the car, I slam my door on the antenna so that the end dangles, destroyed. I was sad and mad and somehow I associated that with church. I didn't go again for probably two years.

Moments earlier, before we left the house, my mom took this picture of me posing with the Boombox on my shoulder. And the truth is, I was posing. I was a total nerd. As far as I can remember, I grew up listening to two vinyl records in our home: the Star Wars soundtrack by the London Symphony Orchestra, and various versions of the Canadian national anthem.

When my wife, Megan, and I go out for breakfast or a drink, one of her favorite pastimes is to quiz me about the songs playing at the restaurant. "Jim, what's this one?" or "Oh, I love this song! Reminds me of middle school. Do you know who this is, babe?" Occasionally I'll surprise her, but I rarely ever get better than 20%. In all the best ways, it brings her great joy to watch me struggle and squirm. If I can get past my mildly bruised ego, then I'm able to revel in her delight and experience my own.

At some point, I acquired a 45 of The J. Geils Band's, "My Angel is a Centerfold," but trust me, that was very far from my lived experience. Really, I was a nerd. I know that's a surprise, right? Truth is, I listened to classical music while I studied and even had my favorite DJs on the local classical station. (This appreciation for classical music did pay off at Megan's 50th birthday dinner, when we were the only patrons at a fancy downtown restaurant, and the Belarussian pianist essentially gave us a private show when he discovered I knew a little of what I was talking about. She doesn't make fun of me quite as much anymore. Progress!)

I was enough of a nerd that I also played Dungeons & Dragons. That's the other thing that happened when I was 13. I met a foursome of friends that played D&D and they brought me in. Three of them are friends to this day. Please understand, this was before GenCon and World of Warcraft© and Game of Thrones mainstreamed fantasy role-playing. This was the 80s when a fantasy gamer might still get beat up by the jocks. Not only did I simply play D&D, but I was the "dungeon master." Seeing that in print is almost enough to make me blush, but there it is. I was the DM, as it was commonly known, and I loved it.

I learned a lot about life from D&D. Certainly it helped me with my SAT scores, becoming fluent in more complex words, and learning to thoughtfully read and engage with texts. As a kid who was (and in some ways, still is) naturally shy by temperament, it was a huge boost to my interpersonal skills, giving me real-time role-playing experience interacting with others in diverse situations. And by virtue of my role in the group, I developed capacity for telling stories as well as learning to envision what didn't yet exist and communicating that compellingly to others. I'm convinced that playing Dungeons & Dragons increased my capacity as a leader and for missional living.

Yet that's not how everyone in the 80s saw fantasy role-playing games. At the time I had no Christian identification. In fact, I thought the polytheism of the D&D universe seemed as plausible as any monotheistic or scientific explanation on offer. But my friend Corey, who invited me into his group, came from a church-going home and during that time there was a lot of noise from fundamentalist Christians about how bad games like D&D were. These games, the noise said, led to terrible things like witchcraft, Satanism, skipping school, watching R movies, LARPing in the woods, and listening to the J. Geils Band.

Eventually my friend Corey had a conviction about his faith and he decided to go back to church. He also decided to stop playing D&D. When we got together at my dining room table, we stopped poring over the latest module like we used to and started talking instead about faith and Jesus. I tried to talk to him about continuing to play, but his mind was set. He never pressured me, but he was intentional. He was my closest friend and he cared about me. (Even recently he traveled from Virginia to Detroit to attend my birthday party, and he's partnered with us in prayer for 25 years and counting.)

The winter of my fourteenth year he gave me a copy of Hal Lindsay's book, *The Late Great Planet Earth*. If you're not familiar, it's the non-fiction version of the books and movie adaptations of *Left Behind*. If you're not familiar with that, well, that's maybe a good thing. Basically, the book is an articulation of the author's understanding of the Bible's teaching about the "end times."

The book is very "mid," as my kids say, and his ideas never took enough root to make a lasting impact on me past high school. But at the end of the book there was a prayer. A scripted prayer that the reader could pray, acknowledging their sins and shortcomings, God's greatness and Jesus' goodness, affirming my need for Jesus and his forgiveness, and committing to him as my Lord and Savior. It's one version of what's often called "the sinners' prayer" in Christian circles. It's nowhere in the Bible, of course, but it's a composite of a lot of biblical ideas and language. When I got to the end of the book and read that prayer, something happened. Unexpectedly, I really prayed that prayer.

Before I say more, let's have some straight talk. The one thing the book was pretty good at was cultivating fear, of the "What would happen to you if you died tonight?" variety. In that way, the author made a strong impression on impressionable minds. It feels almost embarrassing to say, but it seems I was impressionable.

Like I said, I prayed that prayer. I prayed it probably a dozen times over the next month. Standing up, sitting down, on my knees, with tears in my eyes, with serious conviction to make sure it "stuck." Always alone. Almost always in my dining room, weirdly enough, which is where I read the book. (It seems God has something for me and dining room tables!) I hadn't seen this coming. I know now that I prayed this mostly out of fear.

Fear of hell. Fear of being left behind. Which was a serious fear for an only child teenage boy with a single mom and grandma handicapped by polio. Let me put it in my personal perspective. Throughout that year with the Boombox and Members' Only© jacket, I had a regularly recurring dream: my mom and I floated against a black background and then, suddenly, unexpectedly, I would get propelled (though it usually felt like pulled, like a rubber band snapping) away quickly into the dark of the outer void.

The author painted a picture of judgment at the end times. God would come and rescue devout Christians so that they escaped from the hellish trauma that was visited upon the earth in those "last days." It was understandably fearful. I now know that this fear is not the gospel of Jesus. Fear is something we all face. Fear is the fruit of fractured relationships: with God, ourselves, others and creation. Fear flows from all the trauma and pain that humans inflict on one another and ourselves, in our woundedness and loneliness.

This "gospel of fear" is something less than the good news that God birthed into the world with Jesus. The God revealed in the Bible, through Jesus, rarely rescues people from hardship, but is always with us as we experience hardship, suffering and trauma. The whole of scripture, the life of Jesus, and thoughtful reflection upon our lives attest to this. God doesn't leave us behind or abandon us. God seeks us out when we're missing, searches for us when we can't find our way.

Yet, in the often unfathomable mystery of God's wisdom, God used that book, the author's perhaps misguided intent, that prayer, to provoke something in me. To awaken a hunger. A hunger for something More. A hunger for life. A hunger for God.

Over the next seven months I wrestled. I started going to church with Corey. I started reading the Bible, a lot. I remember sitting in 9th Grade World History with Mr. Hughes as he described the cultures and religions of ancient Greece and Rome, and I could sense the sea tide shifting within. I tried, unsuccessfully as it turns out, to Christianize my D&D. I tried to turn Paladins into Crusaders and Priests into, well, Priests, and somehow fit Jesus into my role-playing pantheon. Ugh. It didn't work.

As I've said, I loved Dungeons & Dragons. It was good for me. I learned, grew, socialized. Yet, increasingly, I felt this gentle nudge to let it go. Sometimes less gentle. At the time that nudge might have been fueled by some of that fundamentalist noise. At the time I probably would've called the game "bad." I don't know if I actually used that word, but you get the idea. Now, today, I would use the language of "disordered attachment." I learned this from Ignatius of Loyola. A "disordered attachment" is an otherwise good gift from God, that we unwisely and unhelpfully attach to, cling to, placing it out of order before our joyful and trusting relationship with the good and loving God.

Also during this time, my mom remarried, I inherited two stepsisters and a stepbrother, and we moved into a new house in a neighboring suburb. There was a lot going on.

Shortly after we moved, about a month after I turned fifteen, it happened. I was sitting in my bedroom, and this quiet, gentle, compelling voice spoke to me. I wasn't aware at the time that Christians debated whether Jesus still spoke to us or not. But I immediately knew this was Jesus.

Jesus spoke simply and straight to the point, straight to my heart, "Jim, what's it going to be? D&D or me?"

Then he waited. Patient. Kind. Moments later I knew and I responded, "I choose you, Jesus."

I've tried to keep saying *Yes* ever since.

A year and a half later I was baptized. (In a serendipitous irony, it was exactly 10 years later to the day that I celebrated the other most significant ceremony of my life: my marriage to my beloved, Megan.) Pastor Smith had asked me to pick and then read a verse from scripture as part of the baptism ceremony. So, standing in the water, holding the microphone (!), I read from Philippians:1:20-21, "*I eagerly expect and hope that I will in no way be ashamed, but will have sufficient courage so that now as always Christ will be exalted in my body, whether by life or by death. For to me, to live is Christ and to die is gain.*" I still have no idea how I landed upon that particular passage.

Over time this has become my life verse, giving voice to a deep cry of my heart.

I opened the chapter by saying this book isn't about my family. Yet, as we all know, the people among whom you live your life are an essential ingredient in your story. So I would be remiss if I didn't at least mention the folks that entered my life when my mom remarried. All told, there were five Jims: my father, my step-dad, my father-in-law, my stepbrother and me! My older stepsister, a full decade older, never lived at home with us. Sadly, she's drifted from our family and I haven't spoken with her in many years. My other stepsister is just two weeks younger. In some ways we are wildly different, while in other interesting ways we are strikingly similar. My stepbrother is a few years younger. We fought from time to time during the very short five months that our parents courted (my kids would call it "throwing hands") but in time we developed a friendship rooted in a mutual love for hiking (and later by whiskey, red wine and Jesus).

If this book isn't about my family, it's even less about my kids. They've already endured too much of their lives being shared in sermons and on social media. They'll have their own stories to tell in due time. I like to think of them as an amazing jazz quartet, taking the music Megan and I have given them, and riffing on it to make it their own. The chords and underlying rhythms are there, yet they're adapting the tune so that the song is their own.

Still, a few remarks to give a feel for this foursome that rounds out the Pool Party. Our oldest, Elijah, is a fascinating mix of Megan and I. As a kid he built huge forts and waterfalls out of blankets. A lover of Godzilla, he wrestled in State Finals as a senior. He and I have walked hundreds of miles together in a dozen states, including a single day 52 miler in mid-Michigan.[6]

Esther is our oldest daughter. We adopted her at three days old. Hard of hearing from birth, she's overcome numerous obstacles, playing a lead role on synth with her competitive high school marching band in the State Championships. She's been bullied for being too nice and is the greatest friend someone could have. She's calm and peaceful and will be an excellent early elementary school teacher.

Adventurous Eden is next, my mini-me, with enough personality to require two middle names. Though she might seem bashful at first, she's highly responsible and a born leader. She keeps the house lively, is passionate about her faith, and can't keep a secret from us or follow a recipe to save her life.

Olive is the youngest, a lot like her mother yet with her own flair. She's a deep feeler and even deeper thinker. A creative, poetic writer with a great eye for interior design. She loves cultures, languages and all things traditional. She's also the family queen of one-liners and can drop the mic more than anyone I know when she's in her zone.

---

[6] https://www.freep.com/story/news/local/michigan/2023/06/15/father-son-michigan-woods-north-country-trail-hike/70288361007/

The best journeys are shared with a companion. Jesus sent the apostles out two by two. Frodo and Samwise, C3PO and R2D2: they had each other. Megan and I have been partners on the journey for more than half our lives now. I didn't know until a few years after our marriage that she had watched *North and South* enough as a young girl that she always wanted to marry a West Pointer. We share a love for travel and stability, early morning quiet and French pressed coffee, good books and a sense of place, downward mobility and living purposefully, the serendipity of other cultures. We're both thoughtful, yet she expresses it as deep feeling and me as decisive action. Our companionship has not always been easy, this transformation of two becoming one.

Amidst all the hard work, the arguments, the forgiveness, the sorrows and the celebrations—in other words, the ruptures and repairs—our third strand[7] has been our shared commitment to Jesus and the missional spirituality we've forged and live out together, practiced in maturing relationships of love, honoring health, formation, simplicity and multiplication, infused with curiosity, patience, hope and delight.

In my mid-40's I was reading a lot of Brené Brown, especially on long plane rides. In *Dare to Lead*[8] she invites her readers to articulate their deepest core values, what drives them, in one or two words. Flying over the Atlantic, I journaled into my phone these two words: *Adventurous Overcomer*. These two words convey what was formed in me during my childhood: by nature, nurture, circumstance and choice. They resonate deeply with what I've discovered in all my self-awareness work. These things would get matured in the years to come. The missing piece of my passion and capacity for connections and networking with people would be unearthed in the next season of my life.

---

[7] Ecclesiastes 4:12
[8] Brené Brown, *Dare to Lead* (London: Vermillion, 2018), 187-189

Slowing Down To Catch Up With God

G-Movie

Like most colleges, West Point publishes an annual yearbook for the cadet student body, parents and posterity. West Point's yearbook is called the Howitzer and it's a big deal. Like, literally, a large, heavy book. I've heard that they send a copy to the White House every year as a record of each graduating class. Along with all the other impromptu moments and group photos in clubs, teams, barracks and more, every graduating senior has a head shot with a personal bio. Many cadets will craft this bio on their own. Some, however, will honor a tradition of having your friends write all or part of that bio for you. That's what happened for me when a few friends from Company F-4 (Go Frogs!) sat down with me at the Firstie Club (the only bar on campus, reserved for cadet seniors). Below is what they wrote for me, with a little line of my own at the end.

> *Mahayana—The Enlightened One. Jim's smarts never came between him and the Frogs he loved. Jim was always close with an encouraging word or cheering thought for those in need. G-Movie transformed into a PG flick before our eyes. It is said the most prized possession in life is a good friend. Thanks for making us the richest people on earth.*
> *"For King and Kingdom!"*

This sums up something significant for me about my time at the Military Academy.

Going to West Point was a big deal for me. Maybe that seems obvious. Who would attend West Point casually, right? It's not an exaggeration to say that it was a life-changing experience. Of course. Yet I mean it in another way.

We were a "Michigan family." If you know a Wolverines fan, you'll know what I mean. I come from a long line of Michigan grads. My grandma and both of her brothers had graduated from Michigan. Their mother had worked as a housekeeper in the UMich Law Quad to pay to put them through. My mom and my uncle had gone to Michigan, my mom for both her Bachelor's and Master's Degrees. Since I was in advanced math and science classes in school, there had been conversation for years that I would follow in my great uncle's footsteps and graduate from Michigan Engineering as he had. Nor were we a military family. Besides a short tour in the National Guard for my stepdad, the only other military service in recent generations had been my father, with all the pain that brought our family.

While I was applying to West Point, my grandma literally tried to bribe me to attend Michigan, offering to buy me a new car if I put on the Maize and Blue. When that failed, she hit below the belt, saying it would be devastating to my mom to have me so far away after she had sacrificed so much, for so long, to raise me as a single working mom. My mom had sacrificed so much for so long, and I knew it would not be easy. Thankfully my mom practiced maturity and was committed to releasing me into adulthood. She and my stepdad both blessed my decision. Even the one to forego the engineering expectation and pursue majoring in history.

I had this strong conviction to attend West Point. At that time, new to my faith, I didn't much submit the decision to God. At least not in the traditional sense. Rather, it was this deep sense of intuition that West Point was good for me, the best fit, the right path. It was more like a longing than a reason. My passions were stirred as I considered it. Since then I've come to learn that this is an important way that God speaks to us though I had no language for that at that time.

Though I eventually left the Army, I think I correctly discerned God's invitation to me. Attending and graduating from West Point has opened so many doors, made possible so much of what has happened in my life.

Slowing Down To Catch Up With God

The first day at West Point shook that conviction, though. It is called R-Day, for Reporting Day. Incoming students and their families filed into a gymnasium several hundred at a time. After a short welcome and orientation talk by an upper-class cadet, and 60 seconds to hug and say goodbye, the new cadets file up the stairs and through the open doors into the hallway beyond while the families are dismissed. Once the doors closed, we had our first taste of the 47-month journey at West Point. It involved exactly what you might expect: people packed into a too small hall, trying to stand straight and tall, with lots of high volume instructions. The aroma of anxiety hung thickly in the air.

Eventually, after lots of marching around, getting shots, doing pullups, donning a PT outfit plus black loafers and knee-high dress socks, and filling a giant duffle bag with everything we'd need for the next six weeks, we were ordered to report to the "cadet in the red sash." This upper-class cadet's job is to instruct you in your four responses: "New cadet, your four responses are: Yes, sir/ma'am. No, sir/ma'am. No excuse, sir/ma'am. Sir/ma'am, I do not understand. New cadet, what are your four responses?" After correctly repeating your responses (harder than you'd think), we were then told to head up the barracks stairs to receive our room assignments.

It's late June. I'm sweaty. I've gone from 0 to 100 in the time it takes for a metal fire door to swing closed and then stay at 100 for hours in a row. When I get to my room, I'll have a few moments to meet my roommates before having to change uniforms and then march in our first parade for our parents who've been waiting all day to cheer us on from the bleachers before they head home to worry, write letters and pray. This room will be the closest thing to a safe zone that a new cadet has, so getting that room assignment and into the room was key. I climb the stairs to the fourth floor, walking at attention, clutching with one hand that giant duffle bag filled with gear.

Entering the hallway, I see the poster with the room assignments on it. Stepping in front of it, standing at attention, my eyes roam over the small print, searching for my name. It's not there. My eyes frantically search the list. Still not there. Panic. There's no one around to ask, and even if there were, I couldn't ask a fellow new cadet (we're not allowed to speak in the hallway unless spoken too), and I don't know which of my four responses would cover this situation with an upper-class cadet. I just stand there, stuck, unsure what to do, all my great grades and test scores useless now.

Just then I hear a voice behind, "What's your major malfunction, new cadet?" I make my best attempt at an about face and respond, "No excuse, sir!" "Get over here," he replies. I approach as fast as I can, still carrying my duffle bag in hand. "What's your name, new cadet?" It's literally written in permanent marker, by my hand, above the logo over my heart, but I guess he wants to confirm. "New Cadet Pool, sir!" He takes a step forward, looking first at the name on my shirt, then leaning in close to my face. He lingers for a moment before taking the full sense of me, like an alley cat toying with a mouse. "Pool," he whispers huskily, "Pool. Oh, that's right. I remember you, Pool. You fucked it all up. It's all your fault, Pool. You gave us all kinds of headaches figuring out what to do with you. It's your fault, Pool. I know who you are." He then glanced down at the clipboard he was holding and returned to eye contact, "You're in 504 down the hall. Get outta here!" Entering Room 504, my new roommates turned and paused, asking me if I was okay. I immediately burst into tears.

Thankfully, things got better from there. Little surprise, perhaps, given that the H-2 company motto my first two years was "Happy as Hell!" The Yearlings (so called because they had one year done) who had responsibility for us that first (plebe) year led with a light-hearted touch. They took the role of mentoring us seriously, but not too seriously, and they infused some fun into the system. I still remember meeting our Yearlings for the first time. We had just finished "Beast Barracks" (Cadet Basic Training) and were getting ready to start the academic year. We were standing at attention in front of our wardrobe closets and to kick things off they asked us our names (again, even though they were printed on our shirts). "Sir, my name is Cadet Pool!" I replied with gusto. "No, you're not," he said, smirking slightly. "From now on you'll be Cadet Ool, because you don't want any P in your Pool."

I had some great roommates during those two years: TK, TL, Bryson, Evarts, Shipworth, Dave, and others. Some have remained lifelong friends. (In fact, I had different roommates all eight semesters at USMA.)

Dave and I conspired on some "spirit missions" together with our plebes. During Air Force week we stuffed our visiting Zoomie's flight uniform with newspaper, attempting to hang it up over Central Area. When it fell five flights to the ground, Dave ended up taking the fall for our team and accepting the punishment. Later, during Navy week, our team snuck into the bowels of Arvin Gym, and we joined a large number of other cadets in a midnight lights off co-ed swim. Yet, for all the joys, there was lots of surviving: finding your way while pinging at 120 steps per minute along the walls in the halls while keeping eyes front, navigating plebe boxing, plebe swimming, plebe gymnastics, 0500 morning runs with a classmate out to Thayer Gate and back, the seven minute sprint sans backpacks from Physics class in the bowels of Thayer Hall on one end of the academic area to "Dirt" class (Environmental Science and Terrain Analysis) on the top floors of Washington Hall on the other end of the academic area, and so much more.

Early in my plebe year I joined the Navigators campus ministry. They had a weekly large group gathering and then would break up into small group Bible studies. It was a little like the youth group my friend Corey and I had started at our church in 11th grade, just a lot more intentional. This was the first time I was exposed to the idea of discipleship, as in learning to practice the way of Jesus in our everyday lives, instead of just learning more of the Bible as if I was preparing for a test. I remember having this vague sense, wondering why I hadn't heard about this before.

Now, looking back, it's sad that I had been a Christian for three years and hadn't ever really heard of this dimension of the Gospels and one of Jesus' central commands. I started meeting from time to time with an upperclassman, two years ahead of me, who was leading our Bible study. He was thoughtful, caring, and encouraging for me in all the various ups and downs of those first two years of life at the Academy.

My third summer at West Point, as a rising Cow (junior), I spent eight weeks in South Georgia. Three of them spent running, jumping, and learning to fall in Airborne School. The next five were as a drill cadet, helping a team of amazing, professional drill sergeants run basic training for incoming soldiers. Though West Point no longer offers this development opportunity for cadets, I had a wonderful experience. It was a chance to interact with sergeants and enlisted soldiers that would not be possible as a new Lieutenant, and it was a chance for the junior enlisted soldiers to hear what it was like to be an officer.

When we arrived back at West Point for our Cow year, all of us were "scrambled" into new companies. The Academy leadership did this from time to time at the start of academic years. As an old grad I've learned there is a complex algorithm for when they do it, but as cadets it seemed capricious. At first I was annoyed. Not only did it mean a move into another building, adding more tasks to an already overloaded schedule, but I had many happy moments in "Happy as Hell." Yet, as much as I loved being H-2, I'm grateful now for the scramble. My time with H-2 was both fun and foundational, yet my years with the Frogs of F-4 were far more formative.

Maybe I'm overstating the case, but that Cow class of F-4 was one of those magic moments when everything seemed to synergize. Even to this day, 30 years as of this writing, half of our class leadership team are Frogs. Once the Frog thread gets going, which is about once a week, these Old Grads text like teenage girls. (No offense intended to any teenage girls reading this!) Almost all the Frogs had a nickname: Bruno, Chonger, Tunger, K-Pot, Booger, Brando, Skeeter, Marge, and many more, some perhaps not appropriate for print. A few Frogs were even called simply by their names, like the two Toms, Mindy, Kar and Rolli. This is when I was first called G-Movie. Bruno was the Master of Monikers.

Early that academic year, my friend Jason Prost found me in my new room. We had met in plebe boxing, being alphabetical neighbors of similar height and weight, so we often found ourselves sparring and then chatting in the locker room after. He had introduced me to the Navigators and we had been in a Bible study together the past two years. He stopped by to suggest a trip to his hometown of Atlanta over Labor Day Weekend. Cows had a little more leave, a little more money, and he needed a trip, having broken up with a girlfriend over the summer or something. He wondered if I'd be his wingman. He had bumped into an old high school friend of his while on leave and suggested a double date with one of her friends, along with some whitewater rafting and other fun. Jason's date didn't work out, but that's how I started seeing Ashley.

Ashley was a southern belle from an SEC school with a flair for full-length flowery sun dresses. I'd describe that first date as "good enough" to stay in touch, which was made possible because I had a landline in my room since my roomie was in a leadership position. She was just coming out of a long-term, toxic relationship. We had lots of long phone calls, mostly characterized in those early days by me encouraging her sense of worth and value, something which had been bruised by her last boyfriend.

I didn't see it at the time, but there was a lot of rescuing going on. I had never had a serious dating relationship, so honestly I didn't really know any better. Now, decades later, I can see that my early kindness towards her got confused for intimacy, and her reciprocation awoke some as-yet-untapped thing inside of me. I was hooked. We saw each other only a few times that school year, but we talked often.

I spent the two weeks of summer leave before my Firstie Year at her home in the South. In both my experience and observation, long distance relationships have lots of challenges. A two-hour phone call can be wonderful and feel very intimate, yet it also lacks a lot of context. You're not together in the same way. There's a lack of with-ness, an absence of what in Christianity we'd call incarnation, where the two are together on the good days and the bad. When we're upbeat and confident, as well as when we're frustrated and feeling fat. Then, when the distanced couple finally comes together, I find there's an intense pressure to be on and cram into three days what would normally take three weeks or in two weeks what would be healthier over two months.

It was on that summer leave that the fractures in the foundation of relationship were exposed. It manifested in pressures around physical intimacy. I was a 21 year old with no experience, but lots of pent up passion. She had lots more sexual experience than I did, and her parents didn't seem to mind that we spent lots of alone time together at all hours of the day. It was becoming clear how immature was our relationship.

We first had sex later that year, on Christmas Eve, in my childhood bed. She had come to visit me while I was on leave over the holiday break. The rest of my family had left after dinner to take step-great-grandma back to her nursing home while we stayed behind. Trust me, despite the intentional secrecy and the Barry White CD, I didn't intend on us having sex that night. We had fooled around so many times this felt like just one more escapade. Then it happened.

When I realized it happened, I cried out and literally jumped back, horrified. I was sitting on the edge of the bed, crying. Once we both quickly got dressed, she tried unsuccessfully to console me. We had been dancing across the line of my convictions so many times over the past months, yet this time came with a certain sense of finality. Though it's what I wanted (in one sense), it's never what I had intended, and it could not be undone. But it wasn't the last time we had sex. We did it several more times over that week, as a way of making up whenever we fought. This was the only connection we had left. What rubbed salt in the wounds of my sorrow was that I was trying to break up with Ashley.

Backtrack several months to the start of my Firstie Year. Ring Weekend is a major milestone event in the 47-month West Point journey. My mom is there, along with Ashley and her mom. On a scale of awkward, this one is at 11. After the dinner and dance Saturday night, Ashley and I went for a stroll along one of my favorite parts of the West Point campus: Flirtation Walk. Flirty, as it is sometimes known, is a beautiful old trail winding along the western banks of the Hudson River, famous since the early 1800s as a place where cadets would walk with their dates. At the midpoint, where the river turns to make the strategic western point in the river, there is a large spit of rocks that descends into the river. Sitting atop it together in the moonlit night, we could hear passionate noises closer to the water. It was a gorgeous night. Captivated by the moment I thought to myself, "Man, if I were going to ask someone to marry me, this would be a moment to do it." Here's the problem: I'm a verbal processor. So my self-reflection was actually uttered. "What was that you were mumbling, Jim? Do you really mean it?" Uh-oh!

If you've ever seen the movie Ferris Buehler's Day Off, you're familiar with how he breaks the "fourth wall:" pausing the action and talking directly to the audience. I had one of those moments. Time stood still and I turned to ask myself, "Do I really mean it? Really?" I hesitated for a momentary eternity, then turned and falteringly replied, "Yes. Yes. Yes, I do." "Oh, yay! Of course I will!" And that's how I got engaged. Sorta. Because I didn't tell my parents for weeks, nor anyone else that weekend. And I never got her a ring. Every time I'd see one of those jewelry stores at the mall and try to pressure myself into going in, I couldn't.

Then we started fighting. The Big Fight came when I called to talk with her about where I wanted to post for my first assignment in the Army after graduation: Germany. "What?!?!" she cried. "We can't go to Germany! I'll be so far from my mom." I tried to talk about opportunities to experience adventure in Europe and other such lines of thought. She wasn't biting. "But we'll be so far away, so far from my family. There are plenty of posts in the Southeast. Why don't you pick one of those? What are your options?" That's how I ended up at Fort Bragg in North Carolina.

I also got mad. It was like blinders fell off and I could see we weren't seeing the same things, nor the same way. We had different values, different priorities. I tried to break up. She consented to a pause on our engagement while we figured things out. "Jim, I've already got tickets to come see you in Detroit over Christmas break? And for 100th Night at West Point too. Your friends are my friends now." 100th Night, another one of those milestones, could've been a highlight celebrating only one hundred days until graduation. Instead, it was probably the worst weekend of my life. We broke up during the hourlong ride to Newark airport Sunday afternoon.

Where were my Christian friends during all this time? After I had broken up with Ashley, a few pulled me aside for a private conversation, lovingly and honestly confronting me with my poor choices and inviting me into repentance, healing, and a better way. They didn't know about my sexual choices, yet they could tell I wasn't doing well. I was sometimes drinking more than was wise and my leadership was suffering. I was still involved in the Navigators, leading a Bible study. In fact, through an unexpected turn of events, I became the Cadet in Charge of the club my Firstie year.

The naturally missional couple that had been staff leadership for the past number of years left that summer and the new staff couple had a more direct style. He kept trying to meet with me. Like my classmates, he could tell something wasn't right with me. We would set up appointments in a quiet room of the library. When I showed up I was almost always tight-lipped. Sometimes I didn't even come. I didn't yet trust him, and when I really needed someone who knew me and loved me and was glad to be with me, he seemed to be coming at me with "truth" and accountability. Unfortunately, I never gave him a chance. I'm embarrassed by how I related to him and years later I wrote him a letter of apology. He graciously forgave me and we've since stayed connected.

But what about those Frogs? What was it about them? They were welcoming. I've been to many churches that could learn a thing or two about welcoming from this brood of heathens, saints and agnostics. When I say welcome, I don't mean the sunny, syrupy smile from a greeter at the front door of the church, giving you a bulletin and directions to the coffee bar or children's ministry check-in. I mean, they included me. The Frogs embraced me as their people. It wasn't just me, of course. As a whole we did it for each other.

Though I wouldn't have had language for it at the time, West Point and the Class of '94 was my "tribe," and the Frogs were my "clan." We were saints and sinners, every one of us, and they included me. And when I needed people who were glad to be with me to come alongside me, they were there. I remember fondly how one of the Toms would sing hymns from the top of five flights of stairs, serenading us after his shower or sending us off to lunch formation, while later that night in another room, others would joke about who was winning their masturbation competition. There were tales (and a few pictures) of the senior year spring break trip to Jamaica, frequent trips to the Firstie Club or a family member's home off-post. Long talks on the stoop with Bruno about philosophy, war, religion, and his favorite bands. Late night talks with Collins about philosophy, love, religion and life. We didn't see eye to eye, yet we listened to each other. We respected each other. We loved each other.

Fast forward to the Covid years. Megan and I needed to get $18,000 to a Sudanese American colleague living in Sudan, so that he could staff and supply for another season the three medical clinics and schools he ran for hundreds of internally displaced children in his country. Don't worry, it was all legal. But politics had imposed sanctions on international banking, so the only way our friend could receive his funds was the old-fashioned way: by human mule. The catch was that Sudan had emptied many of their prisons rather than deal with the complexities of Covid in such confined spaces, and crime around the capital was on the rise.

Enter Bruno, who had recently retired from the Special Forces. Telling him about our plans, he pleaded with me for the opportunity to come along: "Jim, please take me. I'll be the big guy in the background looking out for you, making sure no one messes with you. I know you'll probably try to talk to me about Jesus and stuff. That's cool, I don't mind at all. You don't even have to pay me, just cover my expenses. Just give me a chance to help and get in the action." That's what I'm talking about. We made room for each other. We were a people. (In the end we realized it was logistically much easier, and financially much cheaper, to just bring our Sudanese friend to Ethiopia for a few days, where we were already going to be. But Bruno and I still talk about ways we can "get in the action" together.)

The Frogs welcomed me and included me as one of their people. My time with the Frogs also matured me as a human and shaped me as a leader. I know plenty of pastors who go from Christian schools and children's ministry, to youth group and Bible college, then work at a church. These folks, pastors and missionaries alike, charged to serve and love the world, be a light of blessing in it, have never really spent adequate time among everyday people who don't share their convictions. They've never rubbed shoulders, labored and sweated, argued and reconciled, cheered and fêted with them. How can we translate our experience of God to our neighbors if we don't feel their culture, don't know the language of their heart?

I sometimes still struggle at describing what I do for a living these days, yet I guess one way that I'd describe it is that I'm trying to help spiritually curious people experience and know the God revealed by Jesus and what it could look like for them to follow this Jesus in their real, everyday life circumstances. And to whatever extent it might be true that I do this with any success, I give gratitude to the Frogs. These amazing women and men helped me be a better missional leader.

I graduated West Point and joined the Long Grey Line of Old Grads. I reported for duty in the Personnel section of the General Staff of the 1st Corps Support Command at Fort Bragg. It was a great assignment.

I had matured during my time at West Point. I had entered into adulthood, yet I had a lot to learn. I took two years off from drinking. And though I never had sex again until I was married, the few relationships I did have in between were all burdened by my sexualizing them. Counter to my best intentions, I had become what I didn't want to be. It's like I was in a hurry, trying to take what I wanted, instead of trusting God to provide.

Even after more than ten years of marriage, I still experienced shame associated with sex. Often, the first words out of my mouth after we were finished were not, "Thank you," or "I love you," but "I'm sorry." I was embarrassed by how automatic this was. Some of you, friends, might be wondering why I'm bothering to talk about this. It's my experience that "sex is always in the room"[9] yet we rarely ever talk about it. Sex was never easy for Meg and I. She had a severe case of endometriosis in college and was put into a state of early menopause to help combat it. That, combined with my poor choices, and her own past sexual trauma, meant that we've always had to be intentional about it. Yet as we practice patience, understanding and love for one another, plus plenty of time sitting in the presence of Jesus holding this pain before him, we are finding healing and hope.

---

[9] Curt Thompson, *Soul of Desire* (Downers Grove: Intervarsity Press, 2021) 198.

From Parachutist to Pastor

"But what about Ryan," Jenny asked, "how do you think this event will impact him?" "That's a good question," I responded. "I hadn't thought of that. Maybe let's take some time to think about it and pray?"

Jenny and I had met at Church of the Open Door in the single adults Sunday school class. I had been living in Fayetteville, NC, for about nine months now and had found my way to this church not long after moving into town. It was a great fit for me in that season of my life. There was a group of a half dozen of us who spent a lot of time together: a midweek Bible study or two, Sunday School class, and as often as we could, we would go to the Sunday evening service and dinner after. Those bowls of baked potato soup and the conversations that went with it were nourishment to my body and soul. Sometime in the spring the elder leading the ministry asked me to help him sometimes with the class, and then that summer he asked me to lead the Friday night singles' Bible study. The group was larger than that core of six, including soldiers, locals from town, and even a super humble low-key guy we all guessed was a Delta Force operator.

Jenny and I were talking about an upcoming meeting of our Bible study. After some discussion and discernment, we had decided to strengthen our connections by doing a "foot washing" ceremony like the one Jesus had done with his friends at dinner the night of his betrayal. That's why we were talking about Ryan. Ryan was a newer member of our group, a young local guy. He always was wearing Vans and his feet were sorta oddly shaped. The best way to describe it is that they seemed short, like stubby, and thick. We were concerned maybe he had some kind of physical challenge with club foot, and we didn't want to embarrass him or cause him shame, yet we also knew that this kind of experience could foster powerful encounters with God and loving connection with one another, just like what happened with Jesus' friends when he washed their feet at the Last Supper. We decided to press ahead with our plan and work through any strong emotions that might come up.

The day came. We hadn't told the group what we had planned, wanting it to be a surprise like it had been for Jesus' first disciples. Suddenly it was Ryan's turn. Jenny and I nervously glanced at each other as she prepared the bowl of soapy water and I unlaced his shoes. I was the one most surprised: his feet looked just like mine, and the shape came from his habit of folding his socks inside his Vans to get better grip when he skateboarded. He laughed as I told him our story. I was a little embarrassed, but he appreciated our sensitivity. It was a beautiful time together for us all.

I was grounded in my faith again and actively involved in spiritual community too. Nothing will help ground you like volunteering with a group of middle school students, as I had done while I was at my Officer Basic Course and working in the Base Realignment and Closure Office there. Their enthusiasm was infectious, and I found their non-stop questions energizing. It was a gift.

During my Officers' Basic Course I had tried (unsuccessfully) to make a bid to switch my posting from NC to Germany as I had originally desired. I figured, "Hey, we're the personnel people, right? This is what we do." So four of us OBC classmates conspired to make a complex trade, like some NFL multi-team swap just before the trade deadline. No joy. Turns out all it got me was disciplined so that I didn't finish top of my OBC class.

Now I was serving in the G-1 office of the 1st Corps Support Command at Fort Bragg. When I arrived at my unit, they had just returned from serving in Haiti on a humanitarian peace-keeping mission. Morale was upbeat and we had a great G-1 and senior NCO leadership. Our office was basically divided into two halves: the "hard side" of HR, like personnel allotments by specialty, etc., and the "soft side" of HR. I was the #2 on this latter team. My responsibilities included awards processing, congressional inquiries, coordinating with the COSCOM chaplain regarding unit morale, helping liaise with the other staff sections for planning purposes, and other special projects.

Perhaps you're old enough to have been in a business meeting where some presenter says, "If you don't know how to use this new technology, find a 14 year old and they'll help you." Well, as it turns out, I was like the 14 year old in our office. One of those special projects included creating the G-1's monthly presentation to the Commanding General, using an "arcane" program called PowerPoint. It turns out creating the presentation included serving the G-1 as her presentation assistant (which is fancy talk for pressing "next slide"). That, then, developed into actually participating in briefing the CG. Pretty cool for a 2LT to brief the Brigadier General and proof that not all busy-work assignments are bad news.

Another one of my responsibilities was establishing our forward operating section in case of need. That meant that if the COSCOM was deployed to a theater, the G-1, myself, and a small team of soldiers would be on the ground early to set up our operation for when the others arrived and coordinate with other senior leaders on the staff. Because of this, I almost deployed to the Caribbean for two hurricane relief assignments, but the Army decided instead to run our forward operations from Fort Bragg. This meant I still got 12-hour days for weeks on end, but without the beach and downtime in the Caribbean.

Additionally, since the COSCOM supported an airborne Army Corps, the advance units were also airborne. That meant I got to jump. It felt a lot more serious in the Army than in Airborne School. Not only did we jump from several hundred feet lower (which equals more dangerous, because there is less time to respond if your chute doesn't deploy properly), but two soldiers had been seriously injured jumping in the preceding two weeks. I'm very glad I jumped that sixth time, yet I only did it that once. After that, with my boss' permission, I gave my slot over to another junior officer on the other side of the office since he needed the bonus money to feed his family a lot more than I did as a single guy.

The big deal, though, is that I was already beginning to sense that perhaps the Army wasn't going to be a lifelong career for me. I was good at my job (more like a "6-6" instead of a "9-5") and I could certainly see a future. We had a great team of soldiers who worked well together, I had a lot of respect from my section chief, and I got along great with the G-1 who was working hard to advance my career. She told me she had been talking with her friends up at the 18th Airborne Corps G-1, and she had found me a job there for my next assignment in a few months.

Then, right around this time, I heard about something called the Voluntary Early Release Program (VERP for short). Basically, the Army released a small, select number of Regular Army junior officers into the Army Reserves or National Guard to fulfill the remainder of their commitment there. The Army got to right-size it's staffing, and it also helped the Guard and Reserve have a backbone of Regular Army trained officers. I had to act fast as it was first come, first serve, and I needed the signatures of everyone in my leadership chain to sign with their approval.

The VERP appealed to me because as much as I liked my job, I knew deep down that I loved what I was doing on nights and weekends with the church even more. As I sat with the decision in prayer, wondering what I should do, wondering what God would like me to do, it was like a pair of pictures began to form clearly in my mind. The first was of Uncle Sam or one of those little green army men with his hand in the air, waving me on, saying, "Follow me!" The second was of Jesus, simply looking at me, saying, "Come, follow me." They both bid me to come and follow and perhaps to die. As that imagery became clearer for me, I knew what I must do. It wouldn't necessarily be for everyone, yet I knew what was right for me. As much as the Army had been good to me, and as much as I loved my fellow soldiers and my job, Jesus had my heart. I don't know another way to say it, but my allegiance was to him, first and foremost.

I assembled the appropriate forms and began the VERP process. I met first with my section chief, Captain Haskins. He was a stout prior service infantry officer who had branch detailed to AG. He had over 100 jumps including a combat jump in Grenada. We met outside his house. As it turned out, unbeknownst to me, he had planned to go into ministry. The shock of seeing someone die by his hand in Grenada knocked him off that path. I wish I could go back now and walk with him through his trauma, helping him find healing and a way forward. He was more than happy to give me his blessing, said a short prayer for me, and signed the paperwork on the hood of his pickup truck.

Next up was the G-1, LTC O'Leary. She and her husband had often had me over for dinner, helping this single young lieutenant get grounded and well fed. She was disappointed to see me go and tried hard to recruit me for the Chaplain Corps. Yet like any good leader she wanted me to thrive in my passions even if those didn't exactly align with her own expectations. She also gave me a very supportive recommendation.

Last up was the Chief of Staff. He was a fellow West Point grad from the Vietnam era. Some of us around our office called him Colonel Skeletor. I was very concerned about that meeting. Though technically not required, I was sure any lack of support from him would be the kiss of death to my request. Showing up to his office at the appointed time, he invited me into his office and sat me down. After some brief remarks about West Point, "Duty Honor Country," and the value of military service, he asked me what were my plans if I did get out? "Well, sir, my plans are to go into ministry." I think that's the last thing he expected. My sense is he was prepared for me to talk about something much more lucrative, like Wall Street, or some high-paying civilian sector job similar to my Army role. But ministry was perhaps the one job that offered equally high expectations of service and generally with even lower pay. After a few brief remarks, he signed his approval.

I submitted the forms and then waited, continuing my job. In the Army there is a motivational phrase that trainers use with new recruits to get them to move faster: "You're moving like pond water!" It's my guess that whoever invented that phrase had experience with Army administrative bureaucracy.

Two months after my submission, and hearing nothing in reply, I read a report stipulating that the conditions of the VERP had changed such that it seemed I might no longer meet the basic requirements. I was very disappointed yet had come to realize that's how the Army worked. I talked with LTC O'Leary again about the possibilities of posting up in the 18th Airborne Corps G-1. Then a month later I received a call out of nowhere, from a Warrant Officer in the 82nd. He had been at ARPERSCOM (the Army Personnel Command, at the time the second largest building in the DOD) when someone in the office he was waiting in asked, "You're from Fort Bragg, right? Do you know a Lieutenant Pool? We have his VERP paperwork here and all we need is his final signature. We've been waiting. Would you mind taking it back to him so we can finish processing it?" What are the odds?!? He tells me the story, asks me if I'm still interested, and brings the paperwork over later that day. I sign and fax it in, and one month later LTC O'Leary is shaking my hand in an outgoing awards ceremony as I transitioning my service to the National Guard.

My next step was to attend grad school, seminary to be specific. I needed to find a school I liked near to an open National Guard assignment. Some schools were "too hot," others "too cold," but I found one just right in the suburbs of Chicago. There was an available Guard slot nearby, Chicago wasn't too far from home in Detroit, and if seminary turned out to be a terrible idea there was a strong job market to fall back on.

Honestly, I had only the vaguest idea of what I was doing. I was accepted to a one year Master of Arts in Christian Thought program at Trinity. I knew I didn't want to pursue a research program and get a doctorate. I had a clear conviction I needed to grow and learn more. And I had the sense that that I wanted to graduate and "help young people." Maybe that would look like teaching at a Christian high school? Mentoring in some way? I didn't know. The one thing I knew was I did not want to be a pastor.

Trinity allowed me to move into the dorms early so that I could be available for weekends with the Guard. The only other people there were a small group of guys taking college-level summer Greek to prepare for their MDiv program. We became good friends. When they would go somewhere to study, I would tag along and read books that they recommended. I had had little academic Christian preparation, so I soaked it all up. West Point offered two courses in religious thought, both from a historical and cultural perspective. I enjoyed them both, but they weren't the kind of academic preparation most seminarians received.

As the summer wore on and we got to know each other better, Tae and Louis would ask me, "Jim, what are you doing here? What's your degree? What do you want to do?"

"I'm doing the MA in Christian Thought. But, honestly, guys, I don't really know what I want to do. Help young people?"

"Jim," they'd reply, "You gotta switch to the MDiv. You should be a pastor. You'd make a great pastor."

"What?!? You guys are high on drugs! Why would I want to do that? That's a terrible job. Remember the teachers on *Peanuts*? The ones that drone on *Wah Wah Wah Wah*? That's what I think of when I think of pastors."

"Jim, you should be a pastor." And so it went on all summer long and into the fall.

That fall I got a job working as a secretary at a mid-sized local church in the area. Nothing fancy, but the office manager was flexible with my schedule, familiar with seminary students working there, plus it was conveniently located and not too demanding as I studied a whole new discipline. Kay ran the office effectively, taking Jesus and Jesus' mission seriously but the job with humor and grace. And as I've since confirmed, like most good church secretaries, she had a keen insight into people and had a read on almost everything that was really going on in the church.

One of my classes that winter quarter was *Christ, the Cross and the Holy Spirit*. For each of these three subjects, the professor wisely instructed us to read a book from each differing perspective so that we could grow in our understanding, appreciation and development of our own thinking. I had been hearing more and more about the Holy Spirit from some friends, including Tae, who attended the Evanston Vineyard Church on the outskirts of Chicago. The prof published the list of books for us to choose from the last day of Fall Quarter before the Christmas break so we could get started before coming to class in the new year.

I bought one of the books my friends had recommended, *Surprised by the Power of the Spirit*, by Jack Deere. I started reading it immediately. I was engrossed, reading the whole book during break. That first Sunday, the last Sunday of Advent, I was at church sitting next to Kay, who had taken me under her wing. Just as the music was ending and the pastor was walking up to the stage (he was dressed like Joseph since his sermon was from his perspective on the birth of Jesus), a woman cried out, "Jesus! Jesus! Jesus!" from the back of the sanctuary.

I had been reading about how God sometimes visited churches with his presence, in power, by the Holy Spirit. The effect was sometimes overwhelming, even chaotic. Inhaling deeply, I thought, "*Whoa! That's happening here! Wow! It's happening here!*" As it turns out, it wasn't that at all. It was a warm December morning and the heat hadn't been turned off, so a tween boy sitting right under the heat vent had passed out during the singing and hit his head on the pew, opening a cut. His mom was understandably freaked out. Thankfully, he was totally fine.

During the pause in the service as the ambulance responded, I leaned over to Kay and, a little embarrassed, explained to her what I thought had happened with a hushed voice. She laughed, then looked me in the eye. "Jim," she said with a characteristic mix of humor and earnestness, "this church wouldn't know what to do if the Holy Spirit showed up like that!"

I was back a week later, before the winter term started the next day. It was the Sunday after the holidays, and as often happens, the assistant pastor was preaching. His text was from Psalm 133, "*like oil dripping down Aaron's beard is when God's people dwell together in unity.*" He was a sweet man and a good pastor. It was a lovely sermon about a very important topic. Yet all I kept thinking about as I sat in the pew was, *"Who cares about oil on Aaron's beard!?! People are being raised from the dead!"* You see, that Friday night I had finished the book and the author told multiple stories of people being raised from the dead in Africa. Reading that, absorbing that, I sat at my dining room table, alternating between awe, disbelief, curiosity and the desire to take action. So on Sunday morning I kept wondering, *"Why aren't we talking about what God's doing, not just in the Bible, but around the world today?!?!"*

The next Sunday I was at the Vineyard Church of Evanston. I had visited a few times with Tae that fall and I loved what I experienced: the diversity, the passion in the room, how down to earth everything was, and things I didn't yet have language to explain. A few months later I would end my employment at the other church, leaving on good terms, especially with Kay. But that was yet in the future. For now, I was introducing myself to Steve, the senior pastor, who was in the front hallway greeting guests. He attentively listened as I explained how we needed a homegroup (I had been hearing about those from Tae and others too) at the seminary campus.

"Well, there's already one on the college campus," Steve replied.

"Sure, but seminary students aren't likely to cross the street to go there. I've got nine other friends who are interested to start one right now."

His eyes lit up and we agreed to talk next week. Well, next week I was sick and couldn't go. The week after I had Guard duty and couldn't go. So when I showed up at the end of the month, I was sure he would've forgotten me or be mad at me for standing him up. Instead, immediately after the service, he practically ran through the auditorium to find me. He then introduced me to John and Dana, both recent grads, who would be our new homegroup leaders at the seminary campus.

Two months later, in March, I went to lunch with Steve for the first time. Later I discovered that he loved Thai food and cheap Chinese buffet, and that we shared a mutual affection for cheesy action movies.

Yet today it was conversation over shepherd's pie at the local Irish restaurant and now I was sitting on the couch in his office. After small talk while we settled in, Steve launched in, "You know, the Vineyard isn't old enough as a movement to have retiring pastors. We don't really have any transitions yet. So, Jim, if you're going to be a pastor in the Vineyard, you're going to have to plant a church."

This was one of those moments. Do you know what I'm talking about? When time seems to slow, even stand still. This was one of those for me.

You see, though I was opening to the idea, I still wasn't sure I really wanted to be a pastor. I didn't know what the Vineyard was and I didn't really know if I wanted or what it meant to be in it. And I had no idea what it meant to plant a church. Yet, in that moment, as time hung still, I took a deep breath and answered, "Yes. Sure. I'll do it."

I've spent a lot of time thinking about that conversation.

What was going on inside of me in that moment such that I would say "yes" to an invitation I barely understood, and frankly, on the surface at least, wasn't sure I really even wanted?

In one sense, it was because Steve's invitation awoke my deep passion to be an adventurous overcomer. Taking over an established church in an established denomination? Fine for many people, I'm sure, yet where was the adventure in that for me? Take on a challenge I didn't understand in a community I didn't know, to accomplish an unfolding purpose beyond my capacity? Sign me up! This was a way of doing ministry that spoke to the deep places in me, the parts that had been stirred by the epic quests of fighting dragons, jumping out of airplanes, and committing with my life to sacrificially serve for the greater good.

I also believe there was something else. I've spent a lot of time thinking about how people grow. While there is a lot more that could be said about this, one way that I've come to think of this as something I call the Jiu-Jitsu of Jesus.

In the Jiu-Jitsu of Jesus people grow in relationships of joyful loving connection embedded in a community of strong identity practicing healthy loving correction and service to others.[10]

There seems to be a certain flow in this relationship: ***Inspiration*** → ***Invitation*** → ***Imitation*** & ***Information*** → ***Innovation*** → ***Impediment***, leading back to the cycle repeating.

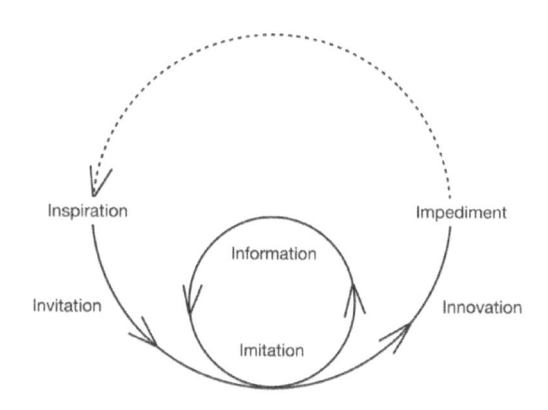

Inspiration — Invitation — Information — Imitation — Innovation — Impediment

We're inspired by the life of someone, moving us to action. They invite us to learn from them or we invite them to teach us. This leads to a cycle of imitation and information working in tandem, and after some time we've developed enough competency and capacity to be able to make that practice our own, innovatively applying it in our own circumstances. As we do so, we bump into impediments and hardships, bringing us back to the learning cycle to go deeper in our growth.

Jesus' school of discipleship is relational, experiential, interactive, holistic and communal. I've observed that in his discipleship dojo, instead of more formally structured settings, Jesus prefers the classroom of common circumstances and the private study of the heart. And again, this discipleship relationship is grounded in loving attachment, with God primarily, and also with our fellow humans, and assumes a longing for another way.

---

[10] To learn more, consider Jim Wilder, *The Other Half of Church*

I say this because that's what I think was happening when I said yes. I was longing for another way. Though it had only been a few months, I had sensed in Steve something I wanted. So when his invitation came to be a pastor and be part of the Vineyard by planting a church, I said "yes," because I experienced it as a way to get what I sensed he had. At the time I would've described that as finally meeting a pastor I would want to be like. My seminary friends had been trying to talk me into being a pastor, but all I could hear was "*Wah wah wah wah.*" Now I had experienced a pastor who had something that I wanted and who was inviting me into a life that I wanted to live.

I think also there was something even deeper going on, yet I'll save that for later in the story.

In the meantime, having said yes to the invitation, the cycle of imitation and information began. At some point around this time, I have no memory of when, I changed my program from the MA in Christian Thought to a Master of Divinity (perhaps the most pretentious degree title ever!). For the next three years I mentored under him. Satay, Chinese buffet, predictable action films, conferences, and lots of conversation and prayer. I often drove Steve to engagements around Chicago so that we could spend time together, especially debriefing the experience on the way home. To this day, 25 years later, if I'm standing and praying for someone, I'll strike the same posture I watched Steve use (right hand extended, left hand on the backside of the left hip, eyes open and looking intently at the person). His mentoring model was intensely relational and has served as a great example throughout my life. There eventually came a period of supervised innovation during my internship. Then it came time to step out and plant a church.

Doin' The Stuff …

It was early Monday morning and I was running to clock in at the small independent custom closet design and installation company where I worked. Though it was still 15 minutes before start time, I knew everyone else in the shop would've been there for at least 15 minutes already. I had called in sick Thursday and Friday the week before. I knew I had to do better since I would begin drawing benefits next week after my three month trial period at the company. I was thinking about all this when I heard my boss, the owner, call my name.

"Hey, Jim. Good morning! Would you mind stepping into my office for a minute?"

"Yes, sir! Of course. Be right there." Putting my punched time card back in its spot, I turned towards his office with a pit forming in my stomach. He motioned me to sit across from him at his desk as he returned to his chair.

Getting right to the point, he asked, "How do you feel it's been going for you with your job at the company, Jim?"

"It's been going pretty good, sir. I know I've not been developing as fast as you'd hoped, but I think I'm finally getting the hang of it. I'm feeling good."

"Yeah, well, I'm not feeling good about it, Jim. You're not developing fast enough. So we're letting you go."

"Today?"

"Yes, Jim. Right now. And don't worry about punching out. We'll take care of that for you."

I grabbed my things and made the long and lonely 30-minute drive back to our apartment. When Meg got home from her job as the floor supervisor at an area nursing home, I shared with her the news: I got fired from my first job stepping out to plant the church. In fact, the first (and only) job I had ever been fired from. Meg graciously gave me a big hug and reminded me all would be well.

Honestly, the job was a misguided idea from the beginning. An old friend of the family worked at this company and told me they were hiring. Only partially tongue in cheek I thought, Jesus had been a carpenter, so I would try that too. The only problem is that I'm not Jesus, in so many ways, including my inability to use an electric screwdriver, plumb a line or single strike hammer a nail. Also, my friend only worked solo in the shop on Saturdays, and I was full-time with the teams during the week, so we never saw each other. Oh well. It was a start. As one of my favorite proverbs says, *"The wise man is he who when he falls down seven times, gets up eight."*[11] In other words, fail forward. Never give up. Adapt and overcome. I took that attitude.

I soon landed a job as a barista on the weekday opening shift at a new Starbucks 10 minutes from our apartment. It was a great job. I took to it seriously. I was that barista who actually read the "Coffee Manual" during the occasional free moments, who knew which beans paired best with which foods and at what times of day, the origins of the beans in the blends and more. I love coffee, and though I'll drink any cup that's even moderately hot and black, I enjoyed embracing the discovery of coffee.

We had a great team. Anne was our ultimate morning shift supervisor. Polite, professional, punctual. She somehow managed to be both light-hearted and serious, and kept the place clean. There was a whole year where typically three of the four on our shift were members of our fledgling church. Our "morning four" could manage the rush, back in the

---

[11] Proverbs 24:16

days of analog espresso machines, and do so while relating well to one another and our customers. We knew their drinks. I still remember some of the nicknames we gave them, like "Tall Coffee and Muffin Top." He was almost always the first customer of the day and would sit reading the first few pages of the New York Times, drinking most of his coffee, eating only the muffin top, and then heading out to wherever the corporate world took him.

We had lots of fun. Reindeer head gear at the holidays. Dancing and singing working the espresso machine. Sitting down with the kindly older Jehovah's Witness who loved to talk to me about religion. We served many of the Red Wings. Steve Yzerman was a quiet gentleman who ordered his tall latte and blended into the crowd. Chris Chelios came in the early afternoons in his stretch black Cadillac with the red trim, ordering a Venti Americano.

One day I was counting out my till in the back room before going home. My manager, Roy, rushed in shouting, "Jim, we need you out front!" "I'm counting my till, Roy, I can't leave it." The normally punctilious Roy retorted, "I don't give a damn about the till, Jim, just get out here right now!" Wondering what was up, I turned the corner out of the backroom and instantly knew: sitting on the counter between the two registers was the Stanley Cup. Steve Duschesne, #28 on the championship team that year, brought the Cup with him on his daily routine and made sure to stop by and see us. He invited me to come around the counter, personally gave me a tour of the cup, allowed me to lift it over my head, and then the Cup handler took our photo.

Being a barista was great preparation for pastoring. I learned a lot about people. The store was located in what had been not long ago one of the five wealthiest ZIP codes in the US. I witnessed how parents handle the pressure of their kids seeing the tempting candy at their eye level on the lowest shelves. I experienced how folks respond to the hardship of their Mocha's being a few degrees different than they expected, or having to pay for both of the cream cheeses with their bagel, as well as how people respond to seeing one of their peers throw a fit in front of them. A regular once offered me two tickets to the Red Wings (from his office's season tickets) if I gave him free Grande Caramel

Macchiatos in return until the value was matched. When I commented that was stealing and I wouldn't do that, he pressed harder. I said no way, my job (to say nothing of my honor) wasn't worth that. A few weeks later he came in and gave them to me and my coworker as a tip. Working at that store was great training ground for ministry and life.

So were the two years I spent substitute teaching after quitting from Starbucks. I subbed in every building in my local public school district as well as spending a lot of time at a local alternative education high school. What a great window into humanity, both the home and culture. Lots of stories, but the one that stands out is the 10th grade girl in the front row who stopped me during my introduction at the start of class with an uncomfortable look in her eyes, "Umm, teacher, I think maybe you should look behind you at the board?" Turning, I saw that my last name "Pool" had been converted to "Poop" and next to it a student had drawn a perfect turd pile, complete with stink lines and a little buzzing fly. I suspected who had done it, but how he had managed to pull that off in the one minute that I stood at the door during passing time has always amazed me. If only that young freshman put equal effort into his classwork. I hope he is experiencing creative success!

This was how the church got started. We didn't launch with a big budget. We received $2500 in startup funds plus about six months of saved up tithe monies from our personal budget. So while we were planting the church, I worked co-vocationally as a barista and then as a substitute teacher, plus the short stint pretending to be a carpenter. All told it was close to five years, and though it was a long time, looking back I wouldn't change it one bit. After those five years I was able to give my full-time attention to pastoring.

It was around this time that our church community laid hands on Meg and me, commissioning us to a lifetime of ministry. This ordination didn't confer anything on me. Rather, it affirmed what God had already done in me, recognizing the track record of my life and labors.

The ceremony, overseen by our board and facilitated by my mentor, was a true celebration. What a special day it was, including testimonies of blessing from family, friends and fellow pastors, not to mention admonitions, exhortations and plenty of prayer. The core message is summarized in these words from my ordination certificate:

> *As a pastor, it will be his task to proclaim by word and deed the Gospel of Jesus Christ, and to fashion his life in accordance with its precepts. He is to love and serve the people among whom he works and lives, caring alike for young and old, strong and weak, rich and poor. He is to encourage and support the Lord's people in their gifts and ministries, nourishing them in God's grace, praying for them, and lifting them up. He is to preach, to declare God's forgiveness to all people, to pronounce God's blessing, to strive for unity among all races, and unity in the Body of Christ, faithfully using all the gifts and talents the Lord has given him.*

These words are a mashup of scriptural passages from Luke 4, Matthew 9, Romans 12, Ephesians 4, and elsewhere. I took them deeply to heart.

Before I tell some stories of how we tried to live out these admonitions in the areas of being "rooted in God," "growing in community" and "reaching out in love," I'd like to draw attention to a significant, yet easily to overlook, dimension of this call: *"fashion his life in accordance with its precepts."* In other words, my life is supposed to match my message. Or, perhaps better said, while inviting others into the transformational love and power of Jesus, it is imperative that I am submitting myself to his same life-changing invitation. I need the ongoing presence of Jesus' gospel in my life as much as everyone I serve, if not more so. I learned this the hard way.

When I heard these words spoken over me, I was harboring judgment in my heart. A common conversation around the time that we moved to plant the church was about the philosophical and cultural idea of "postmodernism" and what was its impact on church practice and theology. One common response amongst many of my peers was a reaction against large institutional expressions of the church and their perceived impersonal nature. In hot tub conversations and hushed corners of conference lobbies, we whispered, taking it for granted that all they cared about was "bucks, butts and buildings." Plus, perhaps, their egos, as these mega pastors grew larger and larger followings. So we thought. (And, very sadly, we were sometimes right.)

I've long had passion for the underdog, for the small and overlooked, for those perceived to be unable. Our first conference in our new church plant (we weren't yet even 40 people) was on the theme of "Small Churches, Big Impact." So this seed of judgment took root in the fertile soil of my heart. It grew quietly in the dark for several years. Sometimes I'd regret it's presence. Other times it might leak out. Then, shortly before I heard that ordination admonition, I met the pastor of one of the largest churches in my denomination. Over a few years, we became friends. I realized he cared about numbers because people matter to God. I realize he cared about money so that the church could generously support the mission of God in his city and around the world. I came to understand that our hearts were aligned around the same purpose though we might have differing principles and practices around how to live that out. God was working on me.

That year I attended a conference for pastors and leaders. I sensed God gently speaking to me as I took my seat at the beginning of the session, but that quickly dissipated during the frankly boring talk. Then, as the speaker invited people to respond in ministry (which I had no intention of doing), I sensed God nudging me again. *"Fine, God,"* I thought to myself, *"I'll do it because you asked me."*[12]

Standing in front of the stage with many others, my large-church friend and a friend of his came to pray for me. The prayer lasted for some time, and it became clear that this long-harbored judgment had opened the door for a demonic spirit. They cast it out of me as I puked all over the sanctuary carpet at the foot of the stage. (For the unfamiliar reader, these things occasionally go hand in hand.) I got to my feet, still wobbly, and looked my friend in the eye, repenting as I confessed my judgment. He received this with love and then graciously prayed for me again, equally powerfully praying for an impartation of gifts and calling in my life. It was a beautiful moment. I was learning to pattern my life after the

---

[12] Cf. Luke 5:5

merciful and generous Jesus who was quick with forgiveness, understanding and love.

Also, it's important to highlight, we didn't plant this church alone. Obviously, it was God's work, and we had a wonderful team with whom we together partnered with God. Seven of us, including Meg and I, spanning four decades of ages (if you count the newborn). Honestly, none of us knew each other well before we got started, and I'm grateful to be able to say we became friends along the way. We had fun together, playing ultimate frisbee at the park, staying up late to watch the Bush-Gore election results, karaoke, and parties to watch the final episode of Survivor.

We knew some hard times, like the dinner meeting at Bakers' Square where we argued at length about principles of ordination for the by-laws we were drafting. We knew disappointment, like those few sessions of our opening Alpha Course where no one came (hence the games of ultimate frisbee!). Our first project as a church planting team was to invite our neighbors to a book club on *Tuesdays with Morrie*, discussed over four Tuesday nights in February. We made some lasting friends of our neighbors in that book club, talked about some deep spiritual topics, and got to know one another better.

One of our central goals was to be a church that was rooted in God, as our members had the roots of their lives in God, helping them learn to practice abiding in Jesus. In addition to many scriptures that were near and dear to me personally, and formed my convictions professionally, we also came at this commitment through what we learned from biology: in a healthy tree, the biomass of the tree's roots is equal to or greater than the biomass of the tree's canopy. So take a break right now and look out your window at the nearest tree. Our neighbor has a huge cottonwood tree in their backyard. I'm amazed by the mass of roots that nourish, sustain and hold it in place. That's what we wanted the disciples of Jesus that participated in the life of our church to experience.

In the section that follows I'll tell some of the many stories I was privileged to be a part of in my 21 years of serving as a pastor. First, as a Jesus-centered community practicing being rooted in God, growing in community and reaching out in love. Next, what it looked like for us to be a great friend to our city, from our neighborhood to the nations. Then I'll share more about the challenges we experienced.

These stories remind me of these words from the Bible: *"You show that you are a letter from Christ, the result of our ministry, written not with ink but with the Spirit of the living God, not on tablets of stone but on tablets of human hearts. Such confidence we have through Christ before God. Not that we are competent to claim anything for ourselves, but our competence comes from God."*[13]

Rooted in God

I think of Anne, my amazing shift supervisor at Starbucks. Those first few months we always used to open the store together. I remember stacking milk crates and organizing pastries in the walk-in cooler when one day she started sharing about some relationship problems she was having with a guy she was interested in. Then, abruptly, she stopped and apologized, "I'm sorry, Jim, you don't want to hear this."

"No, it's cool, Anne," I replied, "I'm happy to listen." With that invitation, she started pouring out her heart and sharing more of her story. Over the coming weeks, relationship problems turned into some gentle questions about spirituality and her faith background, which then became an invitation to join us sometime if she'd like at one of our gatherings so she could reconnect with God. She did, and kept coming back.

A few months later, at one of those Survivor watch parties, she asked, "Jim, how does the church do what it does? How does it, like, pay for stuff?"

---

[13] 2 Corinthians 3:3-5

"Oh, great question. People give of their money to support the work."

"Really? Can I give?"

That was a highlight moment for me. "Can I give?" Seems like that's how it was supposed to be, right? Instead of feeling pressured to give, Anne asked for the opportunity to give in response to what she was experiencing as she reconnected with God and the love she received from others. A couple years later, before she moved back to Chicago to get married, it was so cool to witness her using her organizational and welcoming gifts to run the hospitality ministry at our church.

Sandra lived across the street from the main hangout house in the early days of our church plant. That's how we met her. Naturally friendly and curious, she wondered about all the people frequently coming and going across the street. She and the homeowner, Emma, met and she got invited to the party. Both of Sandra's parents had died tragically in a tornado when she was a young girl and that had, understandably, negatively impacted her spiritual outlook. Now she was married with a young daughter and was struggling to find satisfaction because of this huge hole in her heart from her parents' passing. She kept coming to the parties and getting loved, and we kept coming over to hang out in her backyard too. Wonderfully creative, her backyard was awesome with this cool treehouse. One day some ladies gathered round to pray with her to respond "yes" to Jesus' invitation. Not long later we had the privilege of baptizing her. Over time she found her healing and she put down roots deep into Jesus, sustaining and holding her in the storms that life would bring. God has formed her, and she's been given a presence and a voice that is regularly a blessing to thousands.

Learning to abide in Jesus often begins while we're still exploring who Jesus is and what it looks like to follow him, and it continues over the course of our lifelong journey.

Nate and his wife Amy, plus their newborn Gabe, were three of the members of our church plant core team. For a season, Nate and I worked at Starbucks together. Sometimes, when we both had a Monday morning off, we'd meet up at Bart's Breakfast Club in our downtown. Monday was the only slow day at Bart's, so we could linger and talk, and in time we got to know our waitress, Karen. If no one was around she'd pour coffees and sit and talk with us. In time she would share more of her story with us. Meg and I would also go sometimes, and as we got to know more of the staff, they'd let our rambunctious two-year old son run around without his shoes on and climb on the railing that divided the dining room from the service area.

After maybe a year of eating some of the best breakfasts I've been privileged to enjoy, the entire BQA (Breakfast Queens of America) team agreed to join us for a Bible study at our home. As it turned out, the manager lived on our block, which made it even easier. It was so fun opening our home to them those evenings, sharing stories, discussing the Bible together, and praying. We've stayed in touch with many of them: one still working at another restaurant around town, occasionally bumping into Karen as we go about our errands, and I even officiated a superbly fun wedding for the manager, Colleen, on the front porch of one our city's favorite local pubs. It was a joy to be part of opening up the possibility of what life with Jesus could look like for these ladies.

Jeff and his fiancé Lisa connected with our church for me to officiate the wedding. They decided to stick around and be part of our church community to support them in their marriage too. Jeff was an alternative education teacher. One of the most passionate and skilled teachers I've met, he loved his kids. In fact, both were teachers and Lisa would move on into administrative leadership in her school (which was no surprise as she was a great leader with a sharp mind). Jeff's specialty was the humanities, but he had the mind of a scientist. He had grown up in the church and knew God, yet he had a hard time embracing all the elements of the Christian faith. We often had long talks about the scriptures.

After the service one Sunday he was complaining to me about back pain. I offered to help, asking the question, "Can I pray for you right now?" This was an area that was hard for him. He shrugged his shoulders as much as he could with his hurt back and agreed. I prayed simply for a few minutes amidst all the noise of kids running around and then asked him what the pain was like compared to before. He surprised himself, I think, by indicating that it was a little less. So I prayed again, just as simply and briefly, and then asked again how it felt. I also wondered if he could move it all? He did a little bit of twisting and turning, which he hadn't been able to do before. So we prayed again, this time a little longer and more intently, as the noise of the families faded. After a few more minutes we stopped and he bent over to touch his toes and stretched his arms far behind his back in ways he hadn't been able to do in some time. It took three times, but he was healed!

Mike had joined our church a few years earlier. Though bonded deeply with those he trusted, he was on the suspicious side by nature. He had his heart set on going to the police academy, yet he had failed the Red-Green color blindness test. An understandably important skill for a police officer! He was heartbroken. I suggested we pray. He agreed. We took some time to pray after a gathering, and while nothing dramatic happened, he rescheduled the test for the next available time slot. A week or so later I got the call, "Jim, you'll never believe it, but I passed the color blindness test! I have the documented evidence that God healed me." I'll never forget his testimony in front of the congregation that Sunday. For Jeff and Mike both, God miraculously healed them, helping their roots grow more deeply into the fertile soil of God's love for them.

I met Bill at a community lunch hosted at the church building that our church plant was renting space from. We would sometimes help prepare and serve the food at these monthly meals. Bill lived in the neighborhood, renting a room with others at a large house in the area. We would hang out and talk from time to time over plates of pasta and Styrofoam cups of weak lemonade. He then started volunteering with our hospitality ministry, helping prepare the coffee and refreshments for our community at our Sunday morning service. He wouldn't stay for the service, but he liked meeting some other nice people and appreciated how his service helped him have some purpose.

Bill had some spirituality in his background, and he was also gay, which had led to pain and hurt with the church. At the end of that year, our church plant ended up moving locations, renting space at a school a few blocks away. That small change disrupted our rhythm and I didn't see Bill as much. We did try to stay connected when we saw each other at a coffee shop around town, and I was able to visit with him in his home after he got into some legal trouble and was on a tether. Then things took a terrible turn for the worse. Still on probation, he had a violent altercation with one of his former housemates, landing him a number of years in prison. Bill was estranged from his out-of-state family and had no one else in his life who really cared for him. He asked me and the church to pack up his belongings in storage and he sent me his wallet and personal effects to keep safe awaiting his homecoming from prison.

Bill and I stayed in fairly regular contact during his seven or so years in prison. Occasionally over brief, emotional phone calls, but mostly through letters. I'd pray for him, encourage him, remind him how much he's loved. I shared with him the good news of Jesus. Sometimes we'd fill up his account with money for snacks, and every now and then we'd send him a book. The friendship was as life-giving for me as I think it was for him.

Bill found us when he was released. We helped him move his stuff into a new apartment down the road from our new church building. We helped him find a job with a friend who ran a busy floral shop. Though Bill still didn't attend services, he volunteered at our food pantry when he was able. He radiated joy. About a year later I got a call from my friend, Bill's boss, while on vacation pumping gas with the family in the van, that he had passed. I was grieved at his passing, yet my heart was not heavy, because Bill had been learning to abide. He knew God had rescued him and he knew he was loved.

I look forward with expectant hope to the day I get to see Bill again in the age to come.

Growing in Community

In our church, we not only wanted to help people learn to practice abiding in Jesus, but also to grow in community together. Our discipleship to Jesus is not an independent affair. You can't follow Jesus by yourself. It takes at least one other to practice all the "one another's," like love, bear with, forgive, and more. So our second priority was to grow in community.

It was Sunday evening when I got the call from Brian. We had just finished up dinner so I answered.

Slowing Down To Catch Up With God

"Hey, Brian! How are you? What's up?"

"I'm just calling to let you know, Jim, that we're leaving the church."

I was shocked. I had recently begun to mentor Brian, a father of three, because of his interest in leaving his job at the factory and going into full-time pastoral ministry. We had even begun talking about the possibility of his planting a church.

"Whoa, Brian! I'm very sorry to hear that. Can you tell me what happened?"

That weekend a friend and I had chaperoned three freshmen, including Brian's son Brian, at a youth retreat. On the Friday ride there, after running out of ways to wrestle with each other while buckled in the back row of the van, they concocted the scheme to ask me who I was going to vote for President in the election a few weeks away. I demurred, saying that wasn't something I shared. They cajoled and pestered me as only teenage boys, or dogs with a bone, can do. Maybe it was the monotonous miles along the backcountry rural roads of southern Michigan, but I relented. I shared. I guessed my choice might be different than what they were hearing about at home. The laughs and lighthearted jokes that came my way seemed to support my guess. Then it passed, like an afternoon summer rain, and we had a great retreat.

I suspect that when Little Brian came home that Sunday afternoon, Big Brian asked about the retreat. Like all 9th grade boys everywhere, Little Brian answers, "It was fine, blah blah blah ... oh wait, you'll never guess what, dad! Pastor Jim said he is going to vote for *X*! Hahaha!" Hence the phone call a few hours later.

"Wow. I can hear how important this is for you. Thank you for sharing, Brian. Can I make one request?"

"What's that, Jim?"

"Would you be willing to show me the courtesy of meeting with me one time, simply to talk, before making this decision? I'd like to meet and talk, and bless you in prayer, out of respect for our friendship."

Brian agreed and I began to pray. Thankfully, God began to give me a sense of direction. We met Tuesday night. After greeting each other with the classic bro-hug, I invited Brian to sit on one of the couches in our storefront meeting space while I grabbed a chair.

"Thanks for being willing to meet with me, Brian. Before we begin to talk about the issues you have, I just wanted to share something with you. I've been praying and I've sensed Jesus inviting me to do one simple thing: I wanted you to know that I'm surrendering my constitutional right to vote out of love and respect for you."

"What?!? Whoa. You don't have to do that, Jim!"

"I know I don't. But I want to. Because I love you. And you and our relationship are more important than my constitutional rights, even my right to vote." He sat there, speechless. I think this was the last thing he expected. "And if you don't mind, I would like us to read just one scripture together. Not to convince you of anything, but rather to help you understand how I'm thinking."

"Sure, of course." We opened our Bibles to Ezekiel 16:49-50, *"Now this was the sin of your sister Sodom: She and her daughters were arrogant, overfed and unconcerned; they did not help the poor and needy. They were haughty and did detestable things before me."*

Here we can see God practicing healthy correction of those who identified as his people. The essence of mature, healthy correction is to remind one another (and for God to remind us) of who we are as the people of God, how we behave as the people of God, and humbly and gently helping us see how we were out of alignment with living as our true and best selves in Christ. We're helping one another discover how we can fulfill the godly longing that's in us with something holy and good rather than destructive that puts something else before God.

I could tell he was absorbing the passage. Like had happened with me a year earlier, perhaps he was really hearing it for the first time. "When you read that passage, what does that sound like?"

"America," he said. "Our country." (As an aside, I've repeated variations on this conversation with several dozen other people when political controversy comes up, and when I ask that question, I get the same answer at least 9 times out of 10.)

"I agree. Interesting, isn't it? And sad. What else stands out to me is that those issues sound a lot like the various concerns on both the Left and the Right. In other words, the social and moral concerns of both political persuasions are topics the Bible—and God—care deeply about."

"I hadn't ever noticed that." Brian then went on to share about the issues that were important to him. It was clear his convictions were deep, thoughtful and heartfelt. I did my best to really be present with him, even as he had done for me. Our conversation managed to avoid being about trying to convince one another and instead to honor and love one another. It worked. He didn't leave the church. Instead, we parted that evening with a big hug; he went into ministry and invited me to lay hands on him at his ordination. We remain friends to this day.

A few years into our church plant, it became apparent that we needed a structure more robust than simply our founding church plant team. So, after some prayer and discussion (I think now we could've used more of both!), we divided up responsibilities. Some of us joined a few others and became ministry leaders in the church while the rest joined together and formed our local church board.

One of those board members was Paul. He was a Detroit native, ten years older than me, and had nurtured a decades long passion to see a Vineyard church planted in his home suburb. Paul was an intercessor, loved mentoring younger guys new to the faith and was passionate for bringing the gospel to those on the margins. He was also a major details guy that thoroughly double checked everything. Whereas I was a "Ready,

Fire, Aim" leader by nature, Paul preferred "Ready, Aim, Double Check Aim, Triple Check Aim, Fire."

I loved to brainstorm and would routinely bring brainstorm ideas to the board meeting, maybe two or three at a time. (I know, now, bad idea.) For each of those ideas, Paul was thinking about the 20 or more things that would need to be done to make it a reality. And I wasn't even necessarily committed to any of them. They were just brainstorms. Paul would ask a hundred questions and get overwhelmed. I would feel shut down and take personal offense. It's a little embarrassing to say it, but it's true. This pattern persisted for several years. Thinking back on it now, I'm absolutely amazed at Paul's patience. Did he lose his cool sometimes? Yes. I got mad plenty of times, too, pace around, then slump in my seat as someone else on the board would suggest we "move on to other pressing matters." The breakthrough came a few years (!) in, when I encountered teaching on how different Meyers-Briggs types tend to function on teams. The dynamic between Paul and I (to say nothing of my wife and me, who shared the exact same pattern) was articulated perfectly by the Brainstormer and Inspector roles. So helpful. It revolutionized the relationship.

What I appreciate about both Paul and Brian is their prioritizing the relationship. And they lived that out as they committed to the practice of listening and longsuffering, patience and being present. That's what helps us grow in community.

Any time you have two or more people in relationship trying to accomplish something interesting or meaningful, there is going to be difference of opinion. Conflict in community is inevitable. True peace is not the absence of such conflict, it is reconciliation and maturing relationship on the other side. Growing in community involves conflict resolution.

Like almost every contemporary pastor, I sometimes showed movie clips during my sermons. Actually, I'm mildly surprised there isn't a seminary class on this practice yet. The only thing I remember on the topic is when our preaching professor instructed us to never let the illustration overshadow the scriptural message. I blew that one Sunday.

Perhaps you're familiar with the Jay & Silent Bob cult classic, *Dogma*. It features Matt Damon and Ben Affleck as fallen angels trying to make their way in the world when the Papacy declares a Year of Jubilee and forgiveness of sins for anyone who makes a pilgrimage to one of a select group of cathedrals around the world. Fair warning: this is not an "all audiences" faith & spirituality channel movie. Yet buried in the movie is, in my opinion, one of the clearest, most compelling articulations of the gospel in any movie I've ever watched. Bartleby, Affleck's angered fallen angel, is speaking:

"My eyes are open. For the first time, I get it. See, in the beginning, it was just us and him, angels and God ... and then he created humans. Ours was designed to be a life of servitude and worship. ... He gave them more than He ever gave us – He gave them a choice. They choose to acknowledge God, or choose to ignore Him. All this time we've been down here, I've felt the absence of the divine presence, and it's pained me, as I'm sure it's pained you. And why? Because of the way He made us! Had we been given free will, we could choose to ignore the pain, like they do. ... These humans have besmirched everything He's bestowed upon them. They were given paradise – they threw it away. They were given this planet – they destroyed it. They were favored best among all His endeavors, and some of them don't even believe He exists! And in spite of it all, He has shown them infinite fucking patience at every turn."[14]

It was such a powerful moment. But I screwed it up. Did you catch it? I forgot to bleep the word. I had set up the clip myself and our sound guy played it. I didn't know how to insert a beep, and when the moment came I didn't even attempt a well-timed dramatic cough. The sermon went on.

But that night I got a strongly worded email from an older member of the congregation. More than being personally offended, he thought that "announcing the gospel of truth with a curse word" was flat out wrong, to paraphrase him. He offered a few biblical quotes and personal reflections. I think he was over-reacting a bit. We've since revisited the

---

[14] https://en.wikiquote.org/wiki/Dogma_(film)

story and I think he'd probably agree. I could've reacted in return, firing off a missive of my own. Something about that didn't sit right. So I acknowledged his email, his feelings and then took the matter to prayer. After a few days of reflection, we exchanged emails and I publicly apologized the next Sunday. Some in the congregation felt I had done nothing wrong, believing it was spot on, yet I was able to see how I could've done more to avoid an offense.

What I appreciate about my friend, Jake, is that while maybe he could've handled it better, at least he didn't stew in his bitterness or, even worse, grouse with others in the church. He came to me quickly and directly to share his offense, to seek understanding and pursue relationship. In churches, especially for the pastor or any leader of any organization, there are many opportunities for this.

About five years later our church merged with a small and struggling church. This involved a building, some new ministries, and involvement in our new hometown. One of my first acts as a leader was to remove the American flag and the "Christian flag" from the stage before our first Sunday. While talking with folks following our second service as a newly combined church, I was approached by Betty, a matriarch of the American Baptist Church with whom we had merged. She asked me (it maybe felt a little more like told me) to sit down so we could talk.

"What's on your mind, Betty?"

"Well, Jim, we noticed that you got rid of the flags. What I want to know is why did you take down the American flag?"

"Ah. Thank you for coming and asking me, Betty. It's a good question. Well, I took down the American flag because our church isn't about America."

"Well, this is America and we're all Americans here."

"Certainly we're in America, Betty, yet actually we're not all Americans. One of the cool things about our church is we've got people in our community from several countries: Ethiopia, Japan, Jamaica and more. Also, I'm sure you'd agree that we'd really like to reach more of our community and help other young people in our city get to know Jesus." She nodded her assent. "I knew you would. Well, I can assure you that if the young people in our city that I know came in here and saw that American flag on the stage, the first thing that they'd think of, before they ever heard anything that we're trying to say, the first thing they'd assume is that we're a bunch of nationalist right wingers."

"Well, I never ..." It was clear that this idea alarmed her. By now a growing group of onlookers was joining the conversational circle.

"Betty, I don't know your politics, and I won't ask unless you want to tell me, but it certainly seems that maybe this idea would be unsettling to you." She nodded again. "We don't want people making assumptions about us, right? Especially before we've even had a chance to communicate our hearts. And while we love America, our church isn't about America, it's about Jesus."

"Okay, I get what you're saying. But what about the Christian flag? If that's true, why did you get rid of that?"

"I appreciate you asking. First, that flag has no real history. It's a modern convention. What's more, think about this: I'm going to guess that, like me, you'd be pretty excited if some of our Muslim neighbors joined us here to discover more about Jesus." She smiled and nodded. "And if one of those Muslim guests saw that flag, I'm concerned that, again, before we ever had a chance to communicate our heart, they'd think back to the Christian flags of the Crusades, or more recently to the anti-Muslim rhetoric following 9/11, and their hearts would be shut before our mouths were ever opened. And besides, we don't need a Christian flag as a symbol of our faith. We already have one, the only one we'll ever need – the Cross – which you'll notice I didn't take down from the stage."

"Well, thank you, Jim. I hadn't thought of those things like that. I appreciate you sharing. But I've got one more question." Grabbing the neckline of my t-shirt she asked, "Would it hurt you to wear a shirt with a collar once in a while?" We laughed together.

Another aspect of growing in community is making space for people from diverse backgrounds, people who've perhaps been marginalized from the community of God's people. We need to create space for them to experience love and encounter God. The church has often thought of the progression being ***Believe → Behave → Belong***. Yet, from my experience and study, I've observed humans flourish most the other way around: ***Belong → Behave → Believe***. It all begins with joyful, loving attachment. As we experience belonging, we begin to live into the practices of "our people." Then our beliefs are shaped and formed to align with our community. Sadly, the other way typically devolves into compliance and control.

Andy came to us through his friend, George. They were both without homes. George had a bike and a little trailer that he pulled behind the bike as he rode around town. Through amazing ingenuity, he had improved the trailer with portions of a tent and more, so that it was a bike RV. George found a place a live, took his bike with him, and left the trailer tent RV for Andy. After a few days we noticed Andy living in the trailer in the back corner of our parking lot. We talked to him, agreed to let him stay with a few basic "house rules," and let him use the address for the church building so he could access his benefits, get an ID and such. Andy loved his new home. Even in the winter when our church hosted a warming center for our homeless neighbors, he would join us for dinner, but head out at night to sleep in the trailer instead of taking advantage of our mats and blankets in the sanctuary. Having grown up on a southern farm, his wisdom was a huge help in cultivating the vegetable garden we grew to augment our food pantry.

Over time Andy grew comfortable in his new environment, and he spent more and more time on the stoop outside our main door, rolling cigarettes and greeting people as they came. He was our unofficial welcoming team. For a while we experimented with a Monday night service we called "Second Chance Church." The idea was to open a space for folks in town that worked in the hospitality industry to encounter God. That never really developed. A few people who slept in on Sunday mornings did come. And one of those was Andy. At first he'd find a seat outside the doors to the sanctuary and greet people as they went in, then listen to what was going on. Eventually he found a seat on one of the pews in the back. And then, one night, I'll never forget, he wobbled down the center aisle to receive communion. From that time forward he'd often join us on Sunday mornings, sometimes sitting among his friends in our congregation, other times alone.

We got him into a 30-day rehab and he did great. Upon his release, he stayed with some friends of our congregation. Then he returned home to his trailer and the streets got the best of him. Within the year he was hit by a car when he stumbled into the street and died not long after from complications. We were grieved by the news. He had no family that we knew of. So our leadership team decided to host a memorial service in his honor. Dozens of our members attended the candlelit evening gathering, weeping, laughing, sharing memories, giving thanks for the privilege of getting to know Andy, trusting in the mercy of God that one day we'd meet again.

Another story involves my friend, Chris. For the 10th anniversary celebration of our church we cancelled our normal sermon and instead heard testimonies from ten people whose lives had been impacted by the church. He had been part of our church community for four or five years at that point. I still remember the first time I spoke with Chris and Jack before the service over coffee and donuts. "We just celebrated our first anniversary this weekend! We bought bikes for each other and took a ride." Within a few weeks they asked to meet with us. Not long after they sat in our living room and poured out their story. Chris was a transgendered female to male, married to Jack, his husband. They had met and married at another church, as Christine and Jack. Jack had known about Chris's gender identity confusion and was supportive of the transition. When they showed up the next Sunday as Chris and Jack, the pastor brought them into his office and demanded Chris change and come back as Christine, or they wouldn't be welcome. Deeply pained, they left and never returned.

Jack remembered me from my season serving as an interim pastor. He had been attending the church during that season, before we closed it. That's when he found a new church and met Chris. Newly married and hurt, they spent a year in various pro-gay churches around the metro area. "Nothing against those churches, Jim, they're full of nice people, but after a year we really just want a church that is centered more on Jesus and not just on sexuality," is what they told me over frosted donuts and coffee at the back of our sanctuary.

As my wife and I continued to meet regularly with the two of them, listening to their story and coaching them in next steps to faithfully follow Jesus, we learned that Chris was a musician. Playing on the worship team was the main way Chris experienced the presence of God in his life. Our standing policy was for interested folks to engage in the life of the church, particularly through participating in a small group, before stepping up to any ministry on the stage. They totally understood and did just that. Six months later Chris approached me about being on the team. I knew that having a transgendered person on our worship team would likely be a big thing for our congregation. Meg and I talked and prayed it through. I had several long talks over breakfast with our worship director. We all agreed to give it a go. Chris played on the team at a community outreach for our neighbors during the holidays and then joined the Sunday rotation. It all seemed to be going fine.

A few months later one of our leaders pulled me aside and asked to meet with me. They shared their concerns about the worship ministry, not just about Chris being on the team, but even more about how I had failed to process the decision with them. It quickly became clear they weren't alone and there was widespread dissent. Caught between a rock and a hard place, my choice to honor Chris's privacy cost me a lot of equity with my leaders. It was an untenable situation.

Around this same time, Chris and Jack were in our membership class at the church. After the next session, I approached the two of them and asked to speak. Verklempt, I told them I needed to make a difficult choice because there were some concerns about Chris's participation in the worship ministry. I asked them to pause their membership process while I worked it out. Jack pleaded for the opportunity to meet with whomever was upset and explain their story. Chris simply cried. It was the lowest moment of my ministry to that point. I explained it wasn't any one person. In fact, it was me who had failed. I had failed them in my leadership, and I had failed the other leaders in my leadership. I needed to make it right, and to do that, it would be best if I had a little space. As painful as it was, they agreed. We prayed. Our hearts were very heavy. I hoped they'd have the patience and graciousness to stay connected during the process. I wasn't disappointed. Though they shied away from the Sunday service because it was so painful, they remained faithfully committed to their small group community. To this day I am amazed at Chris's courage.

Meanwhile, my friend Nate and I started meeting with our leadership team. Over the course of the meetings, we uncovered lots of thoughts, lots of emotions, some clear, others confused. Through it all we had some really important conversations. A breakthrough came when Nate was able to synthesize what we had heard over our times together, "Sure, many of us might be uncomfortable with Chris's participation on the worship team, maybe even his involvement in our church. But think of his courage. He literally wears what he's struggling with right out in the open. How many of us would be willing to come to next Sunday' service with a t-shirt on that listed our secret struggle, our hidden sin, our area of brokenness? Not many, I'd guess. That's what stands out to me, Chris's courage in showing up week after week, seeking God."

The process took longer than I had hoped for, yet I clearly remember the day Chris walked into the office where our new worship director and I sat. His feet shuffled, his face crestfallen. We each took a few moments to appreciate Chris, to recognize his courage, honor his perseverance, acknowledge the messiness of it all. Then we invited him back on the worship team. We apologized for the delay yet expressed gratitude for the hard work that had been done by our team. I'm not sure I've ever seen a bigger transformation from a pastoral meeting. He walked out that door with a bounce in his step and smiling ear to ear.

Less than a year later he stood up at that anniversary service and shared how he had finally found a church, a community, where he was welcomed and loved. The kind of church he had hoped existed, where God was taken seriously and people were loved deeply. He wasn't the only one crying. He stayed with us for ten more years.

As I reflect on Chris's story, what stands out to me is his faithfulness to his small group. What I've discovered is that the main way people grow in community is through smaller communities where you can gather face to face in loving, joyful relationship. We made a pretty good start of this in our church plant, yet as it grew and progressed, we struggled. There was one season (Chris's season), where we had four groups: three of which were led by guys with Masters of Divinity degrees, and the other was an avid reader who would become a church planter.

This was not sustainable. The standard for small group leaders could not be theological degrees and/or full-time ministry if we were going to maintain and grow our community. If I think about the "Breakfast Queens of America" and our later youth group, they all had pre-existing community outside of our church bubble, and we introduced the "Jesus dimension" inside of that. We did have some programs that could have been engines for developing groups, but the culture of the church post-merger, plus a denominational shift towards semester-based groups (which functioned more like classes) presaged trouble in maintaining healthy, growing community.

Reaching Out in Love

For several years our church rented the fellowship hall, some classrooms and an office from a big church on Main Street in our urban suburban community. That city hosted the annual AIDS Walk for metro Detroit. One Sunday morning every September, more than five thousand people passionate to help those who have suffered from the devastating effects of HIV and AIDS walked right by our building as they approached the end of their route in the city center. That first year, as I considered the people proceeding by our front door, I thought to myself, *"What are we doing?"* We care about the plight of those suffering from AIDS. We want to bless those who have the courage to walk in their support, to march in memory of those who've passed. These were exactly the people we'd love to serve in love, in Jesus' name, and here they were walking right by us as we were shut up in our building. Instead of serving them, we were having a service. So at the end of our gathering that Sunday, I announced that next year we'd do something different and take advantage of the opportunity. People were excited.

Next year came and we decided to invite people walking by to come back to our building after they were done for a free lunch after our service. A few friendly folks came, and our team was generous, but honestly, it was pretty lame. I had settled for an option that was safe, not courageous.

For the third year, we delivered on our promise to do something different. In place of our service, we threw a party right in our front courtyard: grills cooking hot dogs, chips and cookies, water for humans and dogs alike, tables for people to rest and our band playing cover tunes, plus members from the church cheering people on and giving high fives of love. It was amazing. Our team did such a great job! We did all this with permission from the AIDS Walk organizers. We had reached out to them telling them we wanted to participate by throwing a party. They were cool with that. But our party exceeded even our expectations. So around lunch time, one of the event organizers showed up, wondering why the walk was going slower than normal that year. I mentioned that we had asked permission and apologized if we had caused any problems. He looked around, a little amazed at the sight. "No, it's not a problem at all," then, with a slight pause, "You did all this for us?"

"Yes, absolutely. We did it because we love you."

He turned and looked at me and offered a simple, "Thank you." Starting to walk away, he turned again and invited me to the after-party at one of the gay bars in town.

"Thank you. I'd love to come. I'll see what I can do."

After helping the team clean up and praying for a few folks who had some needs, I walked over to the bar. Walking in, I noticed the bar was pretty empty with just a few couples quietly enjoying their drinks. The back patio was the scene of the action. It was so jammed with bodies there was no way I was getting in. I strained to stand as high on my toes as possible to see if I could see the guy who invited me. No luck. I suddenly became very aware of my bright red t-shirt with our church logo specially made for the day. I felt the bright glare of imagined spotlights highlighting me as a Christian and wondered what the barflies would think. After a few awkward moments deciding what to do, I sheepishly returned to my car at the church building and drove home.

In that moment I realized the courage of every LGBTQ person who has ever visited our church, seeking God and a community of love.

There is a brief teaching of Jesus, spoken while a guest at a "see and be seen" dinner party, that has convicted Megan and I since we were dating, *"When you give a luncheon or dinner, do not invite your friends, your brothers or sisters, your relatives, or your rich neighbors; if you do, they may invite you back and so you will be repaid. But when you give a banquet, invite the poor, the crippled, the lame, the blind, and you will be blessed. Although they cannot repay you, you will be repaid at the resurrection of the righteous."*[15] This is bracing stuff.

For us that banquet has always been Thanksgiving. We love Thanksgiving. For me, it's got all the good stuff: good people, good food and drink, plus a few days off, without any of the religious responsibilities. Several pastors in our municipal clergy group tried to launch an ecumenical Thanksgiving service. I told them to go for it if they wanted, but I wouldn't be there, and I wouldn't advertise it so there'd be no expectation I attend since it's the one major holiday we really get off! I digress. A good Thanksgiving for us is when our table is overflowing with a wide assortment of people. If you've been to our home for Thanksgiving and reading this, trust me, you were one of the upstanding guests! Yet we tried also to have plenty of people over who couldn't repay: teenagers whose parents were working and had nowhere else to go, homeless, addicts, ex-Jehovah's Witnesses, troubled pastors, and more. We tried our best to bless people who otherwise would be lonely, hungry and without the warmth of love and laughter on that day, to give them at least one thing to be thankful for that Thanksgiving. Every year, for Megan and I, one of our gratitudes was those guests. Always.

After ten years of pastoring in one suburb, bouncing around between an apartment building community room, a senior community center classroom, a storefront, a church fellowship hall, and an auditorium-type space at a middle school, we finally moved to a neighboring suburb and acquired a permanent building by merging with an aging congregation. More on that to follow.

---

[15] Luke 14:12-14

After a year of getting grounded in the new building with the merged congregation, we launched a sermon series we called *Mission Possible: Ferndale*. It would kick off our second full year in the building post-merge. Each sermon in the five week series would touch on some practical ways to love our neighbors. Nate & I brainstormed ideas to make it awesome. He came up with the awesome idea that for that first sermon, he'd introduce me and I would run up to the stage to the *Mission: Impossible* theme song. I loved it. I took it one step further: I would rappel into the sanctuary and then run up to the stage to that song. I had rappelled before at West Point.

Above the back of our sanctuary was a youth room that may have once been a choir loft. It was walled in with just one small window opening. We decided to do it. I bought the rope, Nate secured a point to tie off to, and our friend George was on belay. Nate introduced me, the theme song played, and I rappelled into the sanctuary. Since no one knew to look up behind them, a number of people didn't even know what was happening. It took me twice as long to squeeze through the window as it did to rappel down, which meant my butt was the only thing people could see of me for like 30 seconds. It was easily the most ridiculous thing I ever did as a pastor. Mercifully, it was a holiday weekend and attendance was low.

Still, it was awesome and I would do it again in a heartbeat. A few people in the church thought I was crazy, and I've often been made fun of by my pastoral friends. Yet as I type this, I'm reminded of a story of King David, who danced with abandon in gratitude for all God had done. As David said in response to those who didn't understand, I would gladly *"become even more undignified than this, and I will be humiliated in my own eyes,"*[16] if only it meant I could honor God and encourage Christians to love their neighbors with generous and gracious abandon.

The people of that church took seriously loving their neighbors. Together, we sought to be a great friend to our city. We wanted to be "the best friend our city ever had."

---

[16] 2 Samuel 6:22

Our food pantry team has served well over a hundred people every month for more than two decades, sometimes even a hundred families. During the Covid shutdown, we bought a shed so that check-in workers could be outside and stay warm during the winter months, reconfigured our distribution process, and kept carts full of groceries in the back of our sanctuary so that guests could stay fed. The pantry team was routinely recognized by our primary partner agency, and one year a local non-profit recognized the director as one of the "Good Neighbors of the Year." We partnered with fifth grade classes to pack Thanksgiving feasts and taught the kids about the importance of food security. To supplement our pantry offerings with healthier food options, we converted some open space into a vegetable garden tended by members and friends of the church, under the watchful eyes of Andy.

We also hosted a seven-to-fourteen-day shelter for our homeless friends around the turn of the calendar each new year. We housed as many as 110 women and men each night, offering a hot meal, a safe place to sleep, and most important of all, the warmth of friendship. Not to mention occasional haircuts, a quick look over by a nurse, and eventually a fully stocked clothing closet freestore. Our shelter leadership built a large enough and committed enough volunteer team that we were able to consistently encourage volunteers to visit with guests and share a meal with them. This was a highlight for guests and hosts alike. Our team routinely heard we were the favorite stop on the shelter circuit. If there were enough openings, I'd volunteer two nights with whomever of my family wanted to join me, and I loved cooking up beef stroganoff and my own favorite Sloppy Jim recipe served over spaghetti. Sure, someone once tried to fight me and every year had its headaches, but we loved when we learned that guests were not returning this year because they had found a way to get off the streets. One of my all-time favorite memories is of my friend, Terry, a middle school technology teacher at a local charter school, taking the shoes and socks off of a guest passed out in drunkenness, and weeping as he washed his feet.

One of the heroes behind all this work was my friend, Janet. Janet was very hard of hearing, even with hearing aids, and had maybe 50% function in only a very narrow field of vision at the center of her eyes. Yet she served at the pantry every week and was at the warming center every night we were open. Her mother had been the first church secretary.

A few folks gave some money to our benevolence fund to bless Janet in some way. A close friend of hers had a great idea to buy her new hearing aids. I had another possibility: taking Janet with our team on the church's next trip to Ethiopia.[17] Janet had been a lifelong supporter of missions and missionaries, both with prayer and finances. We decided to ask her and give her the choice. When I mentioned the possibility of Ethiopia to Janet, she responded with "Oooh!" and her eyes smiled with all the assent I needed. What a team that was! My twelve-year old son and I, a newlywed couple, a few others, and Janet at 70 years old, making her first mission trip. Her calm and joyful presence mediated the presence of God and to see her walking with our Ethiopian partners, arm in arm, was a delight I'll never forget.

I'd like to close this chapter with a story that I think ties together so much of what we were trying to do. I first met my friend Rod at our warming shelter for our homeless neighbors. He had gotten involved through another friend. Both lived in town and attended one of the many recovery groups that our church hosted at our building. Occasionally we'd see each other around the building before or after his group and we'd chat. We would often talk at the shelter while he staffed the smoke break door for our guests and volunteers. He was a thoughtful, compassionate, young, gay atheist. He was funny and kind and a gracious volunteer. Rod was curious and we would sometimes talk about Jesus and his Way. He found the AA meeting too theistic, so he moved on to a Zen Buddhist AA group in town. Yet he continued to volunteer at the shelter.

One day I was serving at the shelter and was headed to the basement kitchen to wash the dishes and clean up when I saw Rod walking my way. I asked if he'd like to join me. Always helpful, he agreed. Descending the stairs, we started talking. "You know, Pastor Jim," he opened, "though we like each other, there is a lot we don't agree on."

---

[17] https://vineyardusa.org/vineyard-missions-highlight-take-janet-with-you/

"Yeah, I know," I replied, "and I appreciate how we've always found a way to be respectful to each other."

"Yes, of course," Rod answered, "we don't see eye to eye on so many things. Yet, you know, I defend you."

"I'm curious. What do you mean by that, Rod? I'm interested to hear more."

"Well," he continued, "I'm sure you know, that there are lots of people around town that don't like you."

"Yes, I'm aware. Very aware."

"Yeah, they really don't like you, Jim. I hear them talking about you and saying all kinds of things about you."

"How many of them do you think have ever asked me about those things, Rod?" It seemed he had never thought about that and we talked about how, in my experience, some people made a lot of assumptions about me. A few of them true, perhaps, and others false, with most somewhere in between.

"I'm sure that's true, Jim. But that's not really the point. Here's what I'm trying to say. A lot of people I know, whom I do agree with, don't like you. And yet I find myself defending you, even though I disagree with you." He was very emphatic at this point. Clearly this was touching an emotion. "Do you know why?" he continued, "because of this …" At which time he pointed to all that was going on around us. "I defend you because of your service to the community, especially to the poor and homeless and hungry. Even though there is a lot we don't agree on, Jim, you and this church really love and serve others, and so I defend you to my friends." Now it was my turn to be emotional as we continued to scrub the pots and pans together.

Slowing Down To Catch Up With God

Where's Waldo?

I checked into Facebook and noticed that I had been tagged in a post. A friend of mine had seen me walking around town and posted a photo of me, along with some remarks about how I was always walking. Queue the comments as friends of mine, and friends of those friends, chimed in about my walking habits, observing that I might be seen anywhere. In fact, it had become fairly normal for people to honk, even yell out my name through open windows, when they saw me walking down the street. So much so that to this day, if I hear an unexpected honk, my reflex response is to turn to see what friend might be passing by.

One of the comments was my friend Cora, wife of a well-loved high school teacher, "You're like the Waldo of Ferndale. We never know where we'll find you." After a few jokes about this, Cora commented next from the checkout line at the craft store, where she had gone to buy red and white yarn so that she could engage her skills in knitting me a Waldo-style hat. Despite the obvious irony of my vocation, I'm not particularly religious, but I wore that hat religiously for several years. I still have it today, though I've shifted to the warmer beanie cap that was given as swag from my 25th reunion at West Point.

86

Our Neighborhood ...

The first ten years of our church plant we spent a lot of time cultivating the practice of reaching out in love. We did that both as a community and in our family's living out the Way of Jesus. It wasn't until we relocated our church gathering from Royal Oak to the neighboring suburb of Ferndale, the city where many of us lived, that we pursued the habit of being a great friend to our city. Perhaps it was the hometown advantage or maybe the smaller population and geographic area. I'm sure a key dimension was that the American Baptist Church with which we merged had a steady history of serving the poor of the community through the food pantry and warming center I've previously mentioned. We didn't invent these ministries, we simply helped what was already happening faithfully through tremendous effort, to be a little more efficient, a little better resourced, and hopefully a little more fruitful.

Shortly after our church merger, Megan and I were walking through the downtown and wondering how we'd be able to best serve our city. Lots of churches focus on the schools, due to a shared sense of educating the young. What's more, churches like having families around because they're understood to bring stability. We got that, but we didn't want to compete with any of the churches already serving in that space, and since we already had kids in the local schools, that felt sorta natural. As we approached our dinner date destination, we wondered, "What about the business community?" Alongside the schools, businesses are an engine of well-being for any city. I talked it over with our Board Vice President the next Sunday. Carmen heartily agreed, saying she had long thought it would make sense for us to get involved there. So we became members of our local chamber of commerce.

I really appreciated our participation in this group. The chamber held twice monthly "coffee connections" where local business owners mingled with community leaders from other sectors of society—municipal, non-profit, education—for networking, relationship building and such. Then we'd circle up and share our 30-second elevator pitch of what we were about or what we had going on. I was often the only member of the clergy represented. I'll tell you what: it was definitely soul-stretching to stand in that circle and come up with 30 seconds of something to say to a room of people who really didn't care what we were doing and didn't understand what we were about. That's why I kept going. It was a great opportunity to get creative in communicating who we were and translating it for secular and non-churchgoing spiritual people.

A big boost to our efforts at reaching out in love came at a chamber of commerce meeting one day. A new friend, Nancy, approached me with an idea. She had seen that I was active on Facebook and wondered if we could start a Facebook group that would replicate, in a digital space, the best of what we were experiencing in this face-to-face chamber coffee connection. The goal would be to bring people together, both residents and contributors from all around the community, to get people out of their silos and seek our city's success. We opened the group and each invited 100 friends to join. It grew daily, hitting nine thousand members in two years. We heard that realtors recommended the Forum to home buyers as one of the best places to find out what was going on in the city. Two months after launching, there was a big flood in our area and the Forum was a great resource. Our church became a drop-off point for generous residents contributing cleaning supplies to others in need and our church was one of several hubs for coordinating volunteer clean-up efforts for residents needing a hand.

The next year I made the commitment to walk every street in my city. In retrieving archived files after my laptop crashed, I stumbled upon an old digital note I had made to myself with a word I had heard God speak to me several years earlier when we first merged the church. I sensed God saying he meant it as more than a good idea, so I printed off a map of our city, secured a highlighter and started marking off the streets I walked. Several months and more than 100 miles later, I completed my project. I was shocked by the amount of attention I received, in the form of local articles online and in print. As others pointed out, election volunteers, postal workers, and our local newspaper delivery people, walk the city far more often.

Far more than the attention, the main effect of all this walking was what it did in me. I discovered that one sees the world differently when walking, specifically when I slowed down to walk. I don't just see cars,

I see people. I noticed my neighborhood and all the cool little hidden gems in it, like the houses that have stone gates with lions, the funky house with the New Orleans Garden District décor, and so much more. In making walking my primary mode of transportation, I began to approach my city with my whole self. In walking around town, I began to keep pace with my soul. Soon I discovered that people I knew around town, restaurant owners and journalists, started calling me the Three Mile an Hour Pastor, as in "Hey, look, it's our three mile an hour pastor." These people had no pastoral relationship to our church.

It's like, through walking, God was bringing into being something that he had whispered to me while I was in a down moment. In one of those very restaurants, while waiting for someone who was late to an appointment, I looked out the window at all the people busily walking by. "How will I ever reach all these people, God?" I wondered to myself. "Our church is so small."

"Don't worry about that, Jim," I heard God gently encourage. "You just be their pastor. Your congregation is 20,000 people. It's just that 19,875 of them don't attend services yet."

A few years later I left administering the Forum, leaving it in more capable hands with my co-founder continuing on. Yet I didn't stop being engaged in the city. On one occasion, Megan and I were invited by our witch friend to participate in a spiritual gathering to promote healing for victimized women, as part of the larger #MeToo movement. We said we'd be happy to help, but that "the only thing we have to give is Jesus. Is that okay?" The three of us met at a local coffee shop and we told her about how Jesus had brought kindness and healing to the woman with the twelve year issue of blood.[18] Our friend loved the story, so the night of the event, I retold it, and then Meg led the women (along with the few men) gathered in a prayer to encounter Jesus in his healing love.

In the wake of the back-to-back shootings in Baton Rouge and Dallas, I reached out to our Mayor about hosting a gathering for hope and healing for our city. He loved the idea and said, "You do it." I took the invitation. I called my friend, Laila, an African American woman on our

---

[18] Mark 5:25-34

city council, and we agreed to co-host an event in our city's memorial park. At the gathering we shared stories, information on ways to get involved, invitations to consider ways we've been harmed and ways we've caused harm, and how we can receive and give help. For those that were interested we also had an opportunity for prayer. I was honored to be part of the experience. Then, when the war in Ukraine began, our business community invited me to help host a candlelight vigil outside city hall. These were all moving experiences.

Somewhere along the way, it seems I became probably the best-known Christian in our city. I'm pretty sure maybe the Bible has some things to say about how that shouldn't be our ambition, so it's not really anything to boast about. Yet it happened. And it wasn't without a cost. My kids were sometimes harassed in school. The marquee outside our church building was changed from "Pointing People to Jesus" to "Pooping on Jesus" and then later to something that's not appropriate for even this occasionally irreverent memoir. Someone took a photo of that marquee and made it the cover photo of another social media group in our city, some of whose members I'd served on school committees with, had over to my home for dinner, prayed for and given money to when they were in hard times. The very group I had helped start turned toxic and after I had been asked to offer a prayer at the onset of our new city council, someone in the group put up a very hateful post about me. As three different friends put it to me, "Jim, they're saying some really terrible things about you, and none of your friends are sticking up for you." I thought to myself, somewhat ironically, *Wait, aren't you one of my friends?*

On another occasion, while walking the streets of our city, I heard this disembodied voice whisper harshly in my soul, "We hate you here, Jim." While worshipping in song during some Sunday service, I had this vision of fireballs being cast against the building of our church, as some dark spiritual power tried to attack us spiritually.

Then I had what I can only be described as a "hairball demon" cast out of me at a Missional Leaders' Conference in the fall of 2016, in what was probably the hardest year of my ministry career. I know the idea of a "hairball demon" might seem like a hairbrained idea to some of my dear readers, but I don't know of another way to describe it.

I was at this conference, that I was on the planning team for, and was scheduled to speak later that evening, in fact. A team of folks started praying for me. The room was thick with the sense of the presence and the power of God. As they prayed, I saw this picture in my mind's eye of myself wearing this metal armor. Like I said, it had been a tough year, and it seems I had unconsciously armored myself up emotionally to protect myself. As my friends prayed, I could see the armor peel away and underneath my skin was covered with a thousand paper cuts. In my spirit I could sense the pain of all that. Not only had I been hurt by people, but as we prayed an image formed in my mind of me walking through my downtown. Emanating out of several storefronts were these shimmery waves, like the heat that rises from a grill filled with a bed of coals, except these were evil spiritual powers, and every time I walked through them I would get a little cut. Eventually, the demonic power behind this attached itself to me. It was relatively weak, yet tenacious, and my friends were able to cast it out of me as I spit up this "hairball kind of thing" into a garbage can.

In time I came to see that all these hardships weren't the consequences of failure, but were, rather, the cost of faithfulness.

A little after all these events, the same mayor that challenged me to host the healing gathering in the wake of the shootings in Dallas and Baton Rouge took me out to one of our local pubs for a Saturday afternoon beer. Our second story table near the windows afforded us a view of our suburb's downtown. He shared with me that he wasn't going to seek another term as mayor but was instead moving on to the county level (he soon became our county executive).

Several years previously I had taken him out for lunch so that I could get to know him and see how my church and I could helpfully serve the city. I told him that a good leader like him surely had, at any given time, a few projects in their back pocket that they would love to accomplish but didn't have bandwidth to take it on themselves. He mentioned to me an idea to help the kids in our school who struggled with food insecurity. He had once tried to rally the other clergy in town around this without success. A few months later, one of our kids' teachers texted Meg and I asking if there was any way we could help with a program she was launching called "Blessings in a Backpack." We helped her strategize and connected her with some amazing friends who formed the foundation of a fantastic team, along with our food pantry coordinator, so that they could share resources with each other. The program grew to include multiple schools under Lucy's leadership. Carson remembered this and then invited me to run for his seat on city council after he vacated it.

I was a mix of surprised and humbled and honored. I didn't feel remotely electable and told him so. He disagreed and encouraged me to thoughtfully pray about it. A few days later after service I was talking to my friend, Barry, our consummate AV tech, about the invitation. "Why would you want the demotion, Jim?" he retorted. Man, I miss that guy! He passed too soon. Barry's wisdom made it easier to receive Jesus' guidance. I kindly declined the offer, but not before expressing my appreciation at even being considered.

In time, I ended up walking every street in our city three times, about once each year. Not long after this, I was lifting my gaze to the wider world of the rest of metropolitan Detroit. At a conference, my friend Dale shared with me that during one of the sessions he had been challenged by Jesus to walk from his home in the suburbs all the way down Detroit's Grand River Avenue to the city's downtown. His grandparents had fled Detroit to the suburbs down that exact same road during the racial tensions of the 60's. He felt that by walking the opposite direction back into the city, it would be one small step at a spiritual level of undoing the curse of that "white flight." We decided to walk it together. It was a powerful experience walking by his grandparents' old house and praying there, and we really hit it off. We decided to circumnavigate the perimeter of Detroit on foot, including several inner ring suburbs too, talking and praying and learning to see the city a different way. All told we walked over 100 miles around the city and had some really meaningful encounters along the way, including bumping into a neighbor of mine from Ferndale and encouraging her as she was assisting some women in need who were being badgered by some well-intentioned but misguided overly zealous religious folks.

There was also the moment when Dale and I were talking about the upcoming trip Megan and I were taking to Ethiopia in a few days. By this time Dale was a regular member of our church's preaching team. "You know, Jim," Dale said, "if you die on this trip, I want to lead the church." We stopped right there on the corner in downtown Canton and filmed a short video for evidence. He filled in for me as pastor while I was away. When I got home he asked me to delete the video because he didn't want the church anymore. "Too much work," he said. The irony is that though Dale was talking tongue in cheek, God heard. Almost exactly two years to the day he became the Interim Pastor, and six months after that we installed him and his wife as the new Co-Lead Pastors in my place.

It was like a handing off the torch, and it all began while slowing down on a walk in the city.

To the Nations.

I woke up with a start, confused and disoriented, strange sounds washing over me from outside the slightly open window: the chirping of unknown birds, the chatter of the occasional monkey, street noise with its persistent honking, the Muslim call to prayer and Orthodox call to prayer alternating for the attention of faithful passersby (and each competing for which could get to a higher pitch of "11" on the scale of 1 to 10), and then the rhythmic chanting of "*und, hulet, sost, arat*" emanating from somewhere on the floors below.

I had arrived late last night on my first trip to Ethiopia. I had gone to bed with a roommate, my new friend Ramon, but he was nowhere to be seen. Still a little dazed from lack of sleep, not to mention feeling dehydrated, decaffeinated and de-oxygenated from Addis Ababa's 7000+ feet of elevation, I got out of bed and suddenly felt all alone. *What was I doing here? Why did I agree to come?* I needed water, but I knew I wasn't supposed to drink from the bathroom sink, and I had no idea where to buy water and no money even if I did. I was starting to panic. A manic anxiety was settling on me. Right in that moment, as if he had been miraculously teleported, I heard a familiar voice behind me, "What's up, man?! It's good to see you up, Cool Pool!"

Ramon had returned. I explained my situation. He could see the desperation on my face.

"Here, have some of this," he said, handing me a liter sized bottle of water, "I went out to get us some. The Amharic word for water is *wuha*." He was already teaching me. I took a big swig from the bottle and wiped the dribble from my face. "Now let's get you some coffee. I know the perfect spot. I already got myself a cup too when I went out to get the *wuha*. The Amharic word for coffee is *buna*."

Walking through the lobby of the guest house, I embarrassingly noticed that what I thought had been the sound of an invading army turned out to be an aerobics class. The "*und, hulet, sost, arat*," was the ubiquitous chant of "one, two, three, four," as a large class of Ethiopians exercised in rows. Ramon led me through the gates of the compound, and the reality of being in Ethiopia hit me like love at first sight. The activity, the energy, all five senses on fire. The guy we passed wearing the Montreal Canadiens hockey jersey. Ever wonder where those clothes go that you deposit in those parking lot boxes? Ethiopia is one place. Ramon skillfully guided me to our destination, sitting us down outside this little roadside café. As he ordered me my first buna, and then another, savoring the moment, I knew I was entering in on a lifelong love affair.

From a young age I've loved adventure. I love maps. One of my graduation gifts from West Point was a globe that lights up from within. It beguiles adventure-minded guests in our living room to this day. It seems part of my nature and nurture. My father had a strong case of wanderlust and my stepdad would often tell me how he regretted not taking an assignment with the National Guard in old Persia.

I wonder also to what extent it was God's plan. As I prepared for my internship under Steve's guidance, he brought in one of the assistant pastors who was known to have a gift and ministry of prophecy. Her name was Angel and she was a hoot. She stepped into the office and looked at me, internally asking God to speak. She then cooed with her characteristic "oooh" as God began to reply. "Jim, your feet will tread in many nations," she shared. After a ten-day ministry trip with Steve to the UK a few weeks before my engagement to Meg (a few fun stories from that trip are below), my feet next landed in Ethiopia. Ethiopia wonderfully occupied the intersection between my paternal family legacy in Africa with my decades-long interest in the Middle East (even my senior thesis at West Point had been on the historical origins of the First Crusade), and connected with the two most prominent minority cultures in Metro Detroit.

What shall I say about Ethiopia? I'm actually sitting in a friend's apartment on the southern edge of Addis Ababa as I write this section. My mind is awash with memories and saturated with the sights, sounds and smells. The people are warm, gregarious, love to laugh and tell stories.

I once asked my dear friend, Woudineh, with whom I'm staying, how Ethiopia had managed to avoid the religious conflict between Muslims and Christians that had characterized so many other countries in the region. His reply, only half joking, "We prefer to sit together and drink coffee." And the coffee! Ethiopian buna. Forget the coffee culture of Seattle, Ethiopia is where it's at! Coffee, espresso, macchiato. Thank God the Italians tried to conquer and failed, because the coffee culture is that much richer for it.

And the food? The local sour *injera* flatbread, made from the super grain teff, equal parts platter, utensil and food. Lentil stew *shiro*, goat or beef *tibbs*, and the Eritrean bread I've been introduced to this week, stuffed with scrambled eggs and beans. So. Good. Ethiopians are famous for their hospitality. Just today, while waiting for my friend here at his "Airbnb" here in Addis, the young manager insisted on sharing her lunchbox with me: a small Tupperware of lentil stew-soaked injera. Even the Somalis staying down the hall from me invited me to join them on the floor of their room and share from their common plate meal.

My wife and son and I were once in Ethiopia during their Christmas holiday offset one week from ours in America owing to the Orthodox calendar. We were hosting a training for pastors, and rather than cancel due to the holiday (which I requested once I discovered my scheduling blunder), they brought a goat into the retreat center we had rented and we had a feast together! While I continued teaching, my son had the opportunity to participate in learning where his food comes from (let the reader understand), periodically running up to me at the front of the conference room describing the blow by blows of what he was learning. My friend Dawit expertly guided his hand. When the meat was prepared, it was tossed into a large rounded metal pan over the open fire, along with some local butter and salt, and it cooked under the star-laden sky. Everyone gingerly reached in to pick out their pieces as the meat began to sizzle. Earlier that week the pastors gathered round as my son and I took a brief dip in the volcanic lake at the retreat center's shore, with a few of them jumping in to join us.

There are a number of funny stories from our journeys to Ethiopia. The first few trips that we took, we would visit cultural restaurants with our teams. Imagine how an Applebee's might feel to a visiting Ethiopian, except independently owned and operated, and way way better. No offense intended to my friends who like to "Eat Good in the Neighborhood." In addition to the tasty local food, authentic local attire, and aesthetic vibe, there is also music on traditional instruments and dancing. Often this dancing involves trying to get the guests to take a break from their injera and participate. Yep, you guessed it. That's happened to me, twice! And if you engage, they'll take you on stage. It pretty much turns into a "Simon Says" dance off. Yep, you guessed it. That's also happened to me, twice! Apparently I've got the face that says I'll try it, and the body that says I'll lose! Ethiopians are a great judge of character!

On another occasion one of the priests gave us a tour of the visitor center on the Rastafarian Temple grounds (the temple itself is off limits). Yes, there were Bob Marley posters everywhere. Yes, there was one of those high school science class classification posters of the cannabis plant in the back corner of the room. Yes, he was stoned, and yes, he mentioned he had been smoking since he was like five. Yes, there was more than one religious picture of Haile Selassie replacing Jesus on the Cross. And, yes, there was a pink Hello Kitty guest book that we were asked to sign when we left.

On the trip with the Ethiopian Christmas goat, we had the joy of participating in an Ethiopian wedding. We celebrated the love and commitment of a young woman from our church and a young man from the Ethiopian movement we were partnering with. Emma was a close friend of our family. When the day of the wedding came, Meg was prepared for a few hours of getting extra beautiful for the occasion. The only problem was that there was no water for the shower. The only sound was a dull clanking as the pipes were dry. Meg made due and she looked radiant nonetheless. Yet we learned an important lesson about flexibility and learning to make do with what we have.

During another visit we visited a rural church that had a functional farm field attached to it. They grew teff there, to sell at market in the adjacent city. Each of us pastors took turns lining up behind the ox, taking hold of a handful of this mustard-seed-sized grain and then putting our shoulder to the old wooden plow. And when I say old, I mean maybe Jesus might've built it in the days when he was a carpenter. That old. I'll tell you what, I gained a new appreciation for these words of Jesus, *"No one who puts a hand to the plow and looks back is fit for service in the kingdom of God."*[19] I did two rows and I was terrible at it. And when I say terrible, that's not false humility. I mean terrible in the sense that they had to bring in one of the eight-year-old boys from the church to correct my work.

When I think of Ethiopia, I'm most likely to think of my friend, Woudineh. Everyone knows him as Woud (as in Wou-dee). He's great at business and numbers and loves academic theological research. Besides that, we have a lot in common. We can sit and swap stories for hours and he loves a good joke.

His family owns some small ancestral farmland outside of Ethiopia's second city that he helps manage. They have a camel that they use to bear the harvest down the steep hillside to market. He appreciated my love of adventure. On one trip he invited me to take a ride on the family camel. In my pre-ride selfie with the camel, it gave me an unusually pronounced side-eye, which I thought strange given that Woud said that it was used to being ridden. His farm hands gave me a boost up on the camel as he recorded the spectacle on his phone. As soon as it started walking around the alley next to his compound, I started sliding off the back of the camel, so that my bottom was just above the camel's tail. It

---

[19] Luke 9:62

was only after I got off that I learned that the camel was only used for hauling produce and that they had intentionally rigged the saddle loose so that I'd slide around. We had a great laugh!

To honor the ten years of our Ethiopian partnership we hosted a large celebratory gathering in Adama. We took our whole family over for the trip and enjoyed some family time together after the large conference was complete. There was one moment where I was walking between our hotel and the venue and someone driving by honked and shouted out my name, so I think that officially makes me an internationally well-known walker!

At the end of the conference the team put on a huge feast, with all manner of foods, music, presentations (the Vineyard was recognized by the city of Adama for the service it did in the community), and dancing. It was amazing!

The night before that party, we hosted a celebration of another kind: baptism and communion. As I mentioned previously, I love baptism stories. It's customary in Ethiopia to get baptized on a holiday in January called *Timkat*, corresponding with Epiphany. Each of the churches brought the folks to be baptized that year to a spot on the Awash River not far from our venue. There were hundreds of baptismal candidates, all dressed in white, singing, marching, even some running down the gentle slope. All were eager. The team stood in the river baptizing everyone for several hours. We had been told there were crocodiles in the area, but thankfully we didn't see any this year as my friend had in past years.

While everyone was getting organized to head back, my son and I took an opportunity to scamper among the rocks along the bank of the cascading rapids that brought water into the shallow bend of the river where we held the baptism. After maybe 50 meters, we came upon a large boulder that we needed to get around if we were going to continue our exploration. He took the high road and I took the low road. Seeing no way forward around the boulder, I turned to find and follow Eli. I stepped cautiously on a slippery stone and in the blink of an eye my feet were where my head had been and my head was submerged in the water, banging back and forth on the rocks in a little pool among the rapids. It lasted only a couple seconds, but I had that thought, "*Is this where it ends?*" (In fact, I've had that thought many times on various adventures … ask me about the 40-mile perimeter hike around Mount Hood sometime.) Right side up again, I gingerly sat next to the boulder as Eli came quickly, "Dad, what happened? I heard a sound. Are you okay? … Wait, where are your glasses?" To this day I imagine a bespectacled crocodile who's the best hunter in the Awash River. As Meg and I like to joke, that day "A-wash my glasses away!"

Back at the conference venue, my South African friend, Zander, led us in the holiest and most festive communion time I've witnessed. The table was laden with juice and *dabo*, local Italian bread. The large room was packed to overflowing, with the regular participants plus many of the recently baptized celebrants, and friends from the neighborhood too. Hundreds of people. I hadn't really noticed it at the time, focusing on other details, but my friend, Jack, who helped serve, insists that the elements miraculously multiplied. We served everything we had, and more people kept coming, and we never ran out. I can't say for sure, but it sure sounds to me like something Jesus would do.

Deme has been another great Ethiopian colleague. He was pastor of the church in Mugar, a rural-industrial community northwest of Addis Ababa best known for the large cement factory built by the Chinese. I met Deme on my first trip to Ethiopia, at a small conference we held for pastors and church leaders in the area. I prayed for him and after, through a translator, he told me about his desire to travel to the Middle East so that he could do ministry in the hardest places. I was drawn to that passion. His face chiseled by hardship, what stood out to me the most was the intensity of his eyes.

We often traveled to the church in Mugar. That first trip we made a circle tour of the churches in that rural area. The parishioners in Mugar thought we were headed there first when in fact it was our last stop. Undeterred, they had waited six hours or more for us to arrive, and when we finally did the service was intense with spiritual fervor. On other visits we saw Deme cast demons out of church members, as well as gently serve our team popcorn with the ritual coffee ceremony. One year there was great turmoil among the churches of that area as one of the leaders was pulling all the other pastors away to form a splinter movement. When they arrived at the gate to the compound of the Mugar Vineyard, Deme literally wrestled the group down to keep them away from taking control of his church. He was fiercely loyal.

Deme was also deeply committed to his growth. Meg and I once hosted a gathering of pastors to train them in practices of spiritual formation as well as address common questions like how to think about money in church. Deme was there, but was clearly not feeling well. He coughed often and was unusually listless. As we drew the gathering to a close and gave our greetings, we pleaded with Deme to go to the hospital and shared some money to make that possible. Much to our surprise, he died two days later, the day we landed back in the US. He had spent the last days of his life leaning into growth with Jesus, suffering from tuberculosis. Deme was an example to me of dedication to Jesus, and I experienced a sense of brotherhood with him that transcended language.

Another guy I think about is Haile. There was a season where it seemed every other leader was named Haile, so we gave them nicknames. The Haile I'm thinking of was sometimes called "Adama Haile" (since, surprise!, he lived in Adama, not Addis), but I've always preferred "T-Shirt Haile."

A few years into our partnership, a gathering of Vineyard leaders from around Africa was sponsored by the Ethiopian Vineyard churches and hosted in Adama. Some leaders in his church took initiative and made some Ethiopian Vineyard Church t-shirts. And by some, I mean a lot, like a giant carton that could hold a dish washer. They were nice shirts, though sized more for Ethiopians than the Westerners (and other Africans) that were attending the gathering. It was a creative idea and I bought a few for myself, Megan and a couple of leaders in our church most connected to the partnership. A few others bought some, but it was clear there was disappointment.

Every day the carton of t-shirts sat silently in the corner of the conference room where we met, and the leaders who had printed them would come in at lunch to solicit sales. The problem was that many of the leaders there had little specific connection to the Ethiopian Vineyard, hadn't brought cash since they had prepaid for everything ahead of time, and traveled light so they didn't have luggage space to carry many home. Through translation with Haile, I quickly learned that had been the plan: most people would buy 20+ and carry them home to sell in their local churches. A reasonable enough idea, but that had never been coordinated ahead of time. In the end, I ended up giving him most of the remaining cash I had at the end of the trip to at least cover his costs.

Haile was our host and guide many times since we often traveled to Adama. A couple years after the t-shirt incident, our small team was with Haile leaving Adama for a retreat center to participate in several days of training we were facilitating for the Ethiopian pastors in our network. On the way to the bus station, where Haile would negotiate a taxi for the four of us, we stopped for a cup of coffee. That coffee turned into two cups and a mango smoothie. As we sat slurping our smoothies and finishing our coffee, not having paid yet, Haile got a call. The event coordinators were asking for an update on our progress. I thought, *Uh oh! We haven't even paid yet, we still have to negotiate the taxi fare, and it is more than an hour away*. And we were supposed to be there in 30 minutes. I'll never forget Haile's calm answer, "We're on our way." That seemed strange to me because in American culture that means we're on the road and you can expect us shortly, on time. We weren't on our way in that sense. But Haile was right. We had left the hotel and we were on our way to the retreat center. When we arrived at the retreat center maybe two hours later, no one even seemed phased. I was reminded we were in Ethiopia, where the culture is event-oriented, not time-oriented, and relationship is the main thing. It was a good lesson. One I'm continuing to try to learn from.

Haile and his team left that seminar early, missing the final session, discussing our approach to money in the partnership. We were headed back to Adama early in the morning for a long Sunday of ministry in Haile's church: worship service, lunch with the team, an afternoon training on healing and deliverance, then an evening dinner discussion with his elders. By the time we arrived at the home of one of Haile's elders that evening, I was tired. The seminar at the retreat center had been better than expected but was full of LOTS of discussion. An example is when I mentioned that we had made a ten-year commitment to the partnership (which, I'm thinking to most Americans, would seem like a long time), and the universal response of the Ethiopians in the room was,

"What?!?! Only ten years? What then?" with dismay in their voice. It took over an hour of discussion to let them know we wouldn't be abandoning them. I was tired.

As the three of us Americans settled onto the couch in Haile's home, I noticed everyone else was sitting between us and the door. This feeling of unease broke through the fog of my Sunday night exhaustion. After some *tibbs* and *injera*, followed by a brief coffee ceremony, Haile moved to sit across from me. I knew this moment was why we were really here. He handed me a few pieces of paper. On it, he explained, was the budget for the vision he had for his ministry: office rental and equipment, purchase of land for a training compound, salaries for church planters and more. Bottom line: one million dollars. If I had been less tired and discouraged, I might've laughed. Whether by intention or accident, I'll never know, but it dawned on me that all but one of this team had missed that session on money where we had discussed this exact kind of thing. One of my team members graciously tried to engage him, knowing how I was feeling. But Haile wouldn't have it; he wanted to deal with me directly. I don't really remember what I said, but I'm sure it had something to do with how we didn't have that kind of money. We couldn't fund this budget. "Well," he countered, "what could you help with?" It went like that for a while longer. At some point, needing to sleep, I folded up the paper, put it in my pocket and told him, "I'll pray about it." The next day was an awkward visit with him until he handed us off to our hosts for the next leg of the trip.

Less than a year later I was back in Adama again. I had brought $1000 dollars with me to divide evenly between Haile and another leader we were working with at the time. Later that week I found out through a third party (third party mediation is a common African approach to conflict resolution) that they were both mad at me. The second leader just wanted more. But Haile was angry specifically because he had put a new roof on his church building, and I had given him so little when I had agreed to pay for it. The cost had been $3500. You can imagine my surprise when I learned that I had agreed to pay for it given that I didn't remember making any such promise. Through lots of conversation it became clear that in his culture I had promised.

In America, when a Christian, especially a pastor, is approached with an idea and responds with, "I'll pray about it," that's an indirect way of saying No and means it is unlikely. (Consider this a spoiler alert for those whose pastor told them they'd pray about that last idea you shared with them.) However, in Ethiopia, "I'll pray about it" is an indirect way of saying Yes. In their understanding, they've talked to God about their financial needs and so when someone they trust, someone like me, says they'll pray about it, they assume God will tell me what they told God. So they went ahead with part of their plan because I had promised to hear from God and respond accordingly. This was a huge revelation for me: first, to be more direct in future communication, and second in understanding African culture. The reality was, I traveled to their culture and was operating in it. And while he may have had some responsibility to communicate more clearly his expectations with me, I had traveled to them and I felt the burden of responsibility lay with me.

After arriving home I emailed our board. We jumped on a conference call and after thoroughly explaining the situation, they agreed. They had mercy on my mistake and maturely chose to honor our Ethiopian partners. The wonder is that, within a few days, some large bill we had been awaiting finally came in the mail and it was about $3500 less than expected. God had provided the funds almost exactly to the dollar.

One of the most standout features of Ethiopian cities is the frequency of partially finished buildings. Unlike their American counterparts with sophisticated scaffolding and cranes, the Ethiopian variety are surrounded by a warren of dried eucalyptus trunks used as scaffolding, or supports of yet unfinished floors, and may or may not have any noticeable work being done on them. Actually, it is common in commercial buildings for the first floor to be occupied with businesses while the second floor is being completed and the pillars extend upwards to support a third floor in some anticipated unknown future, with iron rebar sticking out like hairs or as if it is the fruit of those concrete trees. At first I was always reminded of Jesus' admonition in the Gospel of Luke, about how no one built a tower without first confirming they had the resources to complete it. *"Well, Jesus,"* I thought, *"it seems everyone is doing that in Ethiopia!"* Then I came to understand the culture better and discerned the wisdom in their approach. Now, years later, I see it as a noteworthy example of "do what you can do instead of not doing what you can't do." So many people I know with compelling ideas get stuck never getting started because they can't do it all at once. These partially finished buildings bear silent witness to me of the value of being willing to go slow to accomplish your goal.

Years before I had ever gone to Ethiopia, in the weeks before my engagement, my first missional trip overseas was to the UK. My mentor, Steve, brought a team of six with him, including two ladies and four of us guys: Nicolas, Jason, Dave and myself. We had lots of great ministry moments, but the memories that stand out were on our free time. Three of us were in our mid-20's and Nicolas at 18 had just graduated from home school. He was filled with all kinds of important knowledge he had discovered during his final term. As we walked around Bath, England, he shared some of these gems, like how much methane cows produce from farting each year and the impact this has on the global environment. After a few more of these, Nicolas and I went in one direction while Dave and Jason did their own thing, because it's a sign of trouble when the ministry team is threatening to beat each other up if the other person keeps talking!

Eventually, peace prevailed amongst us guys and a few days later we found ourselves in Portsmouth. We were finished for the evening and so we decided to find somewhere to hang out. All the pubs were closed but the drumming beats from a basement club beckoned us. It was packed. Dave ordered us all beers and we found a place to stand next to the back stairwell, cautious about leaning up against the sweaty, sticky walls. Wouldn't you know it, here's three handsome mid-20's men and 18-year old Nicolas with his newsboy cap, and all the ladies coming up and down the stairs are flirting with him!

At some point it dawned on us that we had an early morning of ministry again, so we decided it was best to head back to the hotel. Just then the music changed. That very week England was playing in the final rounds of the World Cup in France, and their theme song that year was "Vindaloo," an homage to the spicy curry that Londoners loved. The dance floor was packed and the place went wild. Our exit was across the way. We were a quartet of Yanks in the middle of a British club at the height of frenzied national pride. We put Jason, the spry worship leader up front, military me next, Dave the wrestler in the back, and Nicolas in the middle. The pressure of the moment united us as one and we would leave no man behind. We wove our way through the crowd, shouting "Vindaloo" repeatedly at the top of our lungs, blending in as best we could as we worked our way out. Shared adversity fosters community. That moment bonded us for the rest of the trip and there was no more arguing amongst us. And what's more, later that week we spotted the Queen at Windsor Castle!

In the spring of 2017, I traveled to Arusha, Tanzania for another African Vineyard Leaders' Network gathering. This was probably the most adventurous travel experience I had. The itinerary was complicated because I was first visiting Arusha for the AVLN meeting, then Dar es Salaam to meet with the Tanzanian partnership team, and lastly a brief trip to Addis to meet with our partners there. I was surprised to discover there were two airports in Arusha: one for the city and another for Mount Kilimanjaro. (When I arrived in Arusha, I discovered it to be a significant city of nearly one million people. This often happened to me, betraying my bias, sadly shared by many Americans, about the lack of big cities in the Global South.) I was very distracted when making these plans, as 2016 had been a particularly difficult ministry year, and so I did little research. I knew I wanted to go to Arusha and the Kilimanjaro airport struck me as the boutique destination specific to the trekkers. But I was really confused by why my flights were so expensive. I chalked it up to the itinerary.

I landed in Dar after midnight for an overnight layover before flying to Arusha. Stepping up to the counter to get my visa, I noticed even the border patrol officers were sleeping. They all had their heads down, except the one actively working with another passenger. I stood in front of the window for several moments, wondering if I should gently rap the glass but then wondering what would be the consequence of that. After a minute or two, the officer lifted his head, looked me in the eye, and then put his head back down. No one else was stirring. A few moments later he sat up and beckoned with his hand for my passport. Then he pointed at the fee taped to the glass and beckoned again with his hand for the money. Sliding my crisp hundred bill through the slot produced a forceful stamp in my passport and I was on my way to recover my luggage.

But my bag wasn't on the baggage claim conveyor. It was a skeleton crew servicing the small flight I had been on that arrived in the middle of the night. The young lady serving as the concierge pointed me to the lost luggage department across the way. A glance through the closed service window revealed an empty office. Returning, the gracious woman instructed me, "No, no. you need to go around and knock on the door." The door was slightly ajar. A few knocks produced a flurry of activity as a man and a woman stirred from different hiding places in the office and seemed to be getting dressed. His uniform shirt not quite fully buttoned, the man walked out from behind the desk and directed me to look behind the door. A large pile of luggage didn't produce my duffle bag, nor did it give me much confidence that I'd be seeing that bag anytime soon! I filed my claim with the concierge and went upstairs to the check-in area to await my next flight.

Being maybe 2 a.m. at this point, the check-in counter was closed for several hours, so I was forced to find a bench to sleep on in the secured open-air area. I was a little nervous about the $3000 in cash in the backpack under my head. I said a brief prayer and fell fast asleep. I awoke with a start as a security guard knocked the soles of my feet with his baton. I rubbed the sleep out of my eyes and noticed the bustle around me. It was 7 a.m. I felt genuinely rested. I made it to my gate with some time to spare for munching on the Tanzanian version of sour cream and onion Pringles chips. Breakfast of champions.

The short one-hour flight on the commuter flight of Precision Air (often known locally, I discovered as Imprecision Air) landed me in the Arusha City Airport. Deplaning, I immediately discerned why I had encountered so much trouble with my booking. The terminal was about the size of a shipping container, with bench seating for four and a roof of wood and straw. As the plane repositioned for takeoff back to Dar, a line of five women in colorful local skirts and headwraps, wielding straw brooms, whisked the runway clean of debris. My ride was nowhere to be seen. In fact, there was no one around besides the runway cleaning crew. I oscillated between panic about where I was and how I was going to get to where I was supposed to be, and a sense of joyful wonder at this amazing moment.

Mercifully, my international plan produced a faint cell signal, and I was able to get a short call through to a team member at the retreat center. A driver showed up within the hour and persistently expressed his surprise I would fly in to Arusha City. "Everyone knows Kilimanjaro Airport is the tourist airport internationals use!" It was a great way to get a feel for the city's vibe, and along the way we circled the roundabout with the obelisk marking the midpoint on the one single road that runs between Cape Town, South Africa and Cairo, Egypt. My good friend and mentor in many things Africa, Beau, lent me his spare workout clothes to wear the last day of the retreat. My bag arrived that night, just in time for the next leg of my journey (out of Kilimanjaro Airport, of course!) early the next morning. I was so grateful that the confusion and inconveniences of my muddled plans allowed me to immerse myself in the local culture even in this small way. That's always been my heart, to not be a tourist missionary.

My second to last trip in my role on my denominational missional leaders' team was also among the most significant for me vocationally. We were visiting an indigenous ministry in Sierra Leone that had planted 1,000 churches over the course of maybe two decades and then planted 9,000 churches in the past ten years. I was a third string alternate, joining my cross-cultural mentor and missions boss, Mark, as he hitched a ride with a friend of his to join an already assembled team that was there to explore funding a Bible college and leadership training school that would deepen and strengthen the impact of this ministry for years to come. Mark and I were there as students, observing and discerning ministry principles and practices that we might translate to the teams he led and the numerous contexts where they served. Three memories stand out to me from that trip.

First, the leader of that ministry had been encouraged multiple times to run for president of his country. His reply, "Why would I want to do that? My good friend from school is already president and he's doing a fine job! I have my assignment already." His practice? He would routinely sit anonymously among the group that visited each church and only introduce himself to say a few words as we left. He was perfectly content to make room for those he led to lead and observe them for coaching opportunities after.

Second, one village we visited greeted us with a large welcoming party at the edge of town. They pulled out all the stops. Groups of men, women and children singing and dancing, with greenery and flowers galore. My suspicions were aroused. Though less extravagant, I had experienced moments like this before as churches put on displays of gratuitous hospitality in order to attract Western funds. How wrong I was! As we were seated in the village square and the chief's words were translated, I discovered that all this was an expression of gratitude for the work the ministry had done to bring a government school to the village, educating and empowering the next generation of young people.

Third, we visited a small village in the middle of blood diamond country: a green region of low-lying wetlands where workers one step removed from slavery worked the water to filter for diamonds and other precious stones. The church in this village gathered at the community shelter in the center of town, sort of like a large open-sided gazebo. The 150 square feet of the concrete slab was packed with people, a little over 100 members from the village since the church had been founded 18 months previously. Myself and the other guests were in chairs outside the shelter, in the partial shade of a tree. Our leader, Emmanuel, had an idea as we were preparing to leave. He asked the church planter to stand up and come to the front. He then asked them to identify the "person of peace" they had met in the village who had been the first contact for the church. He pointed to an elderly gentleman who came and stood next to him. Who had he shared with and welcomed to the church? A young man, who had invited a woman, who had welcomed two of her friends, and so on. In two minutes time they had identified eleven generations of disciples among those 100 members, in 18 months.

Part of my job in the Army had been to prepare units for inspections when General Officers came around on tour, so my BS sniffer is very sensitized. I was adept at smelling out dog and pony shows. There was nothing fake here. I was amazed. I had seen nothing like that in all my years of ministry. That visit, and others like it on that trip, were worth the price of the ticket for me. I was in school and I tucked away in my heart what I was learning.

But I did manage some fun! I went swimming near the mouth of the Red Sea in Djibouti. I went swimming with Elijah in Lake Victoria along the shores of Kampala (and with him later that same year in Lake Superior, so that we hit two of the world's three biggest lakes in one year). Then on a 20th anniversary trip in Egypt with Meg, I gorged myself on cultural adventure. I jumped off a boat in Aswan and swam the Nile to the sand dune shore. We rode camels around the Sphinx, climbed into the central chamber of the Great Pyramid of Giza, sat in the hushed silence of the Green Mosque in Cairo, then wondered at the Rock Church in Garbage City where the Coptic faithful would routinely leave behind wheelchairs, crutches and all manner of interior shackles as God healed them in power. We meandered in the Temple of Karnak and the Valley of the Kings, stood astride the Aswan Dam, and savored the baking and breaking of bread in local homes.

Yet, in all of this there was also disappointment. There was, of course, the sorrow of missed opportunities: within 300 miles of Victoria Falls and I never went, on both sides of the Serengeti and never took a safari, three visits to South Africa but never to Cape Town, and I've never yet seen the iconic cultural sites of northern Ethiopia. However, the real hardship, the lingering pain, was in the relationships.

There was one national-level leader of a movement in another African country who would routinely pout when he didn't get his way, playing me and a colleague of mine off against another leader who had less specific involvement but more organizational clout. This leader knew how to play the political card. Despite several visits together, lengthy email and face to face conversations, and plenty of time praying, we could not come to agreement.

I think of one young Ethiopian man, Adamu, who was a sort of coordinator for the group of 12 churches or so in the rural area northwest of Addis. In the youthful days of our partnership when the movement was growing and the team was laying the administrative foundation to support the work, we learned that Adamu had secretly submitted registration paperwork with the government. In hidden gatherings he had gathered 11 of the 12 pastors (all but Deme, mentioned previously) to sign this document, forming a new board and establishing a splinter group that he could use to recruit other rural churches from his ethnic group. Effectively, he was trying to split the movement. He had been invited by Woudineh, the local team leader, to represent the Ethiopian Vineyard churches at one of the African Vineyard Leaders' Network gatherings. I think this filled his heart with ambition. Ethnic, linguistic and cultural nuances were also stirring the pot. Not to mention immaturity. I really liked Adamu and believed he could be a wonderful leader and help to the Oromo-speaking rural churches. But he got it in his heart that he wanted to be in charge, but not to serve. It seemed all he could see were the privileges, not the responsibilities.

The problem was severe enough that an Ethiopian friend and I flew short notice to Addis to meet with the group of pastors. For three days we met, listening, acknowledging our missteps where appropriate, pleading and speaking to his heart. He would not repent. He only budged when some of the pastors who had sided with him heard our heart and came to us in repentance. They were restored by the community of pastors. The registration document failed to meet the government's standards for signatures, so the coup failed. Adamu feigned a return to relationship but soon drifted off into a self-assigned isolation. Last I heard he's alone and not doing well at all. His is a sad story for me.

Even more sad is the story of Ahmed, an indigenous leader from the Horn of Africa. His journey to faith in Jesus is beautiful and compelling. He was bright, confident and gifted. He seemed a natural leader. Sadly, he was promoted into roles well ahead of his emotional and spiritual maturity. This caused great pain for others, and for him.

All my travel has been for a purpose. Angel had spoken God's heart over my life: "My feet would walk on many lands." And that purpose was, and still is, the people. The people are the prize and they've made me experience a richness of blessing that no currency can match.

Midwife or Mother?

It was 2009. I walked around the hills outside some village in Ethiopia with my new friend, Hank. The church he served was one of four or five partners in our work. Like me, he loved spending time around irreligious, yet spiritually open and curious, folks. He was a semi-pro cyclist. He shared stories with me of how he and some of his friends had visited mosques the year following 9/11, offering to clean their toilets as an act of bridge-building love. His church was one of the largest in our denomination at that time. After an hour or two of walking, asking questions and listening to my stories, he shared his own. His church had acquired a building and their grand opening service was the Sunday after September 11th, 2001. The church grew by 400 people that week. They grew year after year ever since. He strongly believed that settling into a building was a critical component of long-term sustainability and growth. He didn't push. He did invite me to consider what that could look like for us.

We had looked for options during the winter of 2006. We began working with a young local realtor, Devon, which led to his conversion and baptism later that year. We talked with a struggling church in our suburban downtown. It was small, with two pastors but only fifteen parishioners, mostly single parents and the elderly. I met with the pastor and broached the topic of purchasing the building. The space wasn't perfect for our needs, yet the location was unbeatable. They suspected something was up when I had visited with two of our leaders. It turned out he and his assistant were both realtors, so they quickly provided me comps and invited us all to a time of fasting and prayer. I was hopeful. The comps matched what the bank was willing to loan us and what my friends and I were sensing from God in prayer. We met with the pastor to name our offer and he countered with a number more than twice as high, one million dollars. I said we didn't have that kind of money and mentioned that if he had a firm number in mind, why didn't he just say it outright. He told me to come back in a week after he had a chance to talk with his board. I wondered, *What board?* but kept that thought to myself. A week later he generously offered the building for $1.5M. I chuckled a little, told him I was standing firm on my offer, to call me if he was ever interested, and to have a nice day. A year later a commercial developer bought it for under a million and tore it down, turning it into a park after an unsuccessful redevelopment effort.

Three years later we looked around again, exploring rental options in long-vacant warehouses.

We explored a nearly vacant property in the downtown of another suburb. The current tenant, a coffee shop, loved the idea of our being there as it would help drive their business. We submitted our zoning change proposal to the board of appeals. It was immediately evident they had no interest in hearing our case. One of our witnesses had to stand up and give testimony on our behalf before my wife stood up instead to defend me from the attacks on my character that one member of the board was making. They actually admitted, in a public hearing, that they could do what we were asking, that it was legally and administratively possible, but they just didn't want to.

As our team congregated in the lobby after the hearing, one member of the board told us that they had met ahead of time and agreed to deny our request. As he left another gentleman, who sat in the front row furiously taking notes the whole meeting, approached us and told us we had a strong case for a lawsuit against the city for religious discrimination. I was familiar with the Religious Freedom Restoration Act that President Clinton had signed into law, but told the reporter, "I don't want my first act of service to the city to be serving them with papers."

Our local school system wouldn't rent to us. A city official told our realtor, "Tell your people they'll never be in our city!" (Ironically, that person no longer works for the city and we've been happily serving the city for over a dozen years now!)

That was the context of my conversation with Hank. I had taken his words to heart, but didn't act on them immediately. I felt I had exhausted every option, and probably, honestly, we had. Then, two years later, another possibility emerged. Friends of ours recommended that we check out a church in our hometown. One of these friends was a retired pastor who served in an advisory capacity on our board. I was familiar, though not deeply so, with the church building they had in mind. My friend Aaron mentioned that they were looking for someone, maybe us, to rent out their vacant children's wing. He knew it wasn't quite what we were looking for, but he wondered if maybe it was a step in the direction of relocating to Ferndale, which he knew was in our heart. Renting space from a church again (it was his church that we had rented space from previously) felt like a step backwards, but I respected him and because of that respect I made the appointment to take the tour and hear them out.

A few days later we met with two representatives from the church: Bob and Pastor Susie. Theirs was an older congregation, in decline and struggling, yet still active in their efforts to serve our city. We walked through the children's wing as they shared their vision. I knew right away it wasn't going to be a good fit: the size was too small, the price was too big, and it didn't lay out right. Yet I found myself curious. Could we tour the rest of the building? The building seemed to be in better shape than I had expected. And the location was great. It was at the intersection of two streets, bordered the downtown and with easy access to most of the schools. One mile north was one of the wealthier suburbs of metro Detroit. One mile south was the 8 Mile border with Detroit and one of the poorest communities around. One mile west was the most racially diverse city on the northern edge of Detroit, and one mile east was the downtown with its bars, restaurants and the center of gay culture in metro Detroit. I told them I'd get back to them.

Walking back to my office after the appointment, I realized I loved it. *But what does that mean, God?* I found myself asking. *Their rental offer won't work for our needs. We can't afford to buy the building, and I don't know if we have what it takes to maintain the building. Yet the location is awesome and the ministry they're laboring to sustain is great.* I called the next day to say we weren't interested in renting and explained why.

Yet I kept thinking about the building. It seemed perfect, we just couldn't afford it. This was top of mind for me. It would come up in conversation all the time with friends. Eventually they got sick of me talking about it and challenged me to do something about it. One of them might literally have told me to "Crap or get off the pot, Jim." Stop talking about it until I had decided which I was going to do. I took this to the Lord in prayer.

Slowly, over the next few weeks, I gained clarity. I discerned the Lord inviting us to have our cake and eat it too. "What if you could have the building and the people to sustain it for free, Jim?" That's what I sensed the Lord saying. God was inviting us to merge our churches together. I talked the idea over with our leadership team and we decided to pitch it and see if God was in it. I called Bob back. Nate and I met with Bob, his wife Agnes, their board chair Linda, and Pastor Susie the next day. A calm came over me as I laid out my vision. They responded with three questions. What did I think about women in leadership in the church? What did I think about homosexuality? How would this affect the experience of their worship service? We dialogued. I knew it was gonna work when, after I described our practice of prayer ministry, 70something Agnes said, "That sounds great!"

They invited me to draft the proposal, which I submitted the next week. Two and a half months later we merged, with our first service as one new church (renamed *Renaissance*) on Christmas Eve. That's how we got our building.

Fast forward three and a half years when my Malawian friend, Akimu, was praying for our leadership team in the youth room. With a prophetic unction in his voice he looked at me and said, "Brother, God has given you this building for free, now go and fill it!"

That's exactly what we set out to do. Having been given the building as a gift, we wanted to put it to use for the sake of God's rule and reign in blessing our city.

I have long been very impacted by the words of God through the prophet Jeremiah to the people living in a strange land: *"This is what the Lord Almighty, the God of Israel, says to all those I carried into exile from Jerusalem to Babylon: 'Build houses and settle down; plant gardens and eat what they produce. Marry and have sons and daughters; find wives for your sons and give your daughters in marriage, so that they too may have sons and daughters. Increase in number there; do not decrease. Also, seek the peace and prosperity of the city to which I have carried you into exile. Pray to the Lord for it, because if it prospers, you too will prosper."*[20] In other words, we had been sent to a place and God's desire was for us to be an agent of well-being for the people and structures of the place where we were sent.

We codified this in our commitment to be *a Jesus-centered community that's a great friend to the city*. One way we expressed that was in our vision for the building to be a community center for our neighbors. We had a foundation of our existing food pantry for the hungry and the weeklong Warming Center for the homeless, plus two or three recovery groups. Over the next few years we added our community garden to supplement the pantry and a number of AA and NA groups to round the total out to at least seven (almost one every day). In our sanctuary we've hosted local dad bands to practice for shows, regular gatherings of co-eds and leaders for a regional campus ministry, plus a screening of a locally produced film on the old Detroit Tiger's Stadium. Some friends we met in the business community expressed interest in my idea for a co-working space in our office area (converted from century old Sunday school classrooms) and they helped me launch the (sadly short-lived) Greenhouse: Ferndale. And when the longest-standing co-op preschool in the city lost their meeting space, they approached us about a partnership to rent a portion of our children's ministry wing since they felt like our values were so aligned. That spawned several other summer community classes run by neighbors to serve neighbors.

One noteworthy way the building got used was as a movie set. One of our members was a regular in the growing Michigan film community, serving as an extra on several sets and an avid online voice. She heard about an independent director telling the story of human trafficking and

---

[20] Jeremiah 29:4-7

a few weeks later the crew was using our office space to film.[21] The main character was played by an actor made famous for his TV portrayal of Superman, yet our family loved him best for his direct-to-streaming work in Airplane vs. Volcano. He was a consummate gentleman, graciously inviting us to watch a day of filming and taking a photo with one of my daughters and I. They even filmed part of our service for the movie and gave me a small speaking part. An unexpected way to serve our city!

It was during this season that our pantry director, Randy, and myself each won "Good Neighbor" awards from one of our local civic organizations, and that Meg and I were humbled with the "Citizen of the Year" recognition. God's vision resonated with folks and through some hard work and lots of connecting the idea was becoming reality. Our church building was becoming a community center for our city and our team was making it happen.

We were filling up the building. It was being used seven days a week. Yet, as you can imagine, this was not without a cost. All that use was hard on a hundred-year-old building. And, as it turns out, buildings are a lot of work! There was always something.

There were nearly constant headaches with the heating system. One cavernous boiler looked like it had been removed from a decommissioned WWII battleship. We also had three newer in-line radiators feeding the classic radiators in the sanctuary and the original half of the building. Ironically, it was these that gave us far more problems. With their little computer motherboards they were finnicky, and it seemed we were often tinkering to get their system right. I'll never forget the Monday morning I went down to check on them after an extra amount of Sunday morning complaints regarding the (lack of) heat in the sanctuary.

The boilers were in the basement in the original part of the building. (The Baptist's had built a children's ministry wing once the Baby Boomers started getting into school, and sadly the church had begun its decades decline in attendance less than a decade later.) I called this

---

[21] *Trafficked: A Parents' Worst Nightmare*

basement the "Zombie Apocalypse Basement," because I was sure, if ever a zombie apocalypse did take place, ground zero would be down there. The original church men's room was down there, now used as a storage room, complete with a window next to the urinals. Who puts a window in the basement? Part of the glass was broken out, of course, and behind it was a vacant space of pitch black darkness beneath the main entrance to the church. It turns out that placing a porch over an empty space leads to a crumbling porch. Further down was a large room, also used vaguely for storage, a kind of final resting space for things we would never use. It had been a coal room, complete with a chute to the outside, and there was one active member of the church who remembered as a young boy watching his dad shovel coal into the furnace.

Well, that Monday morning I took the long walk down the creaky stairs, passed the zombie bathroom, and turned the lights on next to the dot-matrix printer and broken chairs graveyard room. I rounded the corner and imagine my surprise when I see one of the newer boilers with its vent shield lying on the ever-damp concrete floor and flames licking greedily out from the inside, melting all the electronics and wiring on the front face. I hastily turned it off and was in shock. It was an embarrassingly long time before we got it repaired.

The sump pump also gave us lots of trouble. We had two sumps, of course. A residential-sized unit in the Zombie Apocalypse Basement and a commercial unit submerged in a well in the alleyway next to the Children's Wing. How it got there we could never figure out. Perhaps it was a relic from when municipal codes involved a lot more handshakes and who you knew. Also, and more troubling, we could never quite figure out how the water that filled it got there. There were a couple of intake pipes, one from similar wells in the parking lot, and the other maybe feeding from pipes that drained the flat roof over the kids' wing and the sinks and bathrooms in that fellowship hall basement. The commercial sump pump had an alarm, in case of emergency, or at whatever other times were inconvenient or in the middle of the night, that woke up and annoyed the neighbors but communicated nothing to the problem solvers who all lived two miles away or more.

One year, after multiple unresolvable false alarms and disabling the fuse that powered the alarm, there was a massive failure that flooded the fellowship hall with about a foot of water one Sunday morning. We DIY installed two residential units and powered them with an extension cord from the kitchen. For more than a year we cordoned off the well with cones, some yellow tape, and an upside down grocery cart. Few things say "Welcome to our church" quite like that sight fifty feet from your main entrance. Eventually we found a company willing to do the work of installing a commercial unit, and backup, for a price that only mildly abused us.

Speaking of the parking lot. Thankfully it was large enough to serve our needs and mercifully no one had yet tripped and injured themselves on one of the many pockmarks that looked like the crash site of a mini-asteroid. The dominant feature of the parking lot, though, was the slightly sunken impression formed by the once or twice weekly semi-truck that delivered food for our pantry from local grocers and regional food banks. During heavy rains this depression was filled with what we called "Lake Renaissance." On one unexpected late fall overnight freeze we had to make sure the preschool moms didn't have an accidental skating lesson at drop-off. In time we found that the periodic pumping of detritus from the wells mitigated the lake formation and was far more cost-effective than actually leveling and repaving the whole lot.

Yet it was the roof that topped it all off. Pun intended. Actually, it was multiple roofs. We had a small entryway facing the street that was the main entrance in the days when most people walked to church from the neighborhood. In our time it was a large coat closet, with the doors most often locked, since everyone used the back entrance near the parking lot. Whoever had designed that little entryway had never anticipated the rains that came with global warming. Most years, every time we'd get a significant spring rain, we'd get an equivalent puddle in that entryway, often spreading into the main lobby. Not a big deal for Sunday night rains, but a major headache for overnight storms on Saturday. We could never explain why this happened. The puddles became part of our routine.

The bigger deal by far was the flat roof atop the Children's Wing. Its lifespan expired shortly after we merged and moved in. Within a few years, the same kinds of puddles that plagued the under-used entryway started appearing in the very-much-used Sunday school classrooms. The deck under the roof surface was rotting. We had leaks, falling debris and similar things your imagination can fill in. Lacking money to repair the roof, the solution became buckets under the breaches in the ceiling, rearranging furniture away from debris zones, and coming in early to check on things after heavy rains. As you can imagine, all this was a lot of extra work, quite demoralizing, and more than a little unsavory.

After five years of this, we decided we needed to face the problem head on and raise the money for a new roof. Here's how we thought about it: *"What's in a roof? A shelter. A story. A home. That's what's going on under our roof at PVC. We're sheltering the homeless and making room for refugees to feel welcome and learn to discover a new home. We're creating safe space for neighborhood preschool kids, fostering the spiritual lives of adults and kids of all ages, and helping those in recovery find freedom and new stories of healing and hope. We're building a place of belonging, a spiritual home where everyone is welcomed to discover God and themselves, and then join in God's work of blessing in the world. We're honoring a historic legacy from the past and building a bright future together."* I really believed that. People responded and we raised what we needed in just a few months. We hired a company and the adventure continued.

Interacting with the roofing contractors reminds me of the drama around our building renovation project shortly after we merged, as we modernized the social space of our century old red brick building to accommodate contemporary usage. The general contractor started the project a month after he promised it would be completed, so that the church member we had tapped to manage the project on our end had already moved away. Now I was stuck as the liaison. Two months later we were coming home from vacation and my kids asked me, "Dad, do you think the work will be done?"

"I don't know," I replied, "but it will be exciting to see the progress, right?"

The progress for the weeks we were away amounted to zero. No movement. That's when I went for a long walk in the neighborhood and Captain Jim jumped on a phone call, first with the General Contactor and then with the architect. Captain Jim is Just Jim's alter-ego. Just Jim is the name some people gave me after repeated attempts on my part to stop calling me "pastor," as in, "Hey, friend, no need to call me Pastor Jim, just Jim is good enough for me, cause that's the name my mamma gave me." (I always chuckled at "Just Jim," though my favorite nickname after G Movie is hands down Cool Pool. Thank you, Ramon! But I digress.) Eventually the project was finished, several months later, but not in time to avoid sheet plastic hanging everywhere for the big church wedding with two dearly loved members the week after Labor Day.

That's how the roof replacement was for me. More than all summer to finish. Botched work so that the newly installed roof leaked after the first rain. Unpaid bills by the contractor so that a supplier put a lien on our property to force us to get the GC to pay up. Delayed paperwork so that we had to withhold final payment to get them to submit to us the necessary documentation. Lots of difficult phone calls with the contractors, with board members, board members with the contractor, and such. Use your imagination if you'd like to fill in my sketch. The months-long process wore me down, especially when the finished roof still didn't drain well, and there were other indications that it might need a warranty review sometime soon.

Buildings require a lot of work. Even more significant for me was the human dimension of owning a building. I had to squeeze being a building manager into my already crowded calendar. And I didn't even hang pictures in my own house! Many other folks stepped up to help at different times and in various ways. All helpful. Yet the ongoing responsibility to manage all that fell on me. In time I developed what I can only describe as a fairly significant trauma reaction to storms. For most of my adult life I loved rainfall and storms, sitting on the front porch or lying in bed and soaking in the moment. But all that changed. I came to dread rainfall, of almost any amount, and storms would make me anxious, sometimes almost angrily panicky. Instead of delight, I'd get depressed and moody. The effect on me was real.

Everyone had an opinion on the building. Who wasn't locking the doors right and who was leaving the bathroom lights on. I had this idea to repaint the 90's era paneling at the back of the stage. I would've gotten far less pushback in changing our doctrinal statement. And I only once dared entertain the notion of changing the sanctuary flooring, from the stained and worn carpet of indeterminant age to something from the 21st century. Instantaneous conflict. I had heard in seminary that even angels fear to tread on the topic of sanctuary carpets, but I was agnostic on the point. No longer. Everyone came armed with an opinion.

They also often showed up with arms loaded with stuff they no longer wanted in their homes, conveniently dropped off when no one was looking, like an inverted thief in the night. People tended to treat the church building like their communal storage unit, or the cabin "up north" (it's a Michigan thing) where they deposited their 70's paraphernalia or that one holiday purchase when they ignored the caveat emptor feeling in their gut. I would routinely come in Monday mornings and find some candle set or kitschy "faith and spirituality" item in the café area. At first I tried to be nice. Then I adopted the posture of just throwing these deposited treasures in the trash. It sounds harsh, I know. But after a couple of difficult conversations ("You know, you could've asked me first, so that we could together find the right home for your special figurine from Branson, Missouri"), I found decisive action on my part was best. The most difficult choice of all time, the last piece of tchotchke I dealt with, was a painted ceramic of the Last Supper with all black disciples and Jesus. I was tormented at night, wondering if I was a racist if I threw it away. In the end, I left it for the next pastors to sort out.

Yet the human factor in owning the building was most clearly witnessed in our janitor. Oliver was a member of the church who was looking for a side hustle to supplement his part-time job. He was handy and reliable. We hired him to clean the building during his off hours. Over the course of the two years or so he worked for the church, Oliver got more and more frustrated. I'll never forget a conversation I had with him when we sat down one evening.

"You seem frustrated, Oliver. Help me understand what's going on."

"It's all these people, Jim. They're in the way and I can't clean the rooms they're using until late."

"I hear you, Oliver. That sounds hard. Isn't it exciting, though, that the people in these recovery groups are finding freedom, and the kids in the preschool are learning and growing?"

"I guess so. But they get in the way of me cleaning the building. And the building needs to be clean and presentable for Sunday."

"But Oliver, it's only Tuesday. The building is going to be used during the rest of the week."

The conversation continued. Oliver saw people using the building as a problem, because it got in the way of being clean. And that mattered because it needed to be clean for Sunday. For him, and I suspect for many, the building didn't exist to be used, it existed to be clean and ready for those two hours a week.

I guess what I'm trying to say is that for Oliver, and millions of others like him, the building is not a resource that serves the purpose of God's rule and reign. It is a goal of its own. The building isn't a means, it's an end. And that end, at best, is to serve the Sunday service no matter how effective or ineffective that might be at Jesus' mission for the church, and at worst might just simply be to maintain having a building.

Oliver quit not long after and left the church to find one closer to home and more in line with his priorities. The building was never quite as clean, but we also lost the opportunity to bring influence into Oliver's life towards a clearer understanding of the purposes of God.

I had moved back to metro Detroit with the vision from God of seeing churches planted all across the city. That's what all those stars were that covered the map I saw of the city as a 27-year old man. These churches weren't understood as buildings, but as communities of blessing for their neighborhoods, as communities in which people from all backgrounds discovered Jesus and the flourishing life that comes from following him as his disciple.

We bore some fruit. Not only had we planted the Renaissance Vineyard Church née Royal Oak Vineyard Church. We also sent out three other church plants in the metro Detroit area, one of which failed to thrive, and two of which flourished. I was coaching two other leaders at different points in the process in the spring of 2021.

It was in March or April of that year that I invited our volunteer planning team out to lunch at one of the few restaurants open. They were helping me think through pastoral and strategic issues during Covid. After some other discussion, I asked a simple question: "Did our church really carry the vision for church planting, or was it just carried by me and Meg?" I had them think it over while we ate and talked about non-business. As we pushed our plates away, I invited their thoughts.

Though the language varied, the sentiment was unanimous: the vision for church planting was mine, while the church carried the community center vision I described earlier. I knew this was true. Two years earlier I had given our board an early draft of my vision for what I was calling then, "The Motor City Vineyard." It was a strategy for seeing more church planting in our city from our church, and to more effectively release me into my gifts. Only one board member indicated they had ever even read it, let alone embrace it.

This was a clarifying moment for me. It was perhaps the first time I could really clearly see that I was differentiated from the church as a leader and as a person.

God had given me a vision and a call, and he had given another to the church too. They didn't need to be the same.

In fact, for me to try to make my vision their vision would potentially be an act of leadership violence, forcing them to pursue my call instead of their own. I didn't want to do that. It became clear that while I had helped give birth to the "great friend to the city" vision of the church, it was as a midwife and not as a mother.

... It Didn't Work

The title of this chapter is a throwback to the chapter titled *Doin' the Stuff* ... In other words, we did the stuff ... and it didn't work. Of course, sometimes it worked. Just not nearly enough, not nearly consistently enough, and not nearly compellingly enough. It didn't produce the effect, *the fruit*, that we desired and expected. My experience was that no matter how hard we worked, no matter how much we prayed or preached or promoted our church on social media, we just weren't seeing maturing, reproducing disciples of Jesus as the result.

My first choice title for this chapter was *Enabling Infancy* or, more provocatively, *Stop Suckling Off My Spirituality*. Because, honestly, that's really what it came to feel like. In fact, after 20 years of preaching and roughly 1,000 sermons, I came to increasingly challenge the congregation with those words, "Stop suckling off my spirituality!"

Easily one of the most controversial scenes in a series overflowing with controversy is from Season One, Episode Five ("The Wolf and the Lion") of *Game of Thrones*. Tyrion Lannister is presented to Lyssa Arryn in the Court of the Vale, while she breastfeeds her eight-year-old son, Robin Arryn. It's a disturbing scene, for obvious reasons. It's clear both mother and son are sick. It's an intentionally provocative scene, because we all know that by eight years of age, children are meant to be capable of feeding themselves. I'm not sure this was my first thought when I watched the show, but I will say that as I've reflected back on the show and my experience, that scene reminds me a lot of pastoring.

There is a scripture in the Bible that reads like this: "*In fact, though by this time you ought to be teachers, you need someone to teach you the* elementary truths of God's word all over again. You need milk, not solid food! Anyone who lives on milk, being still an infant, is not acquainted with the teaching about righteousness. But solid food is for the mature, who by constant use have trained themselves to distinguish good from evil."[22]

"You need milk, not solid food!" Every time I hear a longtime Christian, an otherwise capable and reasonably competent adult, complain about their church by saying, "I'm not being fed," I think about this verse. I think about that scene from *Game of Thrones*. Who needs to be fed? Infants. Children are designed to become adults. When that's not possible it's a sign that something is somehow very wrong. We don't have babies to keep them infants. We raise children to train and release them into adulthood.

We merged and moved into the building in the hopes that this was the silver bullet that would slay the werewolf of our supposed "missional mediocrity." We moved at 100 mph those first nine months, from the day we pitched the vision until the day we ratified the by-laws, legally and officially celebrated the merger. It happened also to be my 40th birthday. Though we were running hard and working long hours, things seemed solid. Everybody and their cousin seemed to be coming to our services. Somehow one hundred plus twenty-five was now equaling 170, 180, even one Sunday of 190+ in attendance. That first Easter Sunday we hosted a sunrise service and two others, and we boasted something like 212 folks celebrating with us. I was pretty excited. There is for pastors a mythic "200 Barrier." Growing church attendance to over 200. It is in church planting lore like the four minute mile. We seemed poised to burst this barrier and join the ranks of the elite pastors. We would've planted churches, been involved in missions, and grown to over 200 in attendance. And that happened in part by merging, which no one believed was possible. Things were looking good. I could smell the ink on the book deals.

I'm kidding. Mostly.

---

[22] Hebrews 5:12-14

We never broke that barrier. A few weeks after my birthday, we went on a three week trip out west, attending our denomination's national leadership conference and taking some much needed family vacation along the way. As the seasons transitioned from summer to fall, our numbers started falling along with the leaves. Instead of a harvest, it was like things were dying on the vine. Okay, maybe that's too dramatic, but we did feel like we were bleeding people as everyone began expressing their dissatisfaction with the merge.

"I don't like the pews and stained glass windows. It's too churchy. I'm leaving."

"I don't like people drinking coffee in the sanctuary. That's not taking God seriously enough. I'm leaving."

And my favorite: "I don't like that we say the Lord's Prayer now. I'm leaving." (Maybe take that up with the Lord whose prayer it is?)

When I apologized to Bob and Agnes, who weren't always sure on their feet, and Janet, who literally lacked the field of vision to see kids running at her feet, they stopped me. "Don't you apologize for that, Jim. This is what we've been praying for all those years. Those kids are life for us and they're the answers to our prayers."

Some people left because there were too many gay people, others not enough. Some left because there were too many homeless hanging around, others wanted us to do more for the poor. Some left because the drums were too loud, others because there wasn't enough drums.

I heard through the grapevine that a number of the people who left ended up at the same church. It was the double-sized, more professionalized, conservative alter ego of our smaller, more bohemian, messy centered-set community. Now that I think about it, that church should have been paying us a referral fee!

What we noticed is that the people who cared more about the form of the church than its function (clothing culture, song style, where the coffee belonged and the type of building), they left and left pretty quickly. Those who cared about the function of the church more than its form, to be a community of people who loved God, one another and others, whether they were young or old, regardless of their denominational background, they stayed. Sadly, there were a lot of the former. People rarely left because of a thoughtfully considered and articulated difference on a core theological topic, nor after a period of prayerful discernment of Jesus' invitation to them and heartfelt conversation with leadership. They left because of personal preferences. Which was, of course, their right. But that's precisely the point, isn't it? The culture of the rule and reign of God is about responsibility and sacrifice. The culture of the empire of America is about rights and preferences. So let's not pretend that their choices were anything other than a consumer approach to the community and cause of Christ.

Even more pressing was that by the end of the first year, every one of the part-time staff (brought together from both churches) had either quit or given their notice. Later that spring we hired a new full-time pastor and part-time administrative assistant. Within three years, first one and then the other of these second round of staff hires were gone.

The following vignettes from the lives of individuals, couples and groups highlight several of the challenges we experienced.

In the first five years of our church plant, we would periodically host these special services to foster more meaningful community engagement and to introduce one another to different traditions of the Church across the centuries to deepen our discipleship to Jesus. We did each quarterly. One was a pot-luck dinner and testimonies service we called "Extending the Table." The other we structured around the prayer services Megan and I experienced at the Benedictine monastery we retreated at. It had a name that I no longer remember, but I do remember one particular Sunday: our "Liturgy of Lament." If you're familiar with the Bible, particularly the psalms, you may remember that prayers and songs of lament make up a significant portion of this sacred book. It should be no surprise, really, since songs of lament fill our airwaves and AirPods today. God is deeply sensitive to our struggles and pain. The Bible gives voice to this in these psalms of lament, encouraging us to openly and honestly express our sorrows and disappointments to God.

One Sunday we decided to do that very thing, with a service structured around songs and psalms and prayers of lament, with a brief homily to tie it all together and make sense of the experience. I'll never forget how, about 2/3 of the way through the service, this young couple got up and walked out of the room. We were pretty small then, so it was awkwardly obvious, especially with the way we had set up the room for this service. They had to walk right by me, as I was talking, on their way to the door. They were new to the church, young, well-dressed, driving a high-end car, recently married. In other words, exactly the kind of people church planters don't like to see walking out the door in the middle of the service. They didn't wait for me to reach out. They followed up the next day, letting me know that they wouldn't be back, explaining how disappointed they were with the service. Their rationale: "church was supposed to make you happy, not sad." They closed the door on relationship.

When we were renting space in the fellowship hall of another church, we often befriended neighbors who would come to the community lunch that we helped host. One woman we met we'd often see around town pushing a grocery cart with all her earthly belongings. There was one occasion, as the weather was turning, that our church offered to put her up for a night or two at the nearby motel. A friend and I drove her over there and paid for her to get a room. As we were getting back into our car, the hotel manager ran out to us. Knocking on the glass, we rolled down the window and he spent the next several minutes berating us about how we weren't really helping this woman, because another church in town had just paid for her to have a couple of nights lodging earlier that week. I noted that he waited to tell us this until after he took our payment.

Slowing Down To Catch Up With God

Whether he was right or not, I don't know, but I'll never forget what he said as he turned to walk away: "Why don't you churches learn to work together?!" He was right. Despite our claims to be one body of Christ, we lived and worked very independent of one another. We were more likely to compete for members and money than cooperate in the cause of Christ. And because of this, the hotel manager knew, people could easily take advantage of our naivete when we smugly thought we were making a difference. I've also heard from our pantry team about the folks who drive up at our Thanksgiving Feast distribution and have to shuffle around the many other donated turkeys in their trunk, in order to make room for what they're receiving from us.

My friend Noah, a troubled young man who had grown up in the church we merged with comes to mind. His family system was troubled and chaotic. He was dual diagnosis with both mental illness and substance abuse addiction. We leaned into loving him. We were for him the several times he went into and out of jail. We hosted him for Thanksgiving in our home several years and our family cherished him. Yet there was the time that Noah, deep in his addiction, thought it would be a good idea to give his drug dealer my personal cell phone number. Noah was in debt and he hoped that the church could pay it off. My refusal to pay the debt was met with lots of profane jabs about what a terrible pastor I was that I wouldn't help my parishioner get free. I wonder if he had some church background growing up because he knew a bunch of the buttons to push.

It was pretty common that we would get anxious questions about significant cultural and political issues. The most common, by far, was homosexuality (including related sexual and gender-related topics), but also sometimes about abortion, guns, immigration and the rest. Think of the topics in a typical presidential debate, but with even less time and opportunity to answer.

Once our church's social media post received a private message response from someone who had recently started attending the church. It went something like, "I love this picture and what you said. And we've really loved the church. It really feels like home. This post makes me wonder what is your stance on homosexuality?" My reply went something like, "Wow. Thanks for all your kind words. And thank you for such a good question. That's an important topic. I'd love to meet with you in person so that we can dialogue about it." I never heard from them again.

On another occasion my wife was serving at the children's ministry check-in desk. A first-time guest was checking in her three kids, commenting on how she had heard lots of good things about the church, loved the space in our building, and how warm the people felt. Then she paused and asked, "Oh, one question, what's your position on homosexuality?" "Oh," Meg replied. The service was literally starting that exact minute and she was distracted by all the hubbub. Taking a deep breath, Meg started to answer. Before she could even finish her sentence the woman had grabbed her kids and walked away, sure that, whatever her position might've been, ours wasn't good enough.

It was sad to see how many people walked away from dialogue, interested only if our stance on their issue succinctly matched their own, regardless of what we thought about Jesus and how we might belong and serve and grow together.

Then there was the woman who visited us a few times after her long-time church had closed. At the close of the service she approached me, saying, "Hey, Pastor Jim, you've got a good thing going here! I like your sermons and the worship team too. I notice that you're also livestreaming. I think the one thing that would make it better is if you had more cameras so that you could stream even better and maybe put it on more platforms. We could get a few professional cameras and put them around the room. That's what my last church had. It was great." I expressed my appreciation for her kind words and enthusiastic reviews of our service. As well as her stepping up to share her ideas. We loved to hear from folks.

"The thing is, though, that by streaming from my phone, which is already paid for, we're saving LOTS of money. Plus, with the Facebook app, it's like designed for this usage. It works well."

"Sure. But these cameras would really make it professional. That's what we had at my old church and it was great!" I kept thinking, *yeah, but your old church closed, so it couldn't have been that great.* Or maybe it was great, but great at the wrong things. We had a little more back and forth. She was passionate about the professionalism. We never saw her again.

These vignettes give a taste of what it was like and the challenges we often navigated in trying to faithfully steward our calling. The following stories, all with people I love and care about, round out the portrait.

I think of my friend Tate. We met at one of our Sunday services while we were renting from the middle school. He lived in the area and had seen our church sign on his travels around town. He came that Sunday in a pretty desperate situation. He also came nervously since he had experienced lots of hurt from churches and Christians in his past, based on his background and personal choices. I can still remember the service. It was a fairly full room for that season of our church. I was preaching from Genesis 14, the story of Abram and Melchizedek, about the biblical concept of tithing and honoring God with our finances. I never particularly liked preaching on money. In those days we didn't even receive an offering. Instead, we simply had a box in the back of the room that I encouraged people to use if they felt this was their church home and they wanted to support our work. Sometimes I would forget to mention it, which drove the board crazy!

That particular Sunday I was pretty excited about the sermon, and I felt like I had really communicated the topic well. Honestly, I sorta felt like I nailed it. I spoke with Tate after the service and he asked to meet sometime that week. Sitting in the chair in my office he opened up, "I think I enjoyed the service. People seemed pretty loving. But I really had no idea what you were talking about. Your sermon made no sense to me." As he tried to remember the passage and pronounce the names, I was crestfallen. I still had been riding the high, but the wave crashed as I realized my sermon made no sense to exactly the kind of person I most hoped to reach. I lamely apologized, which I wasn't sure was the right thing to do or not. Then I even more lamely tried to explain the sermon, which was a nice gesture as far as it went, but to little avail.

Tate came back a few more times and we stayed in touch. Rather than attend services, he preferred to meet up and talk with me one on one. We did that a handful of times over the next year or two. After a while we lost contact. I'd think about him from time to time, but the press of other people, other problems, would squeeze out my ability to follow up.

Then one day I got a call from his family. Tate had died alone in his apartment. He was found after a few days. The circumstances were mysterious. Unknown. I have my sad suspicions. He led a lonely, troubled, trauma-shaped life. The family asked if I would officiate the funeral. Somehow they had heard about our relationship, understood that I was his pastor.

I still remember meeting Tate's father, shaking his hand as we talked final details before the ceremony began. He thanked me for all that I had done. I felt like a phony. I tried to do what I could do given the circumstances. Tate felt loved. That's significant. Yet I never quite got around to extending a compelling invitation for Tate to become an apprentice of Jesus and his way of life. Instead, I settled for the half-measures of periodically welcoming him to my office, answering his questions, and praying for him instead of teaching him to pray to God for himself.

He longed to find healing from pain and discover hope in place of despair. Yet Tate died alone, not in a community who embraced him in love and was glad to be with him. I never really prioritized the space in my life to winsomely embody and articulate the good news of Jesus. Tate was beginning to feel loved by me, but in those final days I don't really know where he stood with God. God, have mercy. For Tate. For me.

...

At some point I conceived the idea for a small group called "The Bible, A Brew, and You." We called it BBU. The original idea was that this could be any brew: coffee, tea, beer, you name it, trying to reach folks who wouldn't normally participate in a traditional Bible study. But, no surprise, it quickly turned into beers and a bunch of guys. That may have had something to do with our first meeting place: Dragonmead Brewery. Basically, a group of guys who probably played fantasy games as kids got together to brew beer and open a place in a vacant industrial building next to the highway. Cheesy décor, but the beer was good. And expensive enough that we didn't stay there long. Plus, while the environment was conducive to a non-churchy vibe, it was hard to maintain much focus on God and the Bible. But since we had made plenty of room for stories, everyone wanted to keep meeting. So we moved to one guy's basement hang out room. It quickly became apparent that his large TV and extensive catalog of downloaded movies was just as distracting as the bar. So after a few more months we moved the group to my home.

The group started at 10 p.m. This made it more manageable to meet at our house since all the kids were asleep. Our basement had just been finished and we moved some furniture down to accommodate the guys. It was a fascinating group. Definitely not your grandma's Bible study. On one occasion there was a wrestling match that involved a bleeding forehead. Another time half the group brought firearms to clean while we dialogued. The group often went past midnight, with some people staying to discuss and/or hangout until 2 a.m. or later. On several occasions Meg or I would get laundry from the basement in the morning and find someone sleeping in our guest bed. We laughed a lot, argued almost as much, and forgave even more. The group developed its own logo and t-shirts honoring one of our members. It was a special group.

One evening we had a field trip to the basement of another member for a hangout. It was late, after midnight, when one guy in the group made a remark that I felt was racist, about a friend of mine who had recently left. I challenged him about it. He retorted, "Oh, you think that's bad, do you?!? Well, I'm sorry then, Jim, for what I said. But I've got a question for you: What the fuck kind of church is this, Jim? You see, just this last Sunday I talked to so and so about how proud they must be that their son is now on the worship team and doing so well. Then they said, 'Oh, that's not my son, that's my wife.' So that's my question for you, Jim, what's going on here?!?!" He wasn't really mad, just loud, little and Italian. His rant cut through the noise. The whole basement went quiet as they stopped to turn and look. So I circled everyone up at the table and we had a conversation about sexuality, gender, Jesus and the Bible that went until 3 a.m. We talked about how we were a community centered on Jesus, inviting people from all backgrounds to receive his love (including ourselves), respond to his self-sacrificial gift to rescue us from our self-destructive habits, and find flourishing life in following him.

Despite the many wonderful things about this group, I'll never forget the moment it "jumped the shark." (If you're not sure what that term means, YouTube "Happy Days jump the shark" ... it refers to that seemingly innocuous moment when a great thing crosses a line and begins to end.) A group text went out inviting all the guys to gather at a local pub. We met to discuss whether the group would allow new people to join. A few folks had seen us wearing our t-shirts at the service, heard about the happenings, and they wanted in. I asked everyone to share what they thought.

As each person in turn offered their opinion, with shockingly few interruptions, it became clear that this group of guys was completely closed to the idea of new folks. I understand there are moments to have closed groups. Yet here was a group of guys, most of whom had been struggling to find a community, wrestling with God, who were closed to offering that opportunity to others. They were unwilling to share the gift that they had received. It turned out that too much of the group's energy was just so much adolescent enthusiasm. It is the gift and responsibility of adults to make room for others to experience life and blessing. Despite all the time we shared together, all the love and discussions and prayer, this group remained spiritual children, clutching the gift. I was dismayed. Though the group lingered for a while, it disbanded not long after, each person going their own way. Though it took a long time, thankfully they began to grow into mature disciples.

...

I remember the member of our church who I'm convinced robbed from God. Walker was always a little awkward when he visited our church, standing against the wall with a clear line of sight, twitchy with roving eyes. As I got to know him, he shared about his story of seven tours as a sniper during the Global War on Terror, and I chalked it up to trauma related to that. He was a quiet, no-nonsense guy who had grown up nearby and had returned to metro Detroit for work. We had him to our home as part of our Discover Renaissance group. In the spring of 2017 his mom passed away, opening a door for us to take a more pastoral posture towards him as he processed his grief.

One day that summer he called me out of the blue. He told me with his mom's passing he needed to do something with her house and expressed a desire to bless the church in some way. I told him I would get back to him after taking some time to ask God about it. Hanging up the phone, I was in shock. That summer we were beginning to recognize just how desperate was the need to fix our flat roof. We had no money and I was feeling overwhelmed at the prospect of the project. I was just coming off that season in 2016 of feeling so alone.

The day before Walker called, at the encouragement of a trusted friend, I just began to pray directly for God to provide resources to fix the roof. I called him back the next day and explained the situation. He expressed his desire to sell the house and give the proceeds from the sale to the church as a gift. I was floored. Even though it was a small house in poor shape, this would be the largest gift we had ever received, and it would more than cover the expected cost of the roof. He said all we needed to do was form a team to come and clean out the house to ready it for showing. I enthusiastically agreed.

A few weeks later the house was cleared. The team was grateful to be part of this gift for the church. A few weeks later he let me know the house was listed. Months went by and I didn't hear from him. He also didn't show up for service on Sundays. Naively, I trusted all was well. Then I drove by the house. The For Sale sign was gone and new owners were around. I didn't want to believe it, but he had used us. Used me. He made a promise and then robbed God of the gift he had committed. We never asked him to give so generously to the church. He initiated this sacrificial offering. He lied to God and our team. Turns out he had been lying about his tours in the desert as a sniper too. Though he had been hanging around the church for several years, we never really knew him.

...

I dialed the number and waited for my friend to pick up as I paced laps around my basement. (The basement was where I took most of "those" pastoral calls that I expected to be short, whereas the longer ones were reserved for the dog walk park at the end of my block or the neighborhood around the church building, depending on the timing of the call.) Jack answered after a few rings, his voice tremulous, "Oh, Jim, thank you for calling. I don't know what to do! The RV broke down and I had to sell it 'As Is' to a buyer for cash. I rented a U-Haul, loaded in my things with my dog Mr. Wiggins riding shotgun and we've been driving around Florida for the past month, seeing friends as we're able. We've run out of money, Jim, and I don't know what to do! What should I do? Please help!"

Perhaps the clearest example of this spiritual infancy and suckling off my spirituality that I've been trying to articulate is my friend, Jack. You've previously met Jack and his husband, Chris. They were active and engaged members of the church for about a dozen years. They were faithful and committed. They showed up at stuff. They were involved. They walked the path that we laid out for being part of the church.

Jack was retirement age, but Chris was over a decade younger, still in his career. Jack was ready to settle down as a grandpa. Chris was still thinking about partying with friends. Jack was tired of caring for the house, while Chris was thinking about the financial investment he had made in the home from his paycheck. After more than a dozen years of marriage, the marriage hit a really rough spot. Like every relationship I know of, theirs had plenty of fracture lines, but then the pressure of what to do in this next season of life caused it to crack and come apart.

I got a frantic call one evening asking if we'd be able to come and talk. Sensing a crisis, I agreed. We lived in the same neighborhood so I was knocking on their door a short stroll later. The pain and tension in the room was thick. We jumped right in. Jack had discovered Chris posting selfies on a porn site. (How he found out, I still don't know.) Then Jack had stumbled upon Chris having sex for hire in their guest room. I knew Chris's story, had a sense of the sorrow and trauma in his past as it related to sex. Chris loved Jesus and recognized how poor these choices were. He was repentant. He was apologetic. He was also angry. As the conversation continued, sharing his perspective, he unearthed deep-seated pain from nearly a decade earlier, when Jack had kiboshed Chris's dreams. Chris had tried addressing it then, but Jack had been dismissive. He never accepted ownership of his actions nor understood the scope of their consequences. Chris was acting out of this deep hurt. He realized he was wrong and wanted reconciliation, but he wasn't willing to take all the responsibility. Chris was asking Jack to step up and acknowledge his part. Jack couldn't get there. He could only see himself as the victim. They divorced a few months later.

Chris and Jack had had plans to retrofit a school bus into a trendy RV. It seemed that dream was dead. The house was sold in the divorce and, with the market as it was and having to split the proceeds, Jack didn't get nearly as much as he was hoping for. Lingering around the campfire one evening after our neighborhood Bible study he asked me what he should do. He wasn't close with his family in the area, but his relationship with his son's family in the Great Plains seemed solid, so I recommended he hold on to those funds as God's provision of a retirement nest egg and relocate to be an amazing grandpa. He liked the sound of that but couldn't let go of his aspirations for the open road and the idea of visiting old church friends in Florida. So he used what money he had to buy a fixer-upper RV. I understood his longings yet expressed my concerns about his choice.

After a few weeks he looked stricken as he and his dog, Mr. Wiggins, took their place around the campfire. "Jim, I've got terrible news and I don't know what to do! I've been parking the RV at my ex-wife's house while I save up money for the last few repairs I need to make. Well, it was parked on a slight incline, the brake slipped, and it rolled downhill. My ex's house is fine but the overhang of the garage sliced open the roof of the RV. What am I going to do? It's ruined! I don't know if the insurance will cover it." We grieved with him in his loss and prayed with him that night.

A few weeks later, he could barely contain himself as he joined our circle: "You'll never guess what! My insurance accepted my claim! They've totaled the RV and they're going to send me a check for almost the full amount. I can't believe it! I'm so thankful to God!" We rejoiced with him and then discussed next steps, at his request.

"It seems to me, Jack," I replied, "that God has given you an unexpected second chance. A generous second chance. I would take this as an opportunity to start over and relocate to be with family whom you can love and who can look after you as you age."

The next week he bought a smaller used RV that didn't require any repairs. Then he loaded it up and drove to Florida to visit with friends, leaving the falling leaves of Michigan behind.

Sometime that winter I started getting texts and calls from friends about Jack. Because of what had happened in Florida, he started contacting our mutual friends for help and they reached out to me. One guy offered him a one-way ticket anywhere in the US if he took only what he could carry, turned his dog into a shelter, and never contacted him again. He declined.

I called Jack that night to talk with him directly. "What's going on, Jack?" He described his situation. After he ended his frantic, breathless plea, I continued, "I'm not able to help you, Jack, and I'm discouraging our friends from helping you. I wanted you to hear that directly from me. I'm not able to help you because you've refused our help. For the past two years you've routinely reached out to me for counsel. I made space. I listened. I prayed. I took your concerns to heart and shared what wisdom and leading I sensed from God. And at each turn you listened to me and then did the exact opposite of what we talked about. When the house sold, you could've used that money to go be with family who would love and care for you. You didn't. When the first RV was totaled and you received the insurance money, you had a second chance. You didn't take it. When this second RV failed and you received money, you could've driven that U-Haul to be with family or at least to be with friends in Detroit where you've got a social support system, but instead you drove around in circles in Florida until you ran out of money. Jack, at every turn you've refused our wise counsel and so now there is no more help I can give. I love you, Jack, and I commend you to the Lord. I wish you well. Goodbye."

His is a sad story. There is a lot going on in his history, yet whatever that might be, he had been a Christian for fifty years, but he was still a spiritual infant. He sat through innumerable sermons, loved worship and knew the songs, attended retreats and conferences, participated in Bible studies and small groups, served in ministry and went on mission trips, but he never actually grew. Really, he simply kept repeating the same two years of toddler spirituality. Though a sage man, he kept suckling off the spirituality of others, unable to feed himself, unable to rely on himself to make wise decisions towards a mature, flourishing life.

Jack isn't alone. He is merely an extreme version of typical. Most don't try as hard as he did. Most aren't as committed as he is. Yet still he stayed stuck in spiritual infancy.

…

For most churchgoers, Christianity is something they do during an event, at a building, when it happens to be convenient for their already overcrowded schedule, with an extra helping for the holidays or when there's a crisis. They'll feed off the pastor, the worship leader, or the youth or children's workers, and when the milk has an unwelcome taste, they'll leave to find another more palatable source.

<u>Social Living</u>
The images scroll by.
Little windows into worlds
I once knew so well, but now
Enter only through updates.
I settle on one of these icons,
And remember.
I feel the weight of my outstretched arm.
The weightlessness of my open hand.
As soul after soul takes flight.
Trying never to grasp;
Aware my care is never meant to be a cage.
I'm confident my hand is never truly empty.
Long experience teaching me
Some baby bird, with broken wing,
Will roost within my cuppéd hand.
And make of it a nest,
From which to soar.

So many freewill offerings.
Every person knows this Achilles heel of community.
Yet perhaps pastors get the gift in double measure.
Learning the truth of these words,
"Poor, yet making many rich;
Having nothing, and yet possessing everything."

I guess it should come as little surprise that people were equally the greatest gift and most wonderful reward of pastoring, while equally being the source of deepest pain and struggle.

Yet it wasn't just people, it was the professional aspect of the pastoral life that also carried with it hardship and sorrow. I've noticed this is particularly true as it relates to friendships, colleagues, schedule, pay, expectations and how pastors handle stress.

Most pastors I know find it nearly impossible to have friends. All leaders experience loneliness, and pastors more than most. Meg and I were once at dinner with a tableful of seasoned pastors. She and I had been talking about the challenges of friendship that pastors experience. We wondered how they managed. Meg asked the question, "What's your experience of friendship as pastors? How are you able to be friends with people in your church?" One pastor of decades actually laughed out loud. Another quickly retorted, "Why would I want that?" None had a good answer.

<u>Lothlorien</u>
Legendary greatness and
Fabled glory.
Now rumors,
Diminished
In this Fourth Age.
A land of more goodbyes
Than hellos.
Drawn to the East and
Untold opportunities.
Or to the shores of the
Western or Southern Seas.
They are experts at leave-taking

In Lorien.
I know.
I live there.
Steward of stories.
Caretaker of the remnant
That remains.
Faithful against the day when
The world is remade.

Clergy are alone in a crowd. It's hard to be friends with people who aren't Christians because as soon as they find out you're a pastor they always start apologizing for swearing and are hesitant to invite you to the parties because they'll be drinking. Being friends with Christians outside the church can be tough for pastors because you're usually already too busy, you feel a little guilty that you're not spending time with your family or hanging out with the non-Christians ("for the sake of the mission," of course), and there's always a small voice in the back of your mind wondering if maybe they'd like your church better (and there's always a question in the back of *their* minds wondering if you're going to make the ask). And friendship with folks in the church you serve is both easy and really hard. It's easy to be friendly, hard to be friends. You see, friendship involves mutuality, and mutuality is hard when one of you is on a pedestal and the other is unprepared to really hear your real life. Most pastors struggle with healthy friendships.

It would seem that if there was any profession that should do collegial relationships well, it would be pastoring. Nope. I've been to a lot of conferences and pastors' meetings, of all sizes and foci: denominational, geographical, topical. Pastors show up craving connection because they're lonely. Yet they're hesitant because of the burden of comparison. Lots of professions do this, of course. Pastors aren't immune. After the pleasantries about the sports team du jour, the next common question in the liturgy of conferencing is, "How are things?" This seemingly innocuous question is translated as "How big is your church attendance?" Or, if you're slightly more spiritual, "How many baptisms have you had this year?" This is experienced as "What is your value and self-worth and how does it compare to mine?" Comparison is never your friend, as my wise wife loves to say, and it is toxic to healthy loving community. But there it is, always in the room, like the stink of a fart in an elevator.

At one point during the Covid era, I attended a gathering where our denominational leadership wanted to check up on us and see how we were doing. They went around the room and asked people to share what percentage of their pre-Covid levels were they experiencing in attendance and income. As if that was the important thing about how we were doing! I understood what they were trying to do. They really did care, and they were being pressured by their up-stream supervisors. But I knew the toxic possibilities, that this would be experienced as comparison couched in the language of care and accountability. ("Crap," thinks the pastor already struggling with loneliness and shame, "Sally's church is at 75% pre-Covid levels and I just shared we're only at 60%. What are we doing wrong? What's wrong with me?") I refused to answer. I knew they were responsible to someone else, so despite my orneriness, I did email them later with the details. But in the moment I answered with, "We've got money in the bank and people to talk to. I'm fine. We're fine. These are the wrong questions, so I'd like to talk about what we're doing in mission."

Because in my experience of ministerial gatherings, if pastors aren't comparing, they're usually complaining. Complaining about how hard it is. Complaining about whatever. I remember one Tuesday morning that I attended a gathering of local pastors at one of their homes. I was coming from the Chamber of Commerce gathering where there was energy in the room. Businesses were growing, new members were joining, things were happening. When I arrived at my ministerial friends' home, the few pastors were seated around the table of a dimly lit dining room, drinking coffee from ancient mugs, and everyone was sharing about ministries closing because of leaders moving or dying. *What were we going to do?* they wondered. It was sad.

The previous year I had proposed to this same group that we discuss best practices for ministry and mission, each within our own denominational contexts. No one was interested.

I once spoke with a sage minister who had long served as a pastor to pastors. He commented on how many ministers struggled with idleness.

The temptation was to do too little. I suppose there are some of those folks out there. Yet most pastors I know are painfully busy and struggle with overwork. The typical pastor feels the pressure of working during traditional corporate work hours to justify their salary and feed their sense of self-worth, to look like they have a normal job in the eyes of whomever they're trying to please. And because we're in the people business, there is a lot of pressure to work at times when people are available for relationship. This means most work at least a few nights, in between family commitments, when people are off work. Then there is the question of Saturday. People may be available to volunteer in ministry, and they also do social stuff that it would be good to be at with them. And of course there's Sunday with its long hours.

Many pastors take Monday off, which I did for a long time. But most of the best restaurants and fun places are closed, so it was hard to relax well. More significantly, because on Sunday afternoons and Monday everyone in the church seemed to remember God is real and wants to engage with me about him, I'd come in on Tuesday and immediately feel behind and work to catch back up every week. It was so tiring. After several years, I switched to taking Fridays off. More fun places were open that day and, honestly, I was extroverted enough that I never felt the need for a breather come Monday morning. Friday worked better. However, I quickly discovered that my wife was introverted enough that her idea of a day off was a quiet morning of reading, sitting by the gas fireplace, and I was extroverted enough that I ended up responding to emails simply to have some social interaction. Then when Saturday came the kids wanted to hang out, but I was feeling the pressure of needing to "do a little work." The opening of the laptop always brought a frown. Eventually I settled on Saturday as my rest day. It meant I worked six days a week and often had to juggle what to do with Saturday social invitations.

In my iCal, my personal calendar has always been blue and my work calendar green. Frankly, what I felt like I really needed was aquamarine, a "workonal" category. Pastoral work is relational. People invited me into relationship at social events. Because the context of our relationship was often about church, they often asked or talked about church things there, never quite realizing that for me it was a lot like work. Or on other occasions they sorta wanted to show me off as their pastor, hoping that their friends would like me enough to want to join them at their church. It's like I was the bait in some fishing scheme. The pastoral schedule was a hamster wheel.

Another challenge for me as a pastor had to do with my pay. I've come to realize that I felt the board of the church I led was never particularly generous with me in terms of finances. What I did with my time? Yes. But not with money. What's probably a more accurate picture is this: basically, everyone knew there was never quite enough money or as much as we'd like, so the question surrounding my income always seemed to be: "What do you need to live on?" This question generally meant, "What can you get by with?" At a very practical level, this meant that it was me who always suggested my income with the approval of the board. My recommendation was basically always the lowest amount I felt like I could get away with. This went all the way back to the work I did while planting the church and also while in seminary: subbing as a teacher and working at Starbucks while planting, washing storefront windows and as a church secretary while in seminary. For more than half my life I was constantly "selling myself short" and undervaluing my contribution in terms of compensation, asking myself the question, "What's the least amount I can earn, in order to live and do the thing I feel called to do?" This included the core part of my working life as an adult and the expression of my life's work pastoring the church we planted.

I think there was only ever one person on the board that really saw this for what it was and expressed emotion about it. I only ever had one bonus. And other than the transition from volunteer to part-time, and part-time to full-time, my memory is that I only ever had two raises and never any cost of living increases. The one raise that I actually asked and advocated for, members of the board questioned, largely out of their own painful experiences of compensation at their work. From when I was in my mid-20's, I've never had anyone say to me, "We want to pay you this because we think that's appropriate for your contribution," nor "We would love to pay you this, but we can't right now, which you also know, and so we're only able to pay you this. Thank you for your sacrifice." Now, by temperament, life experience, character and conviction, I have been well-suited to this situation. Yet it still stings. I had told Colonel

Skeletor I wasn't going into the ministry for the money, and I guess I was right.

Around the time I started writing this book, I participated in several pastoral ordination celebrations. One of my favorite moments was when one of the newly ordained pastors warned the congregation with these words, "Be careful of pastors." Among other admonitions, he said, "No man or woman can stand as a mediator between you and God because only Jesus can do that," and continued by quoting these stern words of Jesus: *"But you are not to be called 'Rabbi,' for you have one Teacher, and you are all brothers. And do not call anyone on earth 'father,' for you have one Father, and he is in heaven. Nor are you to be called instructors, for you have one Instructor, the Messiah. The greatest among you will be your servant. For those who exalt themselves will be humbled, and those who humble themselves will be exalted."*[23] This is such a timely message.

Yet, despite the powerful message of warning to the congregation, participating in these ordination ceremonies was sobering. Honestly, they had an almost triggering effect on me. I started reflecting back on my own ordination celebration with Megan. At the time it was one of the most beautiful and powerful experiences we had ever had. We felt seen, heard, affirmed, celebrated, loved. My hope is that every disciple of Jesus has that quality of experience in their life, as others affirm them in their life and work and vocation, whether as a pastor of thousands, hotel hospitality worker or volunteer at a rescue dog shelter. Yet my ordination celebration was also bracing, carrying heavy conviction. My mentor read from Matthew 25, Jesus' Parable of the Sheep and the Goats. He also read from Romans 12, how our love is to be expressed in action. He read from other scriptures too. I took these charges to heart.

And as I did so, something interesting happened. A stew took shape, simmering in my soul: the base of a real unction from God, combined with the stock of people's desperate needs, a cup of wide-ranging and often unrealistic expectations from people, mixed with the chopped up bits of traditions and norms around pastors and churches, seasoned with

---

[23] Matthew 23:8-12

the tenacious resiliency that enabled me to attend, thrive and graduate from West Point (the commitment to "adapt and overcome" no matter what). This created a real challenge for me. In one sense, I knew it was never healthy for people to keep feeding off of me. For me to keep trying to feed them. Yet, in another sense, I was willing to work as long and as hard as necessary, to do whatever it took, to see the mission accomplished.

I routinely worked six days a week, often seven. Most every morning as I showered, I would tabulate my hours in my head, to confirm I was working hard and long enough. Even now, I struggle not to apologize to Megan, to myself, when I'm sick and unable to work at my normal pace or need to take a day off.

When God once told me to rest on my day off and trust him to take care of whatever was worrying me, I second guessed him with an inarticulate "ummm" and an interior eye roll. As if I could be a better pastor than God! But that's what my reflex response was. I remember the time that I was grocery shopping with Meg on our day off, pushing the cart with my daughter in the jump seat. An email came from a friend in the church and I answered it, about some ministry question. He shot me back a reply, "What are you doing answering emails on your day off?!?! Don't do that! My email can wait. It's important you spend time with your family." I knew that was true, but I still read his email and thought about how I would reply the next day. That's how I was wired. That was the flavor of my vocational stew. This took a toll on me, of course. How could it not? It could've precipitated a crisis, but thankfully it never got that far.

Honestly, though, I struggled to handle the stress well.

Everyone develops mechanisms for managing anxiety and often these are unhealthy or even self-destructive. One way I came to cope with the pressures of pastoring was alcohol. I love Belgian Abbey Ales and have developed a palate for the wide-ranging flavors of IPAs. I'm no teetotaler. Yet on a few occasions I drank too much.

I remember one evening, probably my most embarrassing pastoral moment. Dear members of our church were coming to our home for dinner a few nights before they moved out of state after retiring. They both had served faithfully in significant leadership for years, were gracious to our family, and were the largest financial supporters of our church. Before they came, I met another leader in our church at my favorite neighborhood pub around happy hour as he was getting off work before the weekend. We had had some trouble connecting recently, so it was important enough to meet despite the awkward timing. We enjoyed a really good conversation over a couple of beers. He shared at a heart level we hadn't experienced in quite a while. The owner walked in just as we were standing to leave and insisted we sit down and chat with him as he ordered us a complementary round. That round turned into another.

Walking into my home, I saw how late I was. Our friends were already sitting down to dinner with my family. I slipped into my bedroom to ready myself to join them. Instead, I crashed out on the bed and slept through the whole evening, waking up in the morning with deep shame. I called to apologize. They were understanding and kind. I saw them two years later when I was in their city with my son to hike. I apologized again and they again graciously forgave me. They hosted us for dinner and a place to sleep and we talked late into the night. There was a lot going on that fateful evening when I passed out. I think that I carried stress about which I was unaware, anxiety about what would happen when they left? *Would the church crash financially? If we couldn't pay the bills would I have to get another job?* This goodbye dinner with them focused all that anxiety and I managed that very poorly.

That was a worst-case moment. Yet I was often anxious. Almost all the time. My kids coined a name for it: "stress calls." They identified different levels of stress calls: 1-10. Think of it as, "Oh no! Dad has a level four stress call!" A level one stress call was a deep sigh as I read an email or a text. You know that sigh. Level three was when I anxiously rubbed my temples, often accompanied by the sigh or a groan. When I did a level five stress call, that was a sign to my girls to find another place to play, because that's when I pounded the table I was working at in frustration.

Then there was that one famous level ten stress call.

I was working at my dining room table, my "home office," conveniently located at the central crossroads of our home. I had a board meeting on Zoom after dinner, and as I sat down to eat and mentally prepare, a member of our church called. I don't even remember the issue, only that they kept going on and on about some small matter, so that I missed my meal and had to hang up hurriedly to log into my meeting. As I opened my laptop to log in, it chose that moment to update and reboot. Wouldn't you know it!?! I had already been grumpy before the unnecessarily long call and wasn't looking forward to the board meeting. I logged into Zoom on my phone and just as it was connecting, my girls came stomping down the stairs, loudly screaming at one another in a playful argument. I lost it as they jumped to the dining room floor, throwing my phone down and shouting, "What the hell, girls?! Can't you see I'm on a work call? Shut up and go somewhere else!" I probably said some other things, too, I'm embarrassed to admit. As I looked around to find my phone, in order to join the call, I discovered that it was ruined. I had thrown it down right on the corner and since I don't use a case, it looked like it had partially exploded from within. But, shockingly, the call was still active. Finally updated, I logged into the meeting on my laptop. "Jim," one of the board members said cautiously, "we heard the whole thing. Let's maybe take a few moments in quiet silence as we begin?" Mortified, I agreed, and let myself be led as the meeting began.

In one sense, these stress calls were meant to be tongue in cheek, and naming them was a way of dealing with the anxiety in a healthy, playful way. However, it was also a sign of a deeper, recurring, problem: the anxiety I was carrying related to my work.

My friend, Barry, introduced me to the idea of pastors being put on pedestals, idolized by their congregations. He used to tell me, "Jim, don't let them put you on a pedestal. That's the worst thing that could happen to you as a pastor. And they'll want to do it. Wait and see." I loved Barry and his no-nonsense wisdom polished by years of being in and out of recovery. He was spot on. The longer I pastored, the more I would try to knock myself off that pedestal. I would preach in shorts and t-shirts. I would preach barefoot. I endlessly used *Lord of the Rings*, *Star Wars* and *Star Trek* illustrations. I once sang a song *a Capella* during the sermon, and on two other Sundays I led worship by myself *a Capella*. I even farted once or twice during a sermon (perhaps accidentally?). Yet no matter how hard I tried to get off the pedestal, people just kept saying, "Look at our pastor! He's great. He's hilarious. He's so down to earth. He farts and enjoys beer and preaches barefoot in shorts and a t-shirt! Let's lift him a little higher on the pedestal!"

In his landmark book, *The Effective Executive*, leadership guru Peter Drucker shares this fascinating insight: if two or more otherwise qualified people take the same job and then repeatedly fail, the issue isn't the person, it's the job description.[24] I've seen this principle at work on several different occasions with a specific job role. Then I got to thinking, what if it applied more broadly to an entire job category: the American church has had generations of men and women who are wonderful, qualified, talented people, take on the assignment of pastor, only to struggle in the role and fail. (Like many of my readers, I'm sure, Meg and I repeatedly get emails and read social media posts about the challenges of the job). We often wonder what went wrong with the person or what was going on in the specific context. But what if Drucker is right? What if the problem isn't the person or the church, what if it is the structure of the position itself?

We did everything we thought we were supposed to do. We tried everything we had been coached and recommended to do, everything we had been told was right. It didn't work enough. It didn't satisfy the longing of our heart. We didn't see our "what" for "why" we had gotten involved in the first place. Actually, to be honest, the problem wasn't so much that we tried and it didn't work. It often did work. Yes, we started and ran a church. Yes, we even ministered God's kingdom. We just didn't adequately make disciples, let alone self-feeding, multiplying disciple-makers. Our work often bore fruit, it just didn't stick, didn't replicate, wouldn't continue without significant ongoing effort. The machine would run only so long as we were in the hamster wheel.

---

[24] Peter Drucker, *The Effective Executive* (New York: HarperCollins, 2006) 79

The Journey Inward

Karen invited the fifteen or so of us seated around the U-shaped table to take out a piece of paper and reflect on the question, "How is your soul as you come to our time together?" It could be anything: journaling, a prayer, a picture or some other creative expression. I settled into a comfortable position and stared at my blank sheet.

In time Karen and her husband, Mark, would become dear friends. For now, however, she was to me simply the wife of the director of this team and the skilled facilitator of our session together. I was the newest member of the Missions Leadership Team, entrusted with responsibility to steward the partnership work of Vineyard USA churches serving in Sub-Saharan Africa. The day before we had wrapped up our four-day annual conference, completed an afternoon debrief and enjoyed a celebratory dinner together. This morning we were strolling leisurely into a weekend of team development and soul care. One of my favorite things about the ten years I served on this MLT was the commitment of time, skill and money the leadership made to the holistic well-being of the team members. It was life-changing.

I sat there with my blank paper seeking to be attentive to God. What I first noticed was sorrow. Disappointment. Tiredness. For the past year back home we had been running to make the merge work. One of our part-time staff, a long-time friend and key leader, had just left the week before. Another part-time staff would leave within a month. I could feel the braking energy in the sanctuary each Sunday, was aware that some of the seats were beginning to empty. Below the sadness and lack of sleep I sensed something deeper: pain. Pain and longing. This took me by surprise. It's like they had been there all along, with God as their attendant, waiting for me to pause long enough to notice. I could feel them. Yet I had no words.

Then, unbidden, I took up my pen, put it to paper, and wrote these words:

How many lives does a phoenix have?
One, two, three, four?
I'm hoping for that, and more.
Let my life be a torch,
Lighting little candles of love,
Ablaze.
I'll go down in the flames if need be,
So that we both may be made new.
"Speramus Meliora; Resurget Cineribus."

This expressed the pain and longing of my vocation the first ten years, especially the past twelve months, articulated most clearly in Detroit's motto: "*Speramus Meliora; Resurget Cineribus.*" "We hope for better things; it will rise from the ashes." As I rested in the ashes of my pain that morning, I came strangely alive.

Sharing the verses and my grief with this new circle of friends, I gently embraced my tears and enjoyed a very meaningful weekend. Home again, I continued my walking around town. Then I saw this giant oak tree aflame with fall colors. The muse struck. I wrote routinely for several years. I discovered that writing poetry was a gift, helping me find voice for the deeper emotions that I otherwise had trouble expressing.

Much of my poetry sprang from pain. Some came with the rush of pleasure or attentiveness to the everyday. Yet I've noticed that many of my urges to put thoughts in verse came when I tapped into the reservoir of pain.

Poetry—whether the verse of joy, devotion or rhyme,
Or the art of living well in the flow of time—
Poetry springs from aerated ground;
Dwells in rooms with open windows wherein is found
Space to breathe.
Forged in the furnace of a passionate heart,
Living experience plays the anvil's part,
Crafted with the hammer of daily discipline.

For some people pain is experienced more naturally. They can sit in it like an ice bath after a long workout. Or they dive in, like Jacques Cousteau, kitted with goggles, air tank and flashlight, exploring the deep. Not so for me. For a plenitude of reasons, pain does not come naturally to me. I'm not so much a stuffer, as I am an evader, like a running back trained to juke, spin and slide past the painful encounter with the opposing tackler. Keep running.

Yet pain is something common to us all. Something we all must face, must all experience. Maybe even embrace. Walking has been part of my story. The bodily rhythm of one foot in front of another became a type of poetry, freeing my mind to process, my heart to think, especially when faced with an emotional situation, a difficult conversation, a hurt or disappointment. And I had always prayed. Perhaps not as deeply as I might, yet conversations with God about matters of mutual concern, being as honest as I could, and asking for help were a lifeline.

God rarely took the whole load, yet my Father in the heavens always eased the burden.

Yet verse took these first steps further. Whether birthed in prayer or worked out while walking, the creative process slowed me down, taught me to pay attention, gave me ways to name what I was experiencing, what I was feeling. Poetry helped me learn to get comfortable with pain, look it in the face and sit with it awhile. Be present. In time to learn to embrace. It helped me to do this sideways, so to speak. Like a pair of teenage boys who can only share their hearts while sitting askance to each other, focus fixed on the screen and their game. Poetry is one of those ways.

The rhythm and rhyme of verse helps me not be too terse, but to take the time, to get inside the pain and feel.

> Out of the Overflow
> *Our hearts are fountains.*
> *We live and move and have our being out of their overflow.*
> *We bless and we curse out of the overflow.*
> *We serve and subvert out of the overflow.*
> *We grudge and forgive, we rage and romance,*
> *We submit and we lead,*
> *We desire and we betray,*
> *Out of the overflow.*
> *Out of the overflow of our hearts,*
> *Our mouths speak, our eyes see, our hands act.*
> *With what does your fountain flow?*
> *Sweet water? Sometimes cool*
> *And refreshing? Other times hot*
> *And purifying?*
> *Fetid and dirty?*
> *Infectious and artery hardening?*
> *Or are you like me, with both taps running,*
> *Making a tepid, lukewarm brew*
> *That satisfies no one?*
> *Jesus invites us to source our fountains*
> *From his spring of living water,*

Crisp and clean,
Deep in the well that will never run dry.

All that's best in what I do—
Serving others, and empowering,
Leading, thinking, communicating
And loving through
Interruptibility and listening—
Happens from overflow,
Not overwork.
Like a spring fed pond
Or a cup running over.
If breakfast is the most important meal of the day,
Then the quiet of morning prayer
Is my Wheaties,
Time with you, Jesus, my breakfast of champions.
Laughter, gratitude, a walk, devotion,
Spontaneous songs of praise –
Hourly effervescence of refreshment
Filling my cup.

Poetry became for me an important preliminary, a necessary prerequisite, in the work God was wanting to do.

I didn't know it yet, but what I would soon discover is that this art of paying attention, particularly to pain, was a wicket gate, beyond which lay the path to being loved and its destination at interior freedom.

The roadmap for that path was provided through spiritual direction. Here is how Megan describes this art: "*an ancient practice of spiritual accompaniment designed to help us deepen our relationship with God, learn to recognize God's activity in the everyday circumstances of our lives, and become more open to the Holy Spirit's guidance and transformation. It's a prayerful space to explore our relationship with God, reflect on life's experiences, be real about the hard questions of faith, and open up an opportunity to grow in our awareness of God's presence.*"

Meg and I had been introduced to the ministry of spiritual direction through our involvement on the Missions Leadership Team. It was modeled as a resource for partnering with God in God's work of spiritual formation.

My first director was referred to me by a friend. A former Ranger in the 82nd Airborne Division and hobbyist body-builder. He pastored a small church in rural southeast Michigan. We would meet monthly for an hour at a Starbucks in Ann Arbor halfway between our two homes. The thing that I most appreciate about that year we spent together was that he was always there first. He was waiting for me, coffee in hand, occupying a table in a quiet corner of the café. It was a visual reminder of how God was waiting for me, holding open a space for us to dialogue. After that year he let me know that he'd need to make a change and it would no longer work for us to meet. I also was feeling like our time together had come to an end. We blessed one another and I set about to find another director. It was a short-lived process. The first person I asked agreed to accompany me and we've been meeting regularly ever since.

I still remember our first session. After several moments of silence to settle and focus our hearts and a brief prayer, he read from this passage and invited me to reflect on it: *"But now, this is what the Lord says – he who created you, Jacob, he who formed you, Israel: 'Do not fear, for I have redeemed you; I have summoned you by name; you are mine. When you pass through the waters, I will be with you; and when you pass through the rivers, they will not sweep over you. When you walk through the fire, you will not be burned; the flames will not set you ablaze. For I am the Lord your God, the Holy One of Israel, your Savior; I give Egypt for your ransom, Cush and Seba in your stead. Since you are precious and honored in my sight, and because I love you.'"*[25]

That first session was about the most directive he's ever been, preferring instead to hold open space for me to set the pace, and for us both to be responsive to the Holy Spirit's direction. Yet that scripture was timely. Vocationally I was in a place where I felt like I was passing through rivers that were in danger of sweeping over me. Internally, the

---

[25] Isaiah 43:1-4

paying attention that poetry encouraged enabled me to discern that there were fires of sorrow, disappointment and more burning below in my soul, and I was in danger of being set ablaze. Also, I desperately needed to know – not multiple choice test knowing, but experiential gut-level knowing – that I was precious in God's sight, and loved. I needed to feel it.

A few years before this, Meg shared with me a picture she sensed God had shown her while she was praying for me. It was really simple, yet it carried the power of what we'd call a prophetic word. In the scene, I was a little boy running up the stairway in the center of our home, holding something I was proud of and crying out, "Daddy, daddy, look what I did!" No one answered. No one came to look. It wasn't about either my biological or step dad, despite neither being around me as a small boy. The scene was God communicating to me, through Meg, how God saw and understood my heart: that I was experiencing God like that little boy. God wanted to change that relationship dynamic.

I cried my way through most of that first spiritual direction session. And for many that followed in the coming months. God was laying the foundation for transforming my understanding and experience of our relationship.

A year later I was on a trip in Douala, Cameroon. I was spending time with my friend, Michel, and the rest of the team he led in the emerging Vineyard movement there. One morning while there, in prayer, I saw this picture of me running up those same stairs in my home, crying out, "Daddy, daddy, look what I did!" As I reached the top of those stairs, I sensed this impression of someone stepping out of the doorway to our bedroom. Though the figure was shadowy, I knew it was Jesus. And so it began.

Week after week, month after month, this encounter with Jesus would clarify and grow. It was most intense those first two years. Jesus moved from being a shadow in the doorway to a solid man at the top of the stairs, waiting for me as I excitedly ran up. Then I'd sit next to him and show him what was in my hand. After a few months, I'd sit in his lap as he held me close and spoke his love over me. Next I'd be older and we'd sit side by side and then we'd sit face to face. Eventually I'd encounter him standing, looking him in the eye as an adult child looks at his father, and he'd put his hands on my shoulders and bless me.

After this time, the encounters seasoned and matured. There was a long period where I'd wake up every morning with a worship song in my mind. I would always encounter God in praying with that song. After a few years, I began to wake up in the middle of the night with one song in my head, then wake up in the morning with another. Both would be very meaningful to me. I began to experience the reality of so many of the psalmists, how God's songs were with me in the night. These encounters progressed over the course of six years, deepening month by month.

All this took place in the quiet pre-dawn darkness of my personal time with God. My prayer life had always been a solid area of strength in my life. Not that the amount of time really mattered, but I had been praying for an hour each morning before breakfast for well over a decade by that point. Yet this was different. I still prayed for an hour each day, but God was accomplishing in ten minutes what had previously taken a month of morning prayers or a year of conferences and retreats. The substance of this time of prayer itself was changing. Instead of talking about what I was doing (which often amounted to fretting), I was beginning, very slowly, to simply be. God and I still talked about matters of mutual concern, but it was shifting from tasks and responsibilities to encounter and relationship.

It began in the context of paying attention to pain and it grew in an atmosphere of vocational hardship. These encounters with Jesus happened at the same time as many of the stories from the last chapter. Alongside my wonderful mentors, the disciplined practice of being accompanied in spiritual direction was a guide for me on the journey. This was no accident in God's agenda. Sitting in spiritual direction opened up space for asking hard questions and reflecting on uncomfortable answers. It was during this season that I began to discern that we had been "doing the stuff" and it didn't always work. I observed that we had done so much of what had been expected of us, so much of what I had been taught was the right way, yet it wasn't consistently producing the desired fruit. And I began to notice how I felt about all this. And, in time, how God felt about it too.

> Psalm XXIII
> *Window into another world.*
> *Crowds gather from every*
> *Tribe and tongue and place and age.*
> *Ubiquitous longing for this*
> *Pastoral scene.*
> *Goodness. Mercy. Comfort. Rest.*
> *Companionship. Provision. Protection.*
> *Stillness.*
> *Weighty words expressing*
> *Profound realities. Experienced*
> *Beside still waters, through*
> *Dark valleys, in*
> *The face of enemies.*
> *At the start of the journey, and*
> *The end of the road.*
> *All along the path.*
> *This abundant, astonishing world*
> *Is shaped*
> *Not by circumstances, but by Someone.*
> *Circumscribed, defined, by a Person.*
> *It is the sublime Shepherd's bountiful creation.*
> *He makes of the window a door*
> *And invites us in.*

In *The Critical Journey: Stages in the Life of Faith*, authors Janet Hagberg and Robert Guelich describe from their research six stages in the spiritual journey, our response to our faith and relationship with God, and what flows and changes with these responses.[26] A defining moment comes in the life of every disciple of Jesus as they transition from a lifestyle of "producing" to making an "inward journey." Entering into spiritual direction marked the beginning of this transition for me.

---

[26] *The Critical Journey: Stages in the Life of Faith,* Hagberg and Guelich

From Pastor to Pioneer

In February 2019, I entered into the Spiritual Exercises. If you're not familiar with them, they're an extended meditation on the life of Christ developed by Ignatius of Loyola in the middle 1500's, using scripture, prayers, and insights gained from his own discipleship to Jesus. A few people choose to do them daily over 30 days on an extended retreat. Most folks undergo them as a "retreat in real life," spending time daily in prayer over nine months, meeting with a spiritual director weekly. It took me ten months to do this nine-month journey. The first few weeks are an introduction, getting used to the rhythms of reflection and prayer, becoming familiarized with key ideas, posturing our heart towards God and attuning our attention to Jesus and the Spirit. While the whole journey was deeply significant and life-changing, definitely the most memorable encounter came at the end of that introductory period.

At the risk of being personal (why stop now?), I've extracted these notes from my journal entries on February 27th and 28th of that year. The first day's experience of meditating on Jesus' interaction with the rich young ruler of Mark 10:17-31 was significant enough that I returned for a second contemplative encounter the next day.

Feb 27. Mark 10:17-27. *I ran up to Jesus: "What must I do to live in and enjoy the age to come?" "You know the commands," Jesus said, "Trust me; abide in me; receive my forgiveness and walk in forgiveness; obey my teachings." "All these I have done since I was young." Jesus looked at me, and loved me. "One thing you lack: go home, raise funds for your support, then come and follow me." Like the rich man, I am eager to follow Jesus: for the beauty of his life, compelling vision, power, courage, the way he looks at me—I'd follow Jesus anywhere for the way he looks at me. Jesus gives the list of commands because they're true and represent walking in God's ways, but mostly I think to root out where the deeper issue is. Without adequately addressing this heart issue, this disordered attachment, it's very hard to enter into the kingdom of God. We must find interior freedom, then we are free to follow Jesus and experience and enjoy the Kingdom. For me, right now, that's asking for help, being free from false attachment to the idea that "I am strong," I can do it, of being responsible. Especially around money and being provided for. And it's love that draws us, not condemnation that compels us. We sit under the loving gaze of Jesus.*

Feb 28. Mark 10:17-27. This man feels a little desperate. He runs to Jesus. I feel the same. Jesus looks at him and loves him. "Go home, ask your put together friends and your messed up friends for help, and then come, follow me." "Go home, lay aside all your appointments and clear your schedule, then come, follow me." The man walked away, thoughtful, for he was strong and busy. "How hard it is for the strong to enter the kingdom of God. How hard it is for the busy to enter the kingdom of God," Jesus said. The disciples were amazed, for they assumed the strong had everything together and the busy were blessed of God. "Man does not consist in the abundance of his ability to be responsible nor in the abundance of his appointments," Jesus said. "With man this is impossible," he continued, "yet all things are possible with God."

There was a lot going on in my life when I heard these words. The church was in another significant cash flow crunch because of expenses related to more boiler repairs and a cold winter. A board member stepped down unexpectedly. My administrative assistant also gave his notice. And so I was alone again in the office. The need to repair our flat roof had become critical. Also, our oldest child was preparing to think about colleges and it was clear the family needed to sort out a new living situation for my mother-in-law who was approaching a crisis in her health.

Jesus was dealing with some significant heart stuff in me in this encounter. He was cutting to a core issue. I heard it and felt it that way, too. Yet that's not quite how I responded. As I walked away from these encounters, I experienced them as an invitation to delegate more, and to raise money for the flat roof over the Children's Ministry wing at our building. It certainly was in desperate need of repair. I don't think I was wrong to hear and respond to Jesus in this way, yet it turns out, as we'll see, that he had more in store for me with these words. Jesus is often like that, circling around our soul like the road down into the mine, returning again and again and again to the same spot, the same thing, just a little deeper down, until together you get to the bottom where what's precious lies hidden.

Another thing going on around this time is that I was being exposed overseas to other expressions and ways of being the church and engaging in the mission of Jesus. The November before that February encounter with Jesus in the Exercises, I had been in Sierra Leone for a week of exploratory learning from local leaders with a team of other folks, including my mentor on the missions leadership team.

A number of years earlier he experienced Jesus speaking to him thusly, "Mark, you've learned to plant hundreds of churches, now I want to teach you how to plant thousands." I was in the room when he shared this vision the next day, and as he shared my heart leapt within me and I heard God speak to my heart, "And you will release dozens of (catalytic) leaders, Jim." I felt like the Lord was not only connecting me to this vision of planting thousands of churches, he was also connecting me to the work my grandparents had done in Nigeria decades earlier: as they had taught many indigenous Nigerian pastors, now I would empower and release many more local leaders. That clarity unfolded over time, of course.

Mark invited several members of his team, including me on a few occasions, to join him in learning another way. We participated in a conference in east Tennessee, visited Kenya and Ethiopia too. That trip in Sierra Leone we witnessed firsthand how it could look different. They had planted 1000 churches in maybe 20 years, then planted 9000 churches in a decade. He set out to find a new way: "You've earned your PhD, Mark, but now I'm taking you back to kindergarten," as God spoke to him through another timely prophetic word. One of the first things that Mark had mentioned was that we couldn't work ten times harder to plant ten times more churches because we were already working too hard as it was.

To give a sense of that work, consider the following two anecdotes.

The denominational community of which I was a part hosted a biennial conference for pastors and other local church leaders. Roughly a decade previous to my journey with Jesus through the Exercises, one of the most attended workshop sessions at the gathering that year was a panel discussion of seasoned leaders about growing your church to over a thousand in attendance. Though most pastors sitting in the auditorium were simply trying to break the more elusive "200 barrier," the 1000 in weekly attendance was, for these leaders, like a holy grail of megachurch identity. I heard from a friend that one of the panel members stated without equivocation that if you wanted to grow your church to over 1000 in weekly attendance you had to commit to work at least 80 hours/week. That same year our denomination began a decade plus long journey of attentiveness to pastoral health and well-being. An anonymous survey in the packet for that conference included the question, "How many hours per week do you work?" The multiple choice answers ranged from "Under 20" to "80 or more." To my knowledge, no one explored the irony of the possible mixed messaging that to grow a church to megachurch big they had to practice a work-life rhythm that was very likely in the unhealthy zone.

The spring of 2017, desperate after a year of loneliness and cash flow challenges, I received a marketing email in my inbox. I've looked high and low to find the email, without success, so I'll have to relate this anecdote from memory. I learned that in the year 2000, the average church attendee that considered themselves "regular" attended services about 3-3.5x/month. There were also some data points for "somewhat regular," "occasional," etc. They did the math for a church of 1000 members (there's that number again!), and that sample church's weekly attendance was like 800 people.

Fast forward to 2015. In those 15 years, the typical Christian who considered their attendance at church "regular" had shifted down to twice a month, with similar adjustments for the other categories. So, taking that sample church of 1000 members and running the numbers again, 15 years later, that church's weekly attendance had dropped to 450! The marketing component then introduced the idea of "texting to give" so that you could continue to get your donations even if people didn't come. But that's not what stood out to me. Notice that this sample church appeared to be shrinking, and probably the staff and board would be routinely wringing their hands, yet actually they still had 1000 members who felt connected to the church and expected care and services. So their span of care had remained the same, yet now it was nearly two times more diffused and they may only have had half as much resource to use. So they're having to work twice as hard, with half the resource, to do the same work! This hit me like a clap of thunder and almost exactly matched my experience.

When I received that word from Jesus in February of 2019, that's exactly what pastoring felt like. I couldn't work harder. I hadn't discovered how to work smarter. I wondered if maybe there was another way.

In July 2017, at another leadership conference in SoCal, I began really asking myself these questions, putting them to writing in my journal for the first time. Here it is in my own words at that time:

*God: "I want to restore your soul, Jim, in ways that might be surprising. It **is** important to me."*

Me: I'm angry. Angry because I feel like we're going nowhere. Expending all this energy with little fruit. I almost feel like I hate our church. I don't feel in a bad place—I feel okay with you, God—but our church seems to suck. I want to make a difference. Are we really?

I'm tempted to leave, tempted to run. But I sense the tattoo on my heart pulsing and I know leaving isn't right.

I have this picture of me plowing my life into the dirt. Like running myself into the ground. Plowing my life, even pouring my blood, into the ground. The Lord asks am I willing to do this? Am I willing to do this difficult thing? Like I'm dying to myself. In reflecting on this I am reminded of Walter Ciszek.[27] *Who did all he did and no one even knew he was alive.*

What I'm wrestling with is the desire to close the church and do DMM.

I'm experiencing a deep sense of shame. That I'm failing. The Lord says, "No," but it's deep.

I feel made for so much more than I'm currently experiencing. Like I'm capable of more than what I can do or currently am doing or have capacity for.

But then I sense the Lord saying—continuing to say: "What if you trust me with that? What if I have another pathway for you? What if your influence will come as you pour your life into the ground? What if it will come as you give your life away, make yourself less? Will you give your best for this little weird church? To love a city that doesn't love you back?"

I say Yes to Jesus. Though it's hard, I will pour out my life for this weird little church, for this weird little town. I will die to myself.

The question of strategy seems somewhat separate. I think I'm struggling inside because it feels so marginally effective. I want to be intentional about multiplication, intentional about life-on-life discipleship, intentional about seeing people far from Jesus draw close and say yes, intentional about raising up leaders and the next generation. What does that look like?

Move to Royal Oak Township?

Reading that through again right now is really raw for me. I remember—can feel afresh—the pain in my soul as I wrestled with myself and God over those several days. Let me briefly describe in slightly greater detail a few elements that I wrote in shorthand.

---

[27] *With God in Russia*, Walter Ciszek (San Francisco: HarperOne) 2017

Slowing Down To Catch Up With God

The tattoo. Several years earlier I had been at a conference when one of the speakers talked about how the Church was called to be a people who made room for others to encounter God, for those who experienced being on the outside looking in. I was deeply convicted. I was struggling with the leadership decision to re-install Chris on our worship team and I realized that fear was driving my decision-making, not love. I had become convicted that we needed to invite Chris back on the team, but I was afraid that if I did so both our biggest donors and my best friend would leave the church. God challenged me through this talk and before it was even half done, I had already walked down to the front of the auditorium and knelt in front of the stage, quietly weeping under God's conviction, waiting for someone to pray for me. As the talk ended a friend approached and said she saw me up front and sensed God speaking to her on my behalf, and she wondered if it would be okay if she shared and prayed? "I saw God stamping a rainbow tattoo on your heart." I immediately broke down in tears. She couldn't have known, yet God did.

Walter Ciszek was an American Jesuit priest who traveled to eastern Europe in the months leading up to WWII so that he could get into Soviet Russia for the sake of serving the people and maintaining a witness for the gospel of Jesus there. Shortly after arriving in the Urals, he was imprisoned for the duration of the war and then sentenced to nearly two decades of labor in the Gulags of Siberia. After his release he helped start several churches in the cities he had previously built before being traded back to the US in exchange for Soviet spies. Everyone had thought he was dead. He had prepared for over a decade and was imprisoned for over two decades, all so that he could have a few brief years of intermittent ministry. And he blessed the land of his captors. You can read his story in *With God in Russia*.

DMM stands for "Disciple-Making Movements." It is one shorthand description for the different expressions of the church and the way of Jesus that I learned about in Kenya, Ethiopia, Sierra Leone and elsewhere. This was the first time I actually admitted to myself the possibility of stepping away from pastoring as I had known it to pursue another way.

So, at the closing session of the conference that week, Meg and I went down for prayer together. Unbeknownst to one another, we had the exact same request for the young man who came to pray for us: "We don't feel like we're taking risks for the sake of the kingdom of God anymore. We don't want to live that way. Pray we stay faithful in taking risks for the sake of Jesus."

Returning home, our first attempt to faithfully respond to God's leading at the conference was to consider moving to the Charter Township of Royal Oak, a small, deeply impoverished community neighboring our own. A little later, the all African-American cadre of pastors there would graciously welcome me into their circle. It was just a few miles away, in the same school district even, yet in many ways it was worlds apart. A realtor friend believed in us enough to front us the money to put a cash offer down on a downsized home and we'd pay her back when our house sold. The seller went with another offer, despite ours being a cash offer, over asking price, for owner-occupancy.

As we talked about this possibility with our kids, our son spoke up. "Mom, Dad," he said, "I think I know what you're wanting to do and I love you. But I don't want to move during my junior year. I would really like to keep a stable home during high school." Thankfully we heard him. Instead of pushing our agenda and ambitions, we listened to him and heard in him the heart of God. It seems God had other ideas for what he wanted to do. Remember, God said to trust him and that his ways might be surprising.

Then came 2020. Obviously (in)famous for Covid, this year has meant a lot to me for other reasons. God spoke to me regularly and compellingly throughout 2020.

That spring I had a dream that I was ministering in a particular city and then traveled across this long bridge to minister in a neighboring city. Think Twin Cities with a much, much wider river. Suddenly in my dream I realized that my plane was departing soon to return to Detroit and that I would never make it back across the river in time to get to the airport. Then it occurred to me that the flight stopped at the small airport on this side of the river too and that I could get there just in time to catch my flight. I made it and relaxed on board while the plane took off. When we landed at the next stop I noticed that no one was deplaning and I got concerned because my connecting flight to Detroit was taking off soon. Finally I got up and found the flight attendant, telling her my situation. All sweet she replied, "Oh, don't worry, honey, this plane doesn't go to Detroit." She smiled and walked away. I turned to head back to my seat so angry in the dream that I woke myself up.

Telling a friend about the dream the next day, he said it sounded spiritual and suggested that I ask God to reveal the meaning. Going to bed that night I asked God to speak to me. For the first time ever I returned to the exact place in a dream that I had been before. I felt a tap on my shoulder and a middle-aged man with a rumpled business suit and a kind smile invited me to sit next to him in the bulkhead row. Taking my seat, I knew in my knower it was God. He said, "Jim, you're not going back to be the kind of leader you've been before. I'm calling you to do a new thing, to be a new kind of leader." I knew it wasn't about leaving Detroit but about not returning to my old ways of leading. A few weeks later I found out from Meg that she had had several dreams over the past month where she was flying to a new city, pregnant, nervous about what would happen when she got there, and when she landed she gave birth.

The big thing for me, though, was this recurring vision from God that developed over half the year. It began in March with a simple reflection on the early verses of the sixteenth chapter of the biblical book of Acts:

Paul and his companions traveled throughout the region of Phrygia and Galatia, having been kept by the Holy Spirit from preaching the word in the province of Asia. When they came to the border of Mysia, they tried to enter Bithynia, but the Spirit of Jesus would not allow them to. So they passed by Mysia and went down to Troas. During the night Paul had a vision of a man of Macedonia standing and begging him, "Come over to Macedonia and help us." After Paul had seen the vision, we got ready at once to leave for Macedonia, concluding that God had called us to preach the gospel to them.[28]

---

[28] Acts 16:6-10

My first observation was how Paul had twice tried to go a different direction, yet God redirected his steps. God was putting up "Road Closed" signs to guide Paul and his friends towards a future better than he could yet imagine. This was just after Covid had shut the world down, cancelling my "goodbye" trip for my assignment in Africa (including visits to Rwanda and Côte d'Ivoire) and my "hello" trip to my assignment in the Middle East (including visits to Georgia and an undisclosed country in South Central Asia; I did get the entry visa, which always seems to throw off the Border Control officers to Canada, "What do you do for a living, sir?" They're always flabbergasted by my reply.) That's how I understood the passage at first, these exciting new adventures being frustrated by the pandemic and the shutdown. Over time, though, I discerned deeper insights. After the dream about the airplane, I connected this passage to that dream: like Paul, God was calling me across to the "other side," inviting me into something new, something different, to something I had not yet known. But what?

God would often bring this scripture up to me in my daily time with Jesus. Sitting on my bed, windows open to the spring and summer sounds of morning, the altered rhythms of lockdown providing more space for prayer. I don't quite know how to describe it, other than that I began to feel the text. I entered into a border country between meditation and contemplation with this passage. I had always assumed that Paul got to Troas (ancient Troy, as I understand it), checked his team into their AirBnB, had the dream that night and left that next morning at first light. But then I began to imagine Paul in Troas. Kept from Asia (and it's important central city of Ephesus), blocked from Bithynia, Paul paced back and forth in his Troas hotel, pent up like a caged lion. Unsure what to do, feeling out of sorts, adrift, longing, waiting. Ephesus was a key cultural center and Paul was eager to serve there. Bithynia was an understandable backup plan, completing the circle of what we now know as Turkïye, visiting the communities colonized by the Greeks on the south shore of the Black Sea long ago. But he couldn't get to either. Then the vision came.

I realized that's exactly how I felt. My Ephesus was Vineyard USA. I longed to serve more significantly in the movement that had helped me grow so much. I had volunteered extensively, informally and formally, locally, domestically and internationally. I had the skills, gifting, experience, capacity, relationships and opportunity to make a meaningful difference. The timing seemed to be aligning and I was being apprenticed. Yet I was kept from this Ephesus.

I looked to my Bithynia, the American Baptist Churches of Michigan. By virtue of our merger, I was a "dually aligned" pastor, with our church a member of the Vineyard USA and the ABC-MI. Their new Executive Minister, hired shortly before Covid with a commitment to renew and plant churches and multiply disciples, called every pastor in the state that he didn't know. When he discovered during our call that I had planted a church, sent out churches, assessed and coached planters and served on a church planting team, he decided we would be new best friends. I really liked him and his heart. The ABC-MI didn't formally require giving, but for the first time in a decade I voluntarily sent them an offering because here was a leader with a vision worth resourcing. He recruited me to form and lead a team to stimulate planting in the state again after a forty-year hiatus. The Holy Spirit said, "I love your heart, Jim, but No. Remember, I've got other plans for you, an invitation into a preferred future that you can't even yet imagine."

And so I paced the secret chamber of my heart, paced in prayer, and paced the pathway of the nearby park. I understood that God was calling me to another way, though I didn't quite yet know fully what that would be. As the months passed, I recognized I was lingering. It's like I was waiting to hear from Ephesus or Bithynia to see if a letter came giving me permission from God to move. Yet that message never came. The only permission God was granting was forward, not back. I wish I was as quickly obedient to the vision of Jesus as Paul, but it took me a little longer.

Finally, in early October I had one of the clearest visions I've ever had. As I ended my time of prayer that morning, God decided to communicate one last thing. I saw this picture of me standing on a beach, looking at an encampment with boats resting on the shore. Then the scene changed in a flash. Storm clouds were clearing and the sun was shining through, illuminating smashed boats and a scattered camp. Jesus was close behind me, his left hand on my right shoulder, and I was weeping. In less than a heartbeat I knew that I had crossed over to

Macedonia, no longer in Troas, but that I had been camping on the shore waiting for news from "the other side." Jesus had taken it upon himself to metaphorically break the boats of my return trip. I was grieved, at the finality of this, yes, but even more at my slowness to obey. Jesus stood with me in my pain. I could sense his love. Then he gently turned me, looked me in the eye, then playfully punched me in the shoulder, saying, "Come on, Jim, it's time to go. People are waiting. And besides, it's not like these are the only boats in Greece!" I turned and walked with him through the tall coastal grass along the shore, heading inland.

I invited the members of the church board out to dinner for our next regularly scheduled meeting after that encounter with Jesus. Nothing like breaking bread with local burgers and beers for a relaxed atmosphere to have an open and honest conversation about what I was thinking. I shared a little bit about my recent experiences in prayer and my growing sense that I was unlikely to continue pastoring the church in the same way that I had been. It was twenty years ago that month that we moved to Detroit to plant the church, and I could feel the winds of change blowing. I explained how leading the church no longer engaged the full range of my passions and strengths and capacity. This meant that I had lots of interest and energy to pursue other initiatives, including the possibility of part-time employment in denominational efforts, or pursuing new initiatives to multiply churches locally in metro Detroit. It was a great dialogue. The board really seemed to hear me. They understood and bore witness to my gifts and call. They were very affirming. They supported me working part-time in other ventures, with the one caveat being that they didn't want me to completely quit the church.

It was not long after this that I finally understood my "Yes" to my mentor Steve all those years ago. You may remember he had said to me, "Jim, if you're going to be a pastor in the Vineyard, you're going to have to plant your own church." Without clear understanding, yet filled with faith, I said Yes. I had always thought that's because I had found a pastor I would want to be like. And in a certain sense, I suppose that's true. Yet not in the way I had thought.

But here's the deeper truth: Something that God had put in me was responding to what God had also put in Steve.

More than pastoring, it was an apostolic gifting and function. That's what I was responding to. What had been buried in me was awakened by what was actively expressed in his life. And now God was calling it forth. Yet I still had some distance to go of learning another way after decades of momentum in the same direction.

This was an intensely stretching season for me. On one hand, my friendship with Jesus was stronger and more intimate than ever. We experienced regular, rich times together in prayer. Also, my wife and I talked often and it was clear we were of one mind. On the other hand, I was facing the disappointment of dreams that would likely go unrealized, I had disagreements of conviction on matters of mutual concern with friends I respected and with whom I had years of collegial camaraderie, and in those moments of intimacy with Jesus he was inviting me to do some hard things. I think two significant supports helped me make it through.

First, slowing. I was slowly learning to slow down. Spiritual direction had started the process, and the Exercises fueled it. The altered rhythms of the lockdown opened a door for more and I was very intentional in taking advantage of that. No late night Netflix and chill for me. I woke up earlier, doubling down on prayer, savoring the silence before the kids awoke for virtual school. Next to my bed is a framed text of the verse from Isaiah 30:15, *"In repentance and rest is your salvation, in quietness and trust is your strength."* Over the door to my bedroom on a wooden slab are the words of Psalm 46:10, *"Be still and know that I am God."* Both are gifts from friends. They each saw something in me that I needed: to be still, to rest in the quiet.

Spiritual companionship also helped me stay sane in this season. I was in regular communication with my spiritual director, my leadership coach and two mentors, each of whom was emotionally stable, spiritually mature, wise and discerning. They each had over 40 years of leadership experience. As a team they were invaluable to me. They gave me space to wrestle and vent and lament without reacting. They epitomized the scriptural admonition to be *"slow to speak and quick to listen."*[29]

---

[29] James 1:19

The Apostle Matthew records this invitation of Jesus, *"Come to me, all you who are weary and burdened, and I will give you rest. Take my yoke upon you and learn from me, for I am gentle and humble in heart, and you will find rest for your souls. For my yoke is easy and my burden is light."*[30] I was learning to submit myself to the easy and light yoke of Jesus. There is a scene in the film Ben-Hur where the title character, the protagonist, trains a team of horses for chariot races in the arena. He understands that when harnessing the team it is wisest to put the steadiest horse on the inside. This horse is the leader, guiding the team not so much through dynamic power but through stability and maturity. Jesus is like that inside horse. I was harnessed to him, yet still on the outside struggling with trying to pull ahead at my own pace. Having responded to Jesus' invitation to do a new thing, I was in danger of rushing God's work and trying to do it my own way. This was not God's way.

In January 2021 I attended a virtual conference to stimulate vision and passion for church planting in our denomination. I participated with a few other members of the missions team in a learning posture in case we needed to run similar events in a virtual space moving forward. From a technical standpoint the two-day event was really well done, with high quality production, high levels of engagement and solid content. But the thing that stood out to me was this: the speakers kept repeating how you didn't need to have a big church or a book contract in order to grow and multiply a church, yet five of the six presenters plus most of the breakout room facilitators were specifically present and promoted because of their books and fast-growing churches.

I couldn't not hear the mixed messaging in this and wondered to myself, *"Is this what multiplying disciples and churches has become?"*

Another thing going on in this season was that a few leaders in our church were developing a fresh vision for our work in Ethiopia yet wanting to express that in a way different from what we had done for the past twelve years. It was exciting to see other members of the church take greater ownership in our mission there. I had prayed for this for years. It was important to me that I work as hard as I could make room for them to get it off the ground. So, a month after that virtual conference,

---

[30] Matthew 11:28-30

Slowing Down To Catch Up With God

I found myself on a peer coaching call hosted by the missions team for pastors engaging in cross-cultural work overseas. I took the evening Zoom call from my darkened parked car, waiting for my son to finish his session with a wrestling coach that would help propel him to the state finals.

When my turn came, I shared with the three or four others on the call about this new initiative our church was considering in Ethiopia, to launch a care point with two of our partner churches in southern Ethiopia to provide holistic community support. My colleagues on the call listened well and asked good questions. After several minutes of discussion, my friend Henry replied, "You know, Jim, it seems to me that you're thinking about a whole lot of stuff over there in Detroit. Have you ever considered doing a Mind Map?" I was familiar with this idea of visualizing on a piece of paper all the things that were, literally, on my mind. I responded that I was familiar with the idea, but that I hadn't ever really given that serious consideration. I said I'd think about it. What really happened is that the whole way home I had this internal dialogue, "You think that's a lot, Henry?!?! That's just one sliver of one of the many things I'm thinking about!" I got home and reported to Megan about the call. "Can you believe it? He's got no idea!" Then in that moment, I remembered this line from Shakespeare: *"Me thinkest thou protestest too much!"*[31] My level of protest was in direct proportion to the truth that Henry discerned. And I knew it deep down.

Two days later, after a little more interior hemming and hawing, I sat down with a blank sheet of paper, drew a small circle in the middle and wrote my name in it. Then I got to work. Several hours later, the page was filled with lines and circles and names, handwritten in small font. I came to call it my "Nine Headed Hydra" because of the nine lines emanating from that central circle, each with appendages of their own. It was like some ghastly monster, both beautiful and terrible to behold. Okay, maybe that's a little melodramatic, but it was jarring and significant. I sat for some time staring at that piece of paper. My dominant thought was simply this: *"No wonder I'm stressed."* Then I asked myself, *"Can I keep doing this? Can I keep living this way? Of*

---

[31] *Hamlet,* William Shakespeare, Act III, Scene 2

course I can. I'm already doing it and I believe I can keep doing it." Then I asked myself a better question: "*Is it good for me to keep doing this?*" I knew the answer: No.

That moment was almost exactly two years to the day after the Lord spoke to me during the Exercises through the story of the Rich Young Ruler in Mark 10. Now I finally understood what Jesus was saying. "Jim, how hard it is for the busy to enter the kingdom of God. I want you to clear your schedule and come follow me." I got it. Then Jesus spoke to me again as I sat with my Mind Map: "Jim, I want you to get rid of all these responsibilities and I'll give back to you what I want you to have." You see, that's another reason why I call it my Hydra, because the only way to kill the mythical beast is to cut off all the heads and burn them with fire. My friend, Tim, a partner with us in our work in Ethiopia, had been telling me as much for years. "You're juggling too much, Jim, you're gonna have to let something go." He was right, of course. It's just that Jesus wanted me to drop all the balls and play a different game.

Leave it to Jesus to be the most radical.

One of my favorite places in my hometown is a wonderfully local pub called The Emory. I've had so many significant conversations there, with Jesus, neighbors and friends. Two months after my Hydra moment, I found myself back at the Emory, sitting with my friend, Neal. He, Megan and I had been talking regularly for the past few months. He had been an assistant pastor at a mid-sized church in West Michigan. Several years earlier he had stepped down to lean into simpler expressions of the church and more intentional multiplying of disciples of Jesus. We met through a mutual friend in the American Baptist circles. He gave me a big hug and then sat on the bench across the table from me, saying, "Okay, Jim, I told my wife I'd be home by 2 a.m., which means I've got until 11 p.m., what do you want to talk about?" It was 2 p.m. We didn't use the whole time, but we did stay glued to our seats until after 8 p.m., experiencing the full gamut of snacks, happy hour, appetizers and dinner. I redirected one appointment to the Emory so that my friend could join in our conversation. Megan also joined us for a while around dinner. It was as the dinner plates got cleared that the crucial conversation came. "Jim," Neal said, "I hear you. Your heart is to multiply. Multiply disciples. Multiply churches. You want to bear fruit. Much fruit.

Transformed lives and more. And I know you know what Jesus said, *'Unless a grain of wheat falls into the ground and dies, it remains by itself alone. But if it dies, it bears much fruit.'*[32] So here's the question, Jim. What are you going to die to in order to bear much fruit?"

I already knew the question. In fact, my guess is I'd probably been avoiding the question for some time. I already knew the answer. I had shown up that day knowing the answer. I think deep down I probably knew the answer from when the Lord spoke to me during the Exercises.

"What will I die to in order to bear much fruit? My job."

There it was. I finally said it out loud. I'd quit my job as pastor, to pioneer a new way of making disciples and being the church. I'd quit my job as pastor, in obedience to Jesus, to discover a more faithful way for me to follow Jesus.

It wasn't just my job I needed to die to. I needed to let die all the old, malformed ways I approached my vocation in my weakness and brokenness, not to mention the accretions of cultural expectations. In particular, I needed to unlearn and let die how I cared for myself by caring for other people. Through lifelong experience I had learned to look out for the well-being of others, emotional and otherwise, being well-tuned to them and caring for them. Combine this with the high level of responsibility I embraced, along with the demands of pastoring, and this was a kiss of death. I think again of my ordination ceremony and the (admittedly good, yet also weighty) words that were spoken over Meg and me. Because I take my commitments seriously, and work very hard by nature, bearing responsibility naturally, this was a burden. I'm sure that left unchecked this would have led to ill health: physically, relationally, emotionally, perhaps even spiritually. Yes, I could've finished well twenty years later. Everyone would give me a pat on the back, and I'd be hollow inside.

I met with the church board the next month, in May, and explained to them I'd be going half-time at the church and giving the rest of my time

---

[32] John 12:24

to missional efforts to make disciples and multiply simpler expressions of the church for every neighborhood of metro Detroit. They didn't seem particularly surprised. We met early in the month to talk high level, then met one on one over the next few weeks, and again as a group at month's end to vote after processing and prayer. We talked ideas for hiring a helper. They were understanding and unanimously supportive. It matched what we had talked about the previous fall over burgers and beers.

The hiccup was Jesus. It seems in my scheming I had forgotten (again!) to take him into consideration.

I labored in prayer about the timing of this part-time transition. Through conversations with my coach and board, the date for going half-time kept stretching out indefinitely into the future. My coach was understandably concerned about a smooth transition. The board was understandably not particularly interested in me transitioning to part-time at all. Though the laboring with God over this question was intense, I soon got an answer.

Pouring a cup of coffee one morning after hours of prayer, the Lord spoke to me an unexpected verse: *"Let the dead bury their own dead, you go proclaim the kingdom of God."*[33] Honestly, I didn't even like this scripture. In fact I had never really understood it. I've always loved what comes soon after, *"No one who puts a hand to the plow and looks back is fit for service in the kingdom of God."*[34] Yet the Spirit chose this verse I would never pick to speak God's heart to me.

Immediately I understood the scripture: sometimes the call of God cuts across and supersedes what would be normal, appropriate cultural norms. As it was appropriate for a son to bury his dead father, it was reasonable for me to go part-time and take a long time to transition. Yet that's not what God was calling me to. God also spoke to me these words: "I thought we were better friends, Jim. I asked you asked to clear your calendar, and you only cleared half. Is that what it looks like for you to obey? Is that how we're friends?" This cut to the core. There was no shaming in his voice, only sorrow since I had disappointed my friend. I

---

[33] Luke 9:60
[34] Luke 9:62

realized I had disobeyed God in going half-time. I discerned I needed to quit my job all the way and do so as soon as possible.

As I continued in prayer I grew in conviction. A few days later Meg and I were on a Zoom call with my coach, Bob. I hadn't really had a chance to debrief Meg what I had been hearing from God, so I took this as the opportunity to share what I heard. She looked at me, maybe slightly surprised, maybe more like excited, and said, "Really?!?" Picking up on that, he asked her, "What do you think, Megan?" Without hesitating she answered, "Oh, he's been ready to be done for a long time, but just hasn't really admitted it to himself yet. And I've been done for several years. So, yes, this is definitely God." We spent the rest of our hour together talking this through. He encouraged us to not tell anyone beyond my director, but just to talk amongst ourselves for the next month and pray. That's exactly what we did.

By month's end we felt even more strongly about this direction. Talking again, my coach asked me, "Jim, it sounds like God is clearly talking to you, so when is the earliest you can respond in faithful obedience?" I told him my sense was that God was inviting me to be done by Thanksgiving that year. We received the blessing of my mentors who had been walking with me through this journey so far. And so, after dropping our eldest off at West Point to start his own Cadet Basic Training, my wife spent the next month in Puerto Rico on a trip equal parts language immersion, ministry, sabbatical and grief support after sending a firstborn son to college. During that time I wrote what I affectionately called the "Fire Myself Plan."

Then, in early August, I spoke individually with each board member. Each of the conversations went basically like this: "Friend, I love you. Remember that conversation we had a few months ago in May, about me going half-time? Well, I know we both agreed to that, but unfortunately, I was disobeying Jesus. So I'm giving you my notice. My last day will be November 21st ... yes, this year. That's my non-negotiable expiration date. But the only thing I'll do between now and then is work 125% to serve the transition of the church, on the administrative and leadership side, as well as the pastoral and relational side with the members. Here's a copy of the plan I've drafted, with my coach's input and blessing, and

I believe it will work. This plan will belong to the board and the pastoral selection team, to be tweaked by you all, and I will serve that process to the best of my ability." Overall these conversations went fairly well. There was some strong emotion, of course, yet each board member was gracious and understanding. They were surprised, yet not completely. For those who knew me best, they understood I wasn't flourishing in my work.

We met again as a team later that month to discuss together the plan I had given them each to review individually. We made some tweaks to make the plan better and that's the one we used until they hired the new lead pastoral team.

I shared my story with the congregation in a sermon a few weeks later, having sat down individually with each member of the leadership team the week before. We then immediately published the news as widely as we could through our communication channels and also posted the job description in multiple places.

The heart of the transition was meeting with as many members of the church community as I could for one-on-one conversations. Over the ten weeks of my transition I had roughly one hundred dialogues, each averaging 90 minutes, a few in groups of 2-10, but most one on one. As I sat down with each person I spent time asking them about their lives, appreciating them, sharing my story, making room for honest reactions and questions and follow up, then sharing how I had seen God work in their lives. They always ended with hugs and often with prayer.

The common flow of these dialogues was this: we're mad (to hear the news), we're sad (to see you go), we're glad (you're so happy and confident in this decision and how good it will be for you), and we love you, so we'll be fine and don't let the door hit you on the way out. This last bit tongue in cheek. I think the only surprise most people had was that our family wasn't moving to Africa. Each of these times together was a precious gift for me, a balm for my soul. Several folks said they had seen many pastors come and go, but that this was the first time the pastor had ever sat down with them to talk it through. I am grateful to God for inspiring the idea to do that. Alongside the tremendously hard and gracious work the Church Board, Pastoral Selection Team, and Interim Pastor did in managing those aspects, I think these conversations of emotionally healthy relational closure were part of the secret sauce of the transition's success. I can (and sometimes do) see these folks at the gas station or grocery store and it's never weird. I was learning from God to slow down and pay attention to the people. These people were the heart of the church.

The Transition Service was a treasured time for me. Most of our church planting core team returned to celebrate with us. Old members made the journey to join us. My church planting mentor, Steve, was on hand, along with several other pastoral colleagues, to bless us and speak words of affirmation to the church. Space was made for family and friends and members of the church to share. We laughed, we cried, we gave thanksgiving. We returned home that day with full hearts.

What would we do now?

As I sat with folks during my ten weeks of transition, or as I'd catch up with old friends online or over a beer, I heard this question a lot. It seems to me that Americans are still a spiritually curious people, despite the rise of the "Nones" in polling data. Just look at the prevalence of yoga studies and reiki healing rooms, not to mention social media influencers with a spiritual bent.

The church as we know it has been decline in the US for some time. And for anyone with the courage to admit it, there is too often an embarrassing inconsistency in helping people develop as apprentices of

Jesus, experiencing the flourishing that comes from following him. Which is, of course, the core mission Jesus entrusted to his people.

Covid didn't create this problem, it merely hastened its growth.

As a society, we remain intensely spiritual, it's just that a growing percentage of folks are not going to walk through the doors of a classic church building to attend a church service in order to satisfy their spiritual hunger or resolve the larger questions of life. Digital media can offer some support, yet online relationships are notoriously thin and the culture of consumeristic on-demand streaming seems to run exactly counter to the wisdom of the great spiritual traditions.

To the extent we think Jesus is beautiful, good, wise and worth following, what can we do?

Instead of buying skinnier jeans and better smoke machines in a vain effort to get people to come, we're opting instead to go. Go where we're already living, learning, working, shopping and playing, helping the folks we already live alongside discover what God's really like and what it could look like to follow Jesus, gathering in spiritual families on mission. These church communities are simple enough to be unburdened by the typical stuff of buildings, budgets, boards, programs and staff, so that we're able to focus on loving God, loving one another and loving our neighbors.

Imagine a sunflower and a dandelion.

As it turns out, a common dandelion plant and a single sunflower stalk have a very similar reproductive potential: between 1200-1500 seeds. Yet few suburban neighbors complain of their yards being overrun by sunflowers. Sunflowers grow tall, reaching for the sky. When they ripen, their large heads fall to the ground. At this point their seeds are consumed, nourishing people and birds alike, which do not become another sunflower. Dandelions stay low to the ground. You might pluck the head, but if you do not remove the root, they'll grow back. And when the time is ripe, their seeds are carried on the wind, reproducing new dandelions near and far.

<u>Minister of Dandelions</u>
Dandelion held loosely in the hand.
A fellowship of
Wispy white gliders
Perched for flight.
My vocation: to blow;
Gently, playfully, lending
My breath, my life.
Each sent seed a womb,
embodying new life;
Carried on the wind,
Borne by the wind,
Seeking fertile soil of its own.
Until I'm left holding nothing,
Except the joy
Of filling this field with beauty.

This all begins with my being a disciple, abiding in Jesus and bearing fruit. My new direction isn't really a new calling, so much as it is taking my original calling and clarifying it, crystallizing it, and stripping it down to the core, and now giving my life to that focus. This assignment isn't really a thing to do. Rather, it's more like a lifestyle to live: "To come alongside spiritually curious people in discipleship and to mentor missional leaders, catalyzing the formation of new simple churches, locally and globally, so that all people may know how good Jesus is and find life in following him."

I Would Walk 500 Miles

I woke up a little worried, trying not to fret and pace too much as Megan packed for the day. After a quick breakfast we'd be checking out of our bed and breakfast on the outskirts of Mazarife, Spain. We had spent the night at the Casa Rural Malino Galochas. It was an absolutely lovely, quaint country location, a former mill, with a bubbling creek running beneath what was now the large dining room. We had enjoyed a festive dinner there the night before, accompanied by most of the friends we had made on our journey to date: Bruce and Allison from Toronto; Olivia and Cathy, two sisters from northern Michigan; Brett and Karen, longtime friends from California; and a German couple whose smiling eyes made up for what words failed to convey. Our hosts served a feast, topped off with a nightcap of homemade cherry brandy. The night was a delight, a memory Meg and I continue to treasure. It was a highlight of our 40-day journey on El Camino Frances.

Now it was time to pay the bill. Hence the fretting. All the places we stopped the day before had only taken cash and now we were in short supply. Not only was I concerned if we'd have enough to cover the treat of last night's spread, I was worried about the day we were just beginning. What if the places we visited today only took cash too? The hostess, as bubbly and inviting as the brook that flowed beneath her home, approached as we finished breakfast to check us out.

"Do you take credit or Apple Pay?" I asked.

"Oh, no, I am sorry. Only cash. The total is 37 euros."

(Permit me to pause before I continue the story. A handcrafted farm-to-table multi-course meal for two, including a bottle of local wine and digestifs, for 37 euros, is an amazing deal! But I wasn't yet feeling that part of the story.) I pulled the cash out of my pocket, counting it up: 36 euros and some change.

"No problem," she said, as she scooped up the money. "It was a joy to host you in our home. Buen Camino!"

Shouldering our packs and heading for the door, we replied, "Gracias! Buen Camino!" and headed out the door.

Six months earlier had been our Transition Service. I still remember that glorious Thanksgiving week that followed. I didn't set an alarm. I managed to get up in time to get the kids situated for school. We'd pray and read and leisurely eat breakfast. I had the same feeling I get when I return to camp after a long hike and finally lay my heavy pack aside. I was experiencing this life-giving lightness and bounce in my step.

The whole month of December it was like we were downshifting from seventh gear to somewhere between first and third. I was beginning to reset. It certainly wasn't a vacation or anything. In the Army we might've called it "Terminal Leave." I had been so wound up for so long that I needed that time to decelerate to something approximating a normal speed. That month provided space for a slowing distance. That space was a gift.

In January we picked back up conversations with folks, both with partners in our work and also those who were interested to learn with us and join us in making disciples and being the church in a simpler way.

We started gathering with another family to be a simple church, rotating between our home and theirs. We experimented with how to engage their young children in what we were doing. We explored together about what it could look like to be the church in a simpler way and what it looked like to follow Jesus without all the supportive scaffolding of the prevailing model of church. We rediscovered the joy of relationship and the gift of beginning to truly understand the 59 "one another" passages mentioned in the New Testament as hallmarks for living in community.

By the end of April we blessed each other to go our different ways: for them to engage more deeply in their own neighborhood and social circles, which was their passion, and for us to do the same. The group didn't last, yet the relationships have. The group didn't go on forever, but that's okay. We grew as disciples and the work was multiplied as we each began to bless our neighborhoods and serve our relational circles. We were learning to trust God with the outcome instead of trying to force it to fit our preconception.

Plus, we were going on the Camino soon, so the timing made sense.

The Camino Frances is the most popular of a number of pilgrim routes across Spain. The 500-mile journey, typically accomplished in about five weeks, begins in St. Jean Pied de Port on the French side of the Pyrenees, traverses the diverse countryside of rural and urban northern Spain, and ends at Santiago de Compestela. By tradition, Santiago is the resting place of the remains of St. James the Apostle. Many tens of thousands of pilgrims have been journeying this route each year for centuries.

Meg and I had wanted to walk El Camino for some time, after hearing the stories of several friends who had walked it in prior years. I had considered including it as part of a sabbatical I never got around to planning, opting to resign and transition instead. My Board knew of my desire to walk the Camino and they strongly advocated that I continue working until the week before our trip. They wanted me to stay on in my role helping transition the church and then use the Camino as my own transition time. That totally made sense logically.

Yet I knew about myself what they didn't fully grasp. I wasn't burned out, but I was done. My expiration date had arrived. Also, I needed to obey Jesus, and Jesus had invited me to be done as soon as possible. And besides, the fact is, no one on the Board really wanted me to go at all, so of course they wanted to delay the inevitable as long as possible. I don't blame them. Not one bit. It made sense.

Still, I'm glad it worked out how it did. Had I stayed on pastoring at the church until the week before the Camino, most of my pilgrimage would've been spent decompressing. Instead, the five and a half months in between my Transition and the Camino gave me room to unwind and then start our new work from a healthier posture. This meant I was able to be fully present for the entire Camino, to myself, to Megan, and also to God whom I desired to encounter more deeply along the Way.

It seems God had a similar idea because the deep work began on Day One. Well, actually, it was Day Zero. We had booked our lodging for the whole trip ahead of time, so we were good to go for a bed and a breakfast every day of the journey. For everything else I had brought cash. We had our Visa and American Express, of course ("Don't leave home without it!" if you're old enough to know what that means), but I hadn't planned on using them except maybe in the big cities.

You see, most of my international travel had been in Africa. At the time of our Camino I had cleared customs in Ethiopia, for example, eighteen times, and I had used a credit card fewer than five times. And never Apple Pay or anything like that. In fact, not being a tech early adopter, I hadn't ever even used contactless payments at home.

So when I walked into the most nicely appointed corner bank on the main strip in the pilgrim (aka tourist) section of St. Jean Pied de Port, I expected an easy process of changing our dollars into euros. I never even considered it would be a problem. I mean, sure, the French and Americans have a notoriously tumultuous relationship, but hey, the Statue of Liberty? They rescued us in our Revolution, and we rescued them in World Wars I and II, right?

"Non, Monsieur. C'est impossible. I am sorry but we do not take US dollars. The closest bank will be in Biarritz [an hour cab ride away]. Why did you not exchange them in the US?"

I had answers to that (probably rhetorical) question, but I knew there would be no explanation adequate to not make me look like the dumb and assuming American that she had already made me out to be. But bigger than the issue of my pride was the problem of how my wife and I would eat dinner in all the rural villages we'd be passing through.

"Perhaps, monsieur, you might be able to exchange your currency in one of the bigger cities you will pass through, like Pamplona, par example. It is just three days away."

"Just three days away" is easy, of course, when you're going home to dinner that night. And, wouldn't you know it, we arrived in all five major cities after banking hours were over on Saturday and while the banks were closed on Sunday. God had other plans.

Day One of the Camino is famously one of the hardest. It's 18 miles up and over the central spine of the Pyrenees, using the same route that Charlemagne had used to confront the Moors and that Napoleon had used to subdue Spain.

The first stop on the Camino is the hamlet of Roncesvalles, population 30, nestled among tall trees at the base of the Spanish side of the mountains. After nine hours of hiking through heavy damp fog, basking in bright clean alpine air, and a steep rocky descent, we were two kilometers out from our goal. Meg requested a breather and leaned back with her pack against a tree to collect herself. I continued on another fifty feet, sat on a large rock, and began to cry. Literally. I had seen Roncesvalles while descending the mountain, a clustered handful of stone buildings many hundreds of years old. There was no way they were going to take my American Express. What would we do? Army training intact, my brain raced ahead to problem solving mode: well, we had bed and breakfast secured, so we could load up on the morning meal and secretly stash croissants and cheese in our packs to snack on during the day. That's how I was thinking. I was panicked.

Meg kept calling out to me, wondering what was going on, how I was doing. I was too busy crying to answer and didn't want her to know. (Yeah, right, like she didn't already know.)

"Jim, do you believe I called you to this trip?" God's voice intruded into my racing thoughts.

"What? Well, 'called' feels a little dramatic, don't you think, God? But I get what you mean. I guess so. Yes, I suppose, we're here at your invitation."

"Did I call the twelve apostles when I sent them out?"

"Yes, of course! Wait, I think I know where you're going with this, God."

"What did they have with them when they went on those journeys?" I knew the answer, but it felt rude to interrupt God. "That's right, Jim, nothing. Or maybe what they had on hand. Did I provide for them, Jim?"

"You know you did, God. I know you did. You provided for them. They were without lack."

"Jim, do you believe that I can and will provide for you? Do you trust me?" God and I both knew the answer. So did Meg, whom I circled into the conversation. She was far less panicky than me.

And so it began. A little over an hour later we were checked into our room and enjoying a glass of wine. Of course they took my American Express. Dinner that night was a delight. At the café nearby our next lodgment in Zubiri, the proprietor enjoyed talking with us so much that he gave us a free drink with our dinner. And at that place I figured out Apple Pay.

For the forty days of our entire Camino we never knew lack. Along the way we met Bruce and Allison, who have become dear friends. We affectionately call them the Peregrinos, the Spanish term for pilgrims. When they heard our currency story over dinner one night, they bankrolled us 50 euros. Exchanging USD was easy for them as Canadians. The next day was the day we stayed outside Mazarife. It was their euros we had spent. After paying the hostess that morning, our first stop was at the Cowboy Bar, a famous waypoint on the trail. Cash only. Before I could figure out what was going on, Meg was already outside exchanging another $100 with the Peregrinos. Those 100 euros lasted us the remaining second half of the trip.

I'm reminded of the scripture in Deuteronomy 8, where God reminds the people how during the forty years of their wandering their shoes did not wear out and their feet did not swell. For us it was forty days, and maybe our feet swelled a little, yet the principle was the same. From Day Zero to Day Forty God provided for us, literally, every step of the Way.

This was a stretching experience for me, to say the least.

Now, you might be thinking, what's the big deal? You had two credit cards, a bunch of cash, and friends willing to bankroll your currency exchange at almost any moment, so how was this stretching? You'd be right. All those things were true. And yet it was still a challenge for me. I had to wake up every day, practically every time we stopped for coffee or a drink or a snack or a meal, and express my trust in God again. I guess I'd say that's a sign of just how deep that hole ran for me.

In one sense, it seems to me this is an occupational hazard. Most pastors I know struggle with worry and anxiety around finance. I remember talking with the landlord of a storefront we rented in the early days of our church plant. He was a pretty big commercial realtor in the metro area, and he owned this building as a side hustle for passive income. He asked me one time, "So let me get this straight, Jim. You depend for your livelihood on people giving money to your church each week or month or whatever, and you get your income from that? How do you do that?!?" It's a reasonable question. Lots of pastors anxiously fret about the weather, wondering how it will impact attendance (and thus, the offering). They're keenly attuned to who might take a job in another city or maybe the quality of car the first-time guests drive. Pastors aren't alone in this as some of the dynamics are in common with retail. Yet no pastor likes to think of themselves as "selling God." I suspect most pastors hate that this is part of what occupies their mind. Certainly, every pastor I know carries at least some scars from this as vocational collateral damage.

In another sense, it is very personal to me. Nature, nurture, circumstance and choice have combined in me to accept high levels of responsibility from a very young age. It literally feels like my default setting. And when I've reached out to ask for help, sometimes I've been let down.

In doing research for this book, I stumbled across a journal entry recounting a moment I had long forgotten. During one of the moments when we were trying to hire staff to support our mission at the church, I had a conversation with my father with whom I had recently reconnected. As I sat in Starbucks on the phone, he described how he would talk to several wealthy friends of his in Texas, men with whom he had done investment business, friends who had helped him out in the past.

"I'll raise that money for you, Jim. We'll do it together."

Six months later he came back to me, dejected. He hadn't raised a dime. I was discouraged. And when he died a few years later, I worked sacrificially to close out his affairs, only to discover there was a non-existent inheritance.

Around this time I would often reflect on Jesus' teaching in Luke 11: *"Which of you fathers, if your son asks for bread, will give him a stone instead? Or if he asks for an egg, will give him a scorpion? If you then, though you are evil, know how to give good gifts to your children, how much more will your Father in heaven give the Holy Spirit to those who ask him!"*

Sometimes I would imagine myself as a young boy sitting in God's lap, and I realized that my attitude was not to even bother to ask God for bread. Instead, I'd wait until our conversation was over and get up to make a sandwich for myself. It's been a long journey of becoming willing to ask God for bread, and the Camino was a 40-day crash course in learning to ask for the whole pulled pork sandwich with fries. I've had to learn to trust that God will provide. I've had to learn to receive.

There was another moment in 2014. A freak storm flooded much of our town. People were kayaking in the street at the end of our block. Our family minivan was totaled when water soaked the engine's computer. We had insufficient savings to buy a new van for our family of six. A board member suggested I ask people in my relational network for help: city, church, denomination, friends and family both. The next morning I was anxiously praying about all this and what to say in my GoFundMe post. Just then my five-year-old daughter, Olive, appeared by my side like a visiting angel. Her large eyes looking at mine she said simply, "Dear Jesus, give daddy whatever he wants. Amen," and then crawled into my lap. A few hours later I crafted the post while tears splashed on my keyboard. In two weeks we raised over $14,000. I wept again as I read the notes people shared. Along with our $4,000, we had just enough to pay cash for the cheapest minivan in America.

Beyond the somewhat artificial environment of the Camino, the way this gets lived out is in my salary. This involves both our income and the compensation process. When I describe to people what I do, one of the most common questions I receive is, "Okay, cool, yeah. I think I see it. But how do you get paid?" I always smile and then make a joke about how the magic gnomes transfer money to my account each month.

Perhaps obviously, perhaps not, people partner with us financially, giving to the small non-profit organization that we started as a legal and financial umbrella for our work. Yet here's the interesting thing, probably half of the people that are part of the simple church community that gathers in our home don't even know that there is an organization. Because that's not the focus. They're just happy to have a place to be together with neighbors and friends learning to follow Jesus and love one another. And that's exactly how I feel too!

I think that's what my question askers are sensing and getting at, "How do you make money when there's no building to pay for, no organization to sustain, and the work is simple enough so that everyday people can do it?"

In the months between my transition and our departure on the Camino, multiple friends of mine, people that cared about me, encouraged me to read a particular book on fund-raising. I discovered it was the industry standard in support-raising ministry circles. The book aimed to help readers develop a solid, robust theology of finances and fund-raising.

There were several things I liked about the book. First, though some of their points felt very stretched, they really did try to focus their teaching in scripture. They had a list of 100 Bible verses to reflect on as an appendix. Second, they highlighted that every time you're talking with a potential financial partner about support, you're really asking God because the money belongs to God and that person is just a steward of God's money. It was filled with programmatic processes and very high on promises. They were confident that if someone like me followed their process "religiously" (pun intended) then I could get to 100% funded in 100 days. I read the whole book and meditated on one of those scriptures per day for the 100 days before the Camino.

The book worked. When combined with the Camino, I did form a robust theology around my finances and fund-raising. It just happened to be the almost polar-opposite approach the book advocated. We have talked to a few people and pitched for them to partner with us. Some even said yes. Most of those gave one time or perhaps for the first year we got started to help us get off the ground. It was like starter capital for our faith-based entrepreneurial adventure. I'm so grateful for every single dollar that came that way. We wouldn't be where we are today without it.

Yet mostly I've chosen to simply talk directly with God. And then wait and watch to see whom God works through.

Often that will look like someone asks me the question, "Jim, how do you get paid?" I'll offer my same lame joke. Then they'll come back with something like, "Well, can I help? How can we support you, your family and the work you're doing?" It's been stretching and amazing to watch God work this way and be together with people who partner with us in this way, because they love God, are responsive to him, and believe in us and want to work alongside us.

What's interesting is that the actual dynamics of my pay are exactly the same now as when I was pastoring in the prevailing model: people give to an organization and that organization direct deposits money into my account every month. In fact, I even use the exact same online giving platform and local bank that we used before. Yet the way it feels is really different. Somehow I feel much closer to the action. It's like the veil that separates me from the process is much thinner. I've discerned that in my prior work, I was subtly putting my trust in the church to pay me. Now it feels much more like I'm directly trusting in God and that I'm in partnership with the folks that God works through as they come alongside us financially.

Sometimes I pause and ask myself the question, *how did I manage all that financial pressure*? Obviously, I know how the mechanics of my pay worked, but at a deeper level I do sometimes wonder, "Really, how did it all work?" As I continue to noodle on that question, I think about three things. All are significant, and probably the first two will seem fairly familiar, yet I wonder if maybe the third point is the least talked about dimension.

First, it seems to be a discipleship issue for church-going Christians. If Jesus' invitation is to express our deep trust in God through a lifestyle of sacrificial generosity, are we as apprentices in his way of life modeling our pattern after his? Second, perhaps the constant anxiety around money in churches, especially in pastors and related to buildings and budgets, is an indication that there's a problem in the system. Jesus, as the Prince of Peace, ushers in peace. His rule and reign is characterized by shalom, non-anxious well-being. The system of the world is characterized by hurry and worry. The near constant anxiety that churches feel in relation to money might point to a problem in the system. Third, though, speaking closer to home, I wonder if the frequent, sometimes crippling, pressure pastors feel around money is an indication of the maturity level of pastors, struggling to experience God's love, struggling to see themselves as God sees them, struggling to embrace their worth and value.

Recently a friend of mine and I were at a party and got to talking about pastors and finances. In his work coaching pastors he was observing what I had also noticed, how seemingly all the pastors we know struggle with matters of finance and compensation. He noticed it because it was something he had struggled with himself for decades. He asks his clients the question he felt God asking him, "What are you worth?" This struck a chord with me.

As I mentioned, for two decades of pastoral ministry, I felt like I never really had someone stand up for me and my worth in the contribution I made as a leader. Sensing this, I suspect, he looked at me and asked, "What do you believe you're worth, Jim?" This has been a tough question for me, and it's been simmering on the back burner of my mind since he posed it.

I'm reminded of a story my mom loves to tell about me. I'm twenty one and she's with me to help me navigate buying my first car. I had recently received a very favorable low-interest loan related to my being a cadet at West Point and I was weighing my options carefully. My mom reminds me how I looked at her and the salesman and said, straight-faced, "You know, this is going to be the peak of my purchasing power." She recalls how she quickly exchanged a knowing glance with the salesman, a little wink or eye roll as if to say, *Sure, sure, son. You'll see one day.* "But you know what, Jim," she continues, "you just might have been right. You knew yourself and what you wanted well."

I've come up with a number in response to my friend's question. But I've wrestled with this idea. I know God treasures me. I've seen his smile and felt the warmth of his gaze. I know people value my contribution. Yet how do I measure my worth?

First, Meg and I have long embraced a pathway of simplicity and downward mobility, and we're at peace with this choice. I was long enough at West Point and in the Army to be comfortable with austerity, as a friend pointed out to me. Second, I can't figure out a way to measure my worth, in terms of compensation, that doesn't involve comparison. And as Meg reminds our family all the time, "Comparison is never your friend." Do I look at other pastors? My West Point classmates who are leading organizations? My neighbors around town? How about my colleagues in Africa, who sacrificially serve in faithful fruitfulness while waiting days in line for fuel or scraping up funds to send bloodwork for sick family members to the hospital? How do I measure my worth? Jesus tells me that our Father in the heavens delights to give me the riches of the kingdom. I've talked to God about the number I've come up with. I've told him I'll receive whatever he would like to give me. And that I'll gladly give it all back in grateful worship, learning to rely on him in daily dependence for what I need each day.

Honestly, I'm still trying to figure all this out. I'm learning to trust God to provide what I need, not take or demand from others what I want. I'm learning to see myself as God sees me and receive from God what God provides.

A New Way

I've never really liked documentaries. That might seem strange given that I'm a history major. In most cases I'd really rather just read a book about the topic if I'm that interested in it. A full-length book will go into much richer detail. Or simply just tell it to me as a fictionalized story. I love stories. But a documentary? Meh. I'm just not that guy. Much to my wife's chagrin, of course, because guess what? She loves documentaries. Which is how I found myself watching *Rat Attack!* a number of years ago.

There are historical records of massive rat packs swarming out of the bamboo forests along the Bangladesh-India border to ravage nearby farms, every fifty years dating back to the early 1700's. *Rat Attack!* documents the research of a team of scientists to understand why and come up with a solution to support the local farmers. Spoiler Alert: it was the bamboo forest. This particular varietal of bamboo would fruit every fifty years. Rich in nutrition, the fallen fruit would fuel a boom in rat population. And just when the rodent community was at a zenith, the fruit would run out, so the scavengers would turn to the farms. Fascinating, right? Strangely, yes.

The big thing for me wasn't the rats, it was the way the narrator described the bamboo forest. I leaned forward as he explained rhizomes and roots and the interconnected multiplication of these shoots. And then I heard it, clear as a best friend whispering a secret in my ear.

"My kingdom is like that, Jim. The kingdom of God is like a bamboo forest."

Consider the growth patterns of bamboo: A single bamboo shoot sends out roots in multiple directions, and every few feet a new shoot rises from each root. With each new shoot, more roots are released and the process is repeated. Though slow at first, in time bamboo grows quite quickly. Soon there is a vibrant, robust, interconnected forest. Bamboo is strong, lightweight, versatile, resilient, persistent, sustainable, and thrives in diverse conditions.

Disciples, families, leaders, and churches can grow and multiply like this.

So now we're leaning in to be and tend the bamboo forest that we believe God is growing and cultivating. I've preached only a handful of times the first year and a half after my transition. I haven't even organized and hosted an "event," other than a few potluck picnics and a block Christmas party in more than a year. I've discovered I'm only now, after three years, feeling detoxed enough to have an appetite for pulling people together for Jesus-y events.

Rather than trying to reach the 16 square miles of our former "parish," we're now focused on loving and serving the six or so blocks of our local neighborhood, plus the places where we routinely shop and socialize.

A group of neighbors and friends gathers in our home each week to be the church around our dining room table. Ours is a liturgy of dialogue and whatever folks happen to bring to eat and drink in communion. We share about our lives, read the scripture together, and ask common questions to facilitate encounter with and discovery of God and one another, fostering response to what we learn.

I meet routinely with a number of other folks – both single and married, younger and older, mostly individually, occasionally in groups – to encourage, resource and coach them to do the same. Nearly half of them are doing so. There's a group of similarly focused folks I'm in relationship with around the US as well, and even now a few in other parts of the world.

All that we're doing now we beta-tested with two different groups during Covid. The first was the Youth Group at the church we pastored. The second was a Neighborhood Group that gathered on our front porch or around the fire on our backyard patio. Our experience with both gave us confident hope that what we were dreaming about just might actually work.

The youth group wasn't big, but it was engaged. Other than our son and oldest daughter, and maybe two or three other kids of families in the church that came occasionally, it was mostly the friends of my son from school. Some of them I had known for a long time, having coached them in community soccer during early elementary.

My son was the ringleader, but he was a fairly typical PK ("pastors' kid") at this point. He would sit down on one of the couches and kick his feet up on the coffee table. His heavy Timberlands would routinely send all the chips and drinks flying. His girlfriend at the time came maybe twice and refused to come again since, in her words, "You're being such a jerk to your parents, who only love you." She might not have been wrong, but thankfully he totally turned around by his junior year.

This was not a churched youth group. That junior year our plan was pizza, soda and the well-regarded Youth Alpha videos. (The Alpha Course is a phenomenal course known worldwide for helping people explore questions of faith in small communities of dialogue and fellowship.) Apparently, our kids didn't get the promotional memos on how awesome the videos were. They kept insisting the two hosts were gay. Even when their wives joined for one of the prerecorded sessions, they insisted it was a front and that maybe they were simply bi. To be fair, they were two of the most metrosexual straight guys I had ever seen (they were British, as the Alpha Course hales from London). After weeks of futile resistance, I caved and after some time connecting over pizza and brownies, I would announce our transition with, "It's time for the Gay Guys' Video." Enthusiastic cheering was the customary reply. The materials, of course, had some assumptions about where the students were starting from, and we routinely found that the foundations they assumed were beyond the actual place the kids were at.

"What do you think of when you think of God?" we asked one week.

"I don't think of anything," Abby answered. "Really. I mean, I know I'm supposed to say that I think of an old man with a flowing white beard or something, but I don't really think of that. I just don't think of anything because I never really think of God. I have no idea even how to pray."

Fun fact, three years later Jesus dramatically rescued her while watching a TikTok video and now she's an active member of the church in our home while being mentored to start one of her own.

Honestly, good as they were, for us the videos were kind of a bust. So when it came to their senior year, we wondered what we would do. Then we recalled how the best conversation we had from the videos revolved around the biblical concept of the "fruit of the Spirit." These nine qualities (listed in Galatians 5:22-23) are a summary expression of the character qualities that the transformative activity of God in your life develops. Instead of any program, we decided, each session let's just read a story from the Bible related to each one of these character qualities, and then have an open-ended, honest, discovery-oriented conversation about what we're learning. Then we can pray.

It was so simple, so straightforward. The kids came right in and sat down and started to talk. They skipped the pool and ping pong tables until after group was done. They shared openly about their desire for self-control, their longing for peace. They started praying for each other, circling around, stretching out their hands, as a conduit of God's presence, love and power. They started growing, maturing. It was beautiful.

The Neighborhood Group developed along similar lines. My wife and I hosted a couple of spiritually interested neighbors from the block, a few church members who lived close by at various places on their spiritual journey, and a former member who lived some distance who was without a spiritual home. It was a wonderfully eclectic group. We ran it along similar lines. Some extended time for fellowship, reading and discussing a scripture passage through open-ended discovery-oriented questions, and then some time for prayer and how we could support one another.

There was the time one of the neighbors walked out mid-meeting in a drunken stumble, only to return ten minutes later to confess his struggles with alcohol. Another guy in the circle shared his story of recently giving up alcohol and then prayed with him, accompanied by tears all around. Rich bonds were formed. Everyone, regardless of their stage on their spiritual journey, interacted meaningfully with the scriptures and community. They were engaged and it was making a difference. We closed the group when we transitioned from pastoring, in order to focus on our new thing. But it was so meaningful for one of our neighbors that she kept asking if we could have a reunion or something.

I answered, "Well, we're thinking of restarting the group but having it on Sunday morning and calling it church. What do you do think of that?" Her request became the nucleus of the church that now gathers in our home.

I'm extremely grateful for the nearly two years we had exploring how this new approach to our ministry could work. I don't know if this would've worked long term as our ongoing approach to small groups or a youth group. Maybe? Some pastors I know are trying that. Time will tell. For us it was a great way to field-test this approach and see if it worked. We were certainly encouraged enough to give it a go because we saw glimpses of what might be possible as we expressed our vocation in another way. Now, after three years, we've living in these new ways to lead, serve, empower and be human.

The holidays can be a hard time for pastors. If they've got a family, not only do they have all the usual commotion that comes with Christmastime with kids, they've got the pressures of the church on top of it. It's not uncommon to try to find time to check-in with members and key leaders, taking a pulse on their engagement level and pitching vision and opportunities for the new year. Plus, in case you've recently migrated from Mars and hadn't heard, churches are heavily dependent on year-end giving to meet their annual budgets.

Pastors and churches know that people get busy at the holidays – work parties, family get togethers for overeating and arguing (politics, sports, social issues, you name it), shopping, college football playoffs, winter break travel, and more. Some people might even try to give back and volunteer to serve.

Knowing this tendency, forward-looking church leaders plan ahead, trying to get their members busy with them before they get busy with someone else, in an effort to get their money to finish the year strong, engage them for the new year, and hopefully help them remember that God is real and that his ways matter amidst the seasonal crush of consumption and consumerism.

I'll never forget two experiences I had at the end of my first full year of our new work.

The first was a dinner at the home of the Adams. They lived in a suburb on the opposite side of Detroit from us, about a 30-minute drive. When we had been leading our old church, we found that people from this city who visited our church never stuck; the distance was just beyond the edge of reasonable and they had to cross several cultural borders to get to us. The Adams were facilitating a simple church of their own and had connected with us through a mutual friend. We were still developing our friendship at the time of our meal. After a pleasant dinner of relating over shared stories, we asked them how their simple church was doing and how we could encourage them. They shared and then the wife asked questions about some specific prayer practices of Meg and I to help her in her discipleship to Jesus. Driving home I noticed this strange feeling in my gut. It was the absence of anxiety.

In my previous system of pastoring, I would have felt a lot of pressure at a get together like this to take advantage of the time, trying to measure their engagement and worrying about their commitment level. I'd be driving home asking myself, "Are they satisfied? Will they stick around?" But instead I was thinking, "That was nice. They're great people. I'm encouraged by what they're doing. And they even asked us about how they could grow in prayer ... that's unusual!"

Instead of trying to get them to be more involved in our thing, we were helping them do their thing better.

I had a similar experience at an ultra-lowkey Christmas Eve Eve gathering we facilitated at the home of one of our friends' parents a few weeks later. As I looked around the room before assembling for a group picture on the stairs, I realized that we had seen a lot less of each other than was normal during that December. And it was okay. They still related with us, still liked Jesus, and still practiced their faith. Instead of trying to force them to be with us more, we made room for them to spend time with their family and friends to practice what they had been learning all year. And it worked!

I was discovering a new way to Christmas.

I soon learned it wasn't just about the holidays. This principle of releasing instead of grasping became a leadership theme.

One of the families that was part of the church that gathered in our home had an opportunity for a new position in the husband's company in another state. They sensed God's invitation to receive it because it made possible a healthier quality of life for their family, especially relating to their young kids. Again, sorrow mixed with joy. We blessed them as they pursued this mature step in their discipleship journey, and also we were excited because this created the possibility of a new simple church in their neighborhood as they got settled and related to their neighbors.

I discovered a refreshing lightness as I developed greater aptitude and freedom for releasing people into their thing rather than carrying the burden of figuring out how to fold them into our thing.

Every pastor I know is familiar with the idea contained in Ephesians 4, about how leaders are given as gifts to the church, entrusted with the responsibility to equip and release people into what God has given them to do. Of course that means the pastors shouldn't be doing it all themselves. That's hard enough. More subtly, though, most pastors I know want to equip and "release" so long as that ministry feeds back into the church's overall vision and ministry. I certainly struggled with this. Even when I didn't want to be, I had always vaguely been in sales mode, trying to empower people by connecting them to our (let's be more honest, usually it was a little more like "my") thing. But I was experiencing freedom from that as I learned a new way of leading.

We're also discovering new ways of being available in blessing our neighbors and friends. It's embarrassing to admit, but the mounting pressures of pastoring inhibited our ability to bless and serve the people in our local circle of relationships. A huge thing for Megan has been walking the dog. With fewer pastoral and relational demands on her introverted energy levels, she had space to not only care for a dog if we bought one (which we did, two weeks before our transition), but also to relate while taking cute little Masha the Morkie on walks. She's met loads of neighbors on several blocks, taking time to chit chat, ask her famously good questions, even sometimes to pray for them.

Occasionally she'll bring a baggie for the poop, and a bag for the trash, picking up garbage along the way. She's also ordered free deliveries of mulch the past two years. The pile fills our driveway. She offers it free to everyone she meets, and to everyone that walks by our house. It's a natural conversation starter, given the quizzical looks of passersby at the mulch pile big enough to hide a car. Mulch is expensive and tending to your yard can be a healthy way to embody cultivating beauty. That's what she tells them. So we got a load big enough to share with everyone in the neighborhood who wants some, all for free.

What we've really noticed, though, is the importance of being attentive to people. We live in a front-porch community. Most people don't have attached garages that they drive into and then from there walk into their home, only reaching out for a moment to get the mail or the most recent delivery order. People park in their driveways or on the street and walk in through their front doors. We even have sidewalks, and people routinely use them. It's not unusual for people to hang out on their front porches. Yet, for all this community potential, when Meg and I walk the dog together each night, I'm always a little saddened by the number of homes characterized by the flickering glow of blue light in the window as people sit alone watching their screens.

Most people we meet are relationally impoverished. Everyone has a deep need to be seen and heard and known for who they are. It's a struggle, even for us. So one way Meg and I seek to serve our neighbors and community is to be attentive to people and foster spaces for community. We set up the fire pit in our driveway and give out candy with our neighbors at Halloween. For the past two years our neighbor, Chris, has even made a "Free Beer" pumpkin for the parents, sticking cans in carved out holes. It's been a great conversation starter. We've hosted an open house holiday party the last two years.

One of our most life-giving activities, though, has been what we call "Spencer Street Tapas Time." As we walked the Camino we noticed that entire towns were out every night before dinner, enjoying fellowship over tapas and red wine. We thought to ourselves, "Hey, we like those things and I bet our neighbors would too." So twice monthly on Sunday summer evenings we set out a circle of chairs in our front yard, and a small table with a bottle of wine and some cheese, crackers and maybe other snacks. Often people will bring their own beverages and snacks. We'll sit and talk for an hour or two. In the unusual event that no one comes it's a great time for Meg and I to spend some quality time together talking and savoring life. We never have a lot of people, but the conversations we do have are always good. We've had next door neighbors meet each other for the first time in our front yard. We seek to ask good questions and be attentive listeners. We want to help people experience being heard and known.

This posture has spilled over into our spaces. I like telling stories and years of preaching has created a comfortability being in the middle of a group of people with some attention on me. Now, however, I'm finding myself more and more drawn away from that. In place of always telling the stories, I'm learning to ask better questions to draw out stories from others. I think of a friend's Army promotion ceremony I attended not too long ago. The whole weekend was fun, but the highlight for me was a pair of quiet conversations I had late Saturday night at the bar with two friends. I was enriched as they honored me by sharing their stories, most especially being honest about the hard parts. It strengthened our connections and it has opened opportunities for relating at a deeper level. But then sometimes I revert to filling the air with the sound of my voice. I'm a work in progress!

When I pastored in the prevailing model of church, my Sundays felt so pressured. It always felt like trying to squeeze too much action into too small a space, and with it often feeling like a lot was on the line. Plus, with four wonderfully rambunctious kids and a wife whose attention was often pulled upon by others in the church community, I got to be a dad on top of that too. Imagine being the lead salesman of a small business and bringing your kids to the sales call with your biggest client every week? Or being the president of a small company and having your kids in the room for your weekly team and investors' meeting? I love my kids. Yet after the hundredth Sunday wondering which of them had climbed the tree between the parking lot and main entrance and what they might be doing as they greeted guests coming in, well, you know. Yet, honestly, that wasn't even the biggest part.

The most challenging part was Sunday morning before the service. I would often wake up super early to pray and ground myself in God. Then I would take a few hours to tweak my sermon. By "tweak" I generally mean "write." For the last five years before my transition I had come to write my sermons Sunday morning. With the press of other demands during the week, I found it increasingly difficult to carve out adequate quiet space to thoughtfully craft a sermon. Sunday morning provided that in a way no other time at my office could. The problem is that it took a lot of focus. On this day that my kids were home from school and available for relationship, I was totally disengaged from them. Sadly, they "knew" not to talk to me. Otherwise it would produce one of those stress calls.

They would always wait for me to leave with them after the service, kids squirming when they were younger, annoyed when they were older, hoping that I'd come home with them. I almost never did. Instead it was a quick "Don't wait for me. I'll walk home, don't worry." They knew I could walk because I walked there every day. Meg and the kids weren't worried about how I'd get home, they just wanted to spend time with me. Sometimes I was physically present sooner, but I wasn't typically emotionally available until at least dinner time. And all that was for the sake of church.

Now I'm discovering a new way to Sunday. I still wake up early to spend more time with God but not as painfully early as before. I read for fun during breakfast. I take a walk in my favorite local park and savor the sights and sounds of creation. I ask God what's on his mind to talk about when our friends gather as the church in our home and also ask God to speak to them about what we should discover that day. We create a hospitable environment. Sometimes I'm just finishing getting dressed as our friends are coming up our walkway. Most other days I'll sit with a cup of coffee in our living room, or on our front porch, and hold open a loving space to welcome each one who joins us.

All in all, Sunday is now a day of peace, of shalom. I'm discovering an expression of being the church that fits within the rhythms of my life, rather than bending my life to nearly the point of breaking in order to do church. It's like what I always would've wanted, without knowing I was desiring it. Words fail me in describing how freeing this is. Three years later and it still feels like that feeling I get walking around after I've dropped my heavy pack after a long hike.

Over the course of the past number of years, I've had the privilege of participating in the ordination of four pastors serving Vineyard churches in Southeast Michigan. In various ways I've been coaching them for many years. Now I'm humbled to see how they're "replicating me" the way a good jazz artist takes what's given and riffs with it until a whole new song emerges with the same underlying rhythm and chords. I'm so proud of these men and women for how they're stepping out in faithfulness and stepping up in courage as they follow God's call.

It's also so exciting to see how the partnership work we helped launch in Ethiopia sixteen years ago has sustained. In fact, it is even growing in some ways, despite no functional formal partnership for the past three years. Meg and I have continued in relationship with our friends there, as has another one of our former partners, walking alongside them in encouragement as we're able. It's always been the case that the Ethiopians initiated and supplied much of the money, vision and effort.

So often while we were in the midst of it, the work seemed so slow and messy, like we were running to catch up (and you know how capable Ethiopians are at distance running!), yet now I see that this was the way, this was the way to sustainable, healthy fruitfulness.

I think my wife Megan says it really well: "It finally feels like my spirituality makes sense." She continues, "I'm living my life with Jesus, living life with others, being in my community, where I actually live and with the people among whom I really do my life." That summarizes it so well.

I think a clarifying moment came for me when I was pruning with Meg. We have a trio of fruit trees in our backyard. They've long been neglected. It was the second spring of my new vocational practice, maybe two weeks before Easter, and we spent most of a Saturday pruning these trees together. She had bought a quality pruning handsaw and I was really loving putting it to use.

Then it suddenly occurred to me, as clear a revelation from Heaven as any prophetic word I had ever received: I would never have been doing this before. Two weeks out from Easter spending an entire gorgeous Saturday pruning and doing yard work? No way. I'd be too busy planning (or executing) our community Easter Egg hunt, or worrying that the final details for our big Easter service were in place, or taking a long walk to pray about what to say on Good Friday. Something, anything, other than pruning all day in the backyard with Meg. I don't have a green thumb, but I loved that day. And it hasn't been the last. Plus, God being God, he still shared with me some insights from that day too, lessons about how pruning, not just in nature but in life and ministry as well, would be a pattern I'd experience again and again. In life and work and relationships, things would grow throughout the year and then how some of them would be pruned to bring more fruit.

My transition hasn't always been easy, honestly. There have been moments of humility. I've had to learn to apologize to my kids, especially my youngest two daughters. As I've slowed down and space has opened up in my life and in my heart, I've come to discern all the ways that my stress was a feature of my parenting them. My most difficult years of pastoring were concurrent with some of their most formative childhood years. I'm now able to see how I wasn't available to them with my best self, I wasn't able to be present to them emotionally, in the ways that I would've liked. A family is a relational system. My stress traveled along the lines of relational network, traveling downstream to them, where they unwittingly absorbed my anxiety. They didn't know any better. How could they? Mercifully it didn't happen every time, but it was often enough to grieve me now. We've been able to sit down and talk this through. I've shared my story, owned my part, listened as they've shared their experience of it all. I've repented. They've forgiven. I'm grateful for their grace. I'm learning that, at the neurobiological level, the repair of a relational rupture can actually make the relationship stronger than if there had never been a break at all. Oh, the wonders of God and the resilience of humans!

I still don't have a very good answer to the question, "What do you do for a living?" In particular, I have a hard time providing a job title. I mean, in one sense, who cares, right? But it's a common enough question that maybe it would be good to come up with an answer. For the time being, I usually stick with pastor because it's a category people can fit me in. However, I'm not particularly comfortable with that box, so I'll often answer with a slight caveat, as in, "I'm a pastor*." The asterisk qualifies it, right?

One of the ways I think about myself is as a partner. I'm partnering with people. This really stood out to me when Meg and I went on our Camino. The day before we left, I sent a text to the various groups of people that we're in relationship with. I included this verse from the Apostle Paul's letter to his friends in Philippi: *"I thank my God every time I remember you. In all my prayers for all of you, I always pray with joy because of your partnership in the gospel from the first day until now, being confident of this, that he who began a good work in you will carry it on to completion until the day of Christ Jesus. It is right for me to feel this way about all of you, since I have you in my heart and, whether I am in chains or defending and confirming the gospel, all of you share in God's grace with me. God can testify how I long for all of you with the affection of Christ Jesus."*[35] The interesting thing is that the day after I

---

[35] Philippians 1:8

sent it, as we boarded the plane for France, I realized that I meant it. I actually meant those words, "*I thank my God every time I remember you ... since I have you in my heart ... I long for all of you with the affection of Christ Jesus.*"

Most pastors I know would probably say that they feel those words about the members of their congregation. I probably would have said that. But now I was feeling what it *felt like* to have those words be mine. And to be honest, as much as I loved the people in the church I served as pastor, and I really did, I don't think I ever felt that way while heading out on vacation. Now I did. And not just for the people we were walking with in relationship as disciples to Jesus and to be simpler expressions of the church, but also for all the people who graciously partnered with us financially, in fellowship and in prayer. They are truly partners, not just donors or supporters. They are laboring and bringing the work into being alongside us. We are doing it together.

I also think of my responsibility as a disciple-maker. I'm not simply pastoring people, helping care for them and sort out their problems, plus all the other manifold things as a pastor does. As important as those things are, I'm now giving focused attention to the commission Jesus gave to his apprentices before he departed from them, entrusting the work to them, with the help of the Holy Spirit. That commission was, as they go to wherever they go, to bear witness to him and his life, coming alongside whomever they meet, immersing them into the Trinitarian community of God, and training them to practice all that Jesus trained us to do as apprentices of his way of life. This is disciple-making. This always happens in relationship. Sometimes that will look like apprenticeship, sometimes like resourcing, and sometimes like coaching, yet always with a dimension of companionship, coming alongside.

A catalyst is an agent that precipitates or expedites a reaction without itself being changed by the reaction. That's another way I'm thinking about myself these days. I'm trying to create change without long-term being involved. That change might be someone's spiritual formation, their family transformation, service to the community, launching a new simple church or seeing a movement form. By coming alongside others to help them do better what they're already beginning to do, I'm serving in such a way to foster change.

That's another expression of my new understanding of vocation: being a servant. I suppose I've always tried being a servant leader, yet as I've mentioned previously, I'm feeling that in new ways. Influence comes in the lives of people; leadership is exercised by serving, more than solving problems. Rather than assuming I know what they need, or posturing myself as the problem-solver, I come alongside individuals and teams to help them discover what their needs and opportunities are and asking how I can serve. It's so refreshing. I could say a lot more about these four fresh understandings, but perhaps that's best saved for another book.

There's a Bible verse that's a favorite of those who love scriptures on magnets that adorn their fridge. It's Jeremiah 29:11: *"For I know the plans I have for you,"* declares the Lord, *"plans to prosper you and not to harm you, plans to give you hope and a future."* That word "prosper" is the Hebrew word shalom, often translated as peace into English.

Its meaning is more robust, though, than simply the absence of conflict or the presence of rest, like a lazy Saturday morning. It carries a deeper sense of well-being. It's more akin to Julian of Norwich's famous maxim: "All shall be well and all manner of things shall be well."[36] This is a reality that I'm beginning to experience. It is not fully realized yet, of course, but it is already beginning to be real. It is not simply a "shall be." I am experiencing a taste of "is now."

The word that I identify this with is *freedom*. Looking up the dictionary definition on my phone, each of these resonate with me: 1) the absence of necessity or constraint in choice; 2) liberation from restraint or the power of another; 3) the quality of being released from something onerous; 4) ease and facility; 5) the quality of being open; 6) boldness of conception or execution.[37] As I've already mentioned, words fail me in providing a clear articulation. Sometimes I experience this as a presence I feel in my gut, akin to joy and power to act according to my desire. Other times I experience it as an absence, like when I've left confined quarters for open space, or when I've been walking into a stiff headwind that suddenly abates.

---

[36] *Revelations of Divine Love*, Julian of Norwich
[37] *Merriam-Webster Dictionary*

Here's how I know this freedom, this *shalom*, is real. Not just real, but something deeply significant. About a year after my transition, I went to bed feeling heavy. As I lay my head on my pillow, I heard an inner voice telling myself that I was a failure. I reflected on what was going on such that I felt that way. I was able to gain some clarity about what it was. Then it occurred to me how startled I was that I had felt that way. I suddenly realized it had been a year since I had felt that way.

You see, before my transition, probably five or six days a week, every week, for at least ten years, I had gone to bed struggling with feeling like a failure. Some people that know me might be surprised to hear that, but it's true. Often I'd think it to myself. Occasionally I'd even mumble it out loud, enough for Meg to ask, "What did you say?" Usually I'd tell her the truth. Usually. Note the math: 300 times per year, for at least ten years in a row, I had gone to bed experiencing a feeling of being a failure. That's 3000 times. After transitioning it happened once in a year. In the few times it has happened since then I have been able to talk myself through it, being kind to myself and speaking truth. Before I was never able to do it.

I'm still seeking understanding about what was going on during all those nighttime routines. I believe I had shame and disappointment that I wasn't living up to the expectation of success in the model of ministry I was pursuing. Some of these expectations were my own, others were fostered and foisted upon me by industry definitions of success. My "shame attendant" (that critical voice in your head that sounds like a parent, Coach Barnes from middle school or even yourself) kept telling me that because I wasn't experiencing success according to these expectations, I wasn't working hard enough, wasn't competent enough, or that I just wasn't good enough.

More deeply, though, I've come to believe that I repeatedly felt like a failure all those nights because I wasn't living authentically to my inner conviction and calling. I didn't yet have language for that conviction and calling, beyond what I was trying to practice, but I could feel somewhere deep down that there was misalignment between my calling and my role and way of being. And the only language available, again provided by my shame attendant, was that of failure. There were times I felt like giving up. But I come from a people that do not give up. I was trained in a way that did not give in, tenaciously adapting and overcoming until we win.

Now I'm learning to be more aware of the desire, the God-curated desire, that is hidden underneath the lurking shadow of shame. As I've come into deeper contact with God, in the silence and stillness, the light of being loved that I encounter there begins to dispel this shadow and offer me another way. Instead of claiming I'm a failure, I'm learning to recognize the longing for beauty and purpose that I'm feeling and pursue that with passion and intention. I'm also learning to receive. Receive love from God, receive grace from myself, receive help from others. The first one is easiest. The last one is hardest. Again, I'm a work in progress.

I frequently ask myself, "How did this—my life—work before?" To be honest, I'm not sure. I can't figure it out. Increasingly, it seems to me that the answer is, it didn't.

Discoveries

During my brief stay in the Army one of the tools that I really appreciated was something called an After-Action Report. I remember standing around a "sand table" map (imagine one of those shoebox dioramas you made in elementary school, only way better) after a training exercise as the Company XO during my cadre tour at Cadet Basic Training. We were all tired and sweaty as each participant shared their perspective on what we experienced during the exercise we had just completed. The basic idea is that following a training exercise, the key people involved gather as soon as they can to review the key details of the event. It's a focused conversation guided by a series of core questions, including items like: 1) "What were we trying to accomplish?" 2) "What went well?" 3) "What didn't go so well or according to plan?" 4) "What can we do to do it better next time?" I love this because it's an institutionalized system fostering organizational reflection, and if it is done correctly, it encourages self-reflection as well.

I've tried to carry this spirit of reflection and ongoing learning into my whole life. It is my conviction that leaders are lifelong readers and lifelong learners. To help me maintain this mindset of self-reflection in my devotional life, one of the most helpful resources for me has been the Prayer of Examen, developed by St. Ignatius of Loyola. There are various ways it can be practiced, but for me I spend some time each morning reviewing the day that had passed. I first spend some time in gratitude. Then I make room for the events and encounters of the day to pass before my awareness, paying particular attention to those moments when I felt a particular sense of God's presence, or when I experienced an awareness of faith, hope, love, joy, and/or peace. I spend time savoring the encounter and giving thanks. Then I do the same for those moments in the day when I felt distant from God or a lack of those gifts. Not to shame myself, but rather to learn and grow and remember that God is with me even when I'm having a hard time experiencing it. I close with a commitment to continue on in my journey. Over time, the rhythm of this habit has helped me to develop a keen awareness of God's presence with me in real time.

Another tool has been journaling. I hated journaling at first. I found it painfully annoying. But then, slowly, over time, I came to love it. I wove journaling together with my prayer, particularly the Prayer of Examen. What was stirred up in this prayer often became material for journaling.

I share that because writing this book has been an exercise in reflection for me and I would like to share a bit about what I'm learning, the discoveries I'm making.

Early in our marriage, my wife joined my step-brother (whose name also happens to be Jim) on a hiking adventure in Glacier National Park. Somewhere along the way between two campsites, my brother spotted a waterfall off in the distance to the left of the trail. It wasn't huge, but it was cool in the way it tumbled over large boulders and then plunged to the creek below that we would soon cross by wooden bridge. As we stopped to gaze at the falling water, maybe a half-mile distant, we noticed a small footpath through the brush that led in the direction of the cascading falls. I could see it on my brother's face. He wanted to go. Not just see it, but climb it and stand atop that boulder and conquer it. He urged us to go. More than his words you could see the passion in his eyes. He had encountered a deep desire. That desire propelled us along that footpath and then compelled us to make our own path to the boulders and then up on top of them until we luxuriated there in the sun and savored the moment. It was desire that drove us. I have experienced this again and again in my own adventures, especially with my son on our many hikes. I'm discovering my life is a journey of desire.

I chose to attend West Point out of desire. I had other options, good schools, closer to home. West Point requires cadet candidates to receive a nomination from a sitting US Senator or Representative. As I sat in my Congressman's office with the four members of his service academy review committee – representing the Army, Navy, Air Force and Marines – they asked me why I had only applied to West Point and not any of the other academies or ROTC programs. "Well, sir," I replied to each question in turn, "I wear glasses and so I can't fly. I don't particularly want to be at sea on a boat for six or more months out of the year. And, frankly, I want to be part of the best of the best. That's why." Brash as I was, I got the nomination. This pride and ambition was part of my desire. So was the realization that West Point would be good for my resumé and whatever future career path I took. Yet below these rational ideas lurked a deeper desire, juvenile yet authentic, to give myself in chivalrous sacrificial service. I didn't want simply a career with stability, I longed for adventure and impact.

I later left the Army and became a pastor also because of desire. It was a continuation of the desire to not just settle for a career but rather to commit to making a difference. I knew I could make a difference through my service in the military, yet I discerned an opportunity to expand and focus that impact through pastoring a local church. The many additional commitments I made in ministry on top of pastoring built on this basic desire. Planting a church. Sending out and coaching other church planters. Serving alongside international partners in mission. Acquiring a building and serving to bless our city. Each of these ministry opportunities helped me experience affirmation from people in my life whom I respected and whose opinions mattered to me. All of these initiatives flowed from convictions and beliefs that I was sure really mattered. Also, each of these commitments expressed one or more aspects of the understanding I had of my desire to make a difference in the world.

As I reflect on these things, I notice that all my language, all my thinking, had been in the direction of doing. I expressed the understanding of my desire by doing. I recognize this is fairly normal for many people through the early stages of their journey, both spiritually and as a leader. But then something happened. I realized it wasn't enough. I think this is why our church building and my early ministry successes in our city (and beyond) are so significant for my story. I had done everything I knew to be right, everything I understood that I had dreamed of, and I reached the end of it.

I discovered that I was merely doing, and that there was something deeper, something more.

I discovered a desire to be.

To practice relationship. To be seen and heard and known and loved. To return these gifts to others.

A desire for a simpler way of practicing my vocation, a simpler way of being a disciple of Jesus.

A desire for a more authentic way of being a mature human.

This desire drew me forward. This desire made it easy to leave behind pastoring for pioneering. Yet this desire to know and be known has not always been easy. The most unexpected part of the journey for me was this discovery of desire. But it didn't happen on its own; it came through a mixture of serendipity and intentional effort.

In addition to desire, another discovery I've made along my journey is what I now call "the Five S's:" slowing, surrendering, suffering, simplifying, and succeeding.

The inward journey and passing through the Wall are a form of transition. In his standard text on this topic, *Managing Transitions*, William Bridges describes a transition like a journey, a road through the desert. It's a psychological, emotional, relational process. He proposes that all transitions begin with an ending, end with a new beginning, and pass through an uncertain, ambiguous middle in between.[38]

For me, slowing and surrender were critical to my ending well. Simplicity and a fresh definition of success were key dimensions of my new beginning on the other side of the transition. Suffering was that challenging season in the middle.

My friend Keith sent me this text not too long ago: "Saw this and thought of you, the 3MPH pastor: *Solvitur ambulando* is a Latin phrase which means "it is solved by walking," referring to an anecdotal, practical solution to a seemingly complex philosophical problem. It is often attributed to Saint Augustine in a refutation of Zeno's paradoxes of motion." I've often found lots of things in my life are solved by walking. A helpful book in this direction is *God Walk* by Mark Buchanan, recommended by my friend, Bruce the Peregrino.

Here is Zeno's Dichotomy Paradox, in brief: a person is standing on one side of a room and with each step they take, they cross half the distance to the other side. When will they arrive? The paradox is that they'll never arrive. I wrote a poem about this once:

My money's on Zeno for getting it right,
At least with regard to this one insight.
I'm sure I can get to where you are.
Yet whenever I step, I never seem to arrive.
I know that I'm closer, but you still seem so far.
How long?
When will I, like Diogenes, rise,
And cross the space to look into your eyes?

---

[38] William Bridges, *Managing Transitions* (London: Nicholas Bealey Publishing, 2017)

I once read (I can't remember where) that upon hearing this paradox of Zeno's, Diogenes, his companion, got up and walked across the room to where Zeno was. You see, it really is solved by walking.

The commitment to make walking my primary mode of *transportation* had an unforeseeable consequence: walking became one of my primary modes of *transformation*.

Walking was key for me in learning to slow down. Walking helped train me in noticing. I noticed my city differently when I walked at 3mph versus driving at 35mph. I saw things I might otherwise have missed. A side benefit of slowing was serendipity. Surprise moments of beauty. Like the two houses in my town that have medieval-esque gate entrances or the walkway shortcut between two streets that's a-flutter with butterflies or the house near the Dairy Queen that has shards from a famous local potter pressed into the sidewalk cement. This serendipity has helped me be more attentive to creativity, like the idea of writing a fantasy novel and another book articulating "the kind of movement I would want to join," as an expression of co-creating beauty with God. Slowing helps me be aware, so that I respond, not react. Respond appropriately to what's really happening and what's really needed, not just what I expect, demand or want. Slowing helps me attune: being present in loving, joyful connection.

When I first read *The Critical Journey* I didn't like it. I reacted negatively. When I read it seven years later, it all made sense. I loved it. What changed?

Me. I had changed.

I was now reading it from a different place, coming to the book as a different person. The authors of this book theorize that somewhere along the path of the "Inward Journey" in our life of faith, we will encounter "The Wall." The Wall is difficult to explain, as it is part of the personalized dimension of the inward journey, yet it is a critical part of part of our spiritual healing. In wrestling with God at the Wall, we meet God face to face and experience another layer of transformation.[39]

<u>Pilgrim's Progress</u>
Steamer trunk trailing behind me.
Wheels fallen off long ago.
Dragging through the mud and dirt,
Catching on roots and tripping me up as it catches my heels.
It's packed down full, cartoon-style, bulging in spots and taut.
It's haphazardly loaded with shame and pain,
disappointments and regret, harbored hurts both real and imagined.
Why do I hold onto this trunk, lug it with me wherever I go?
Are these prized possessions, treasured belongings?
A Traveler appears. Offers to unburden my load.
Removes each item, one by one, donning them.
A strange court jester.
He strips down. Deposits them in the dirt.
"Leave the trunk, too," he says. "You won't need it.
Now come with me."

In the early stages of our spiritual journey, we rush headlong in our need to perform, our desire to achieve. We run from the pain of our unresolved past traumas and race towards the goals that we are sure will bring us the satisfaction we crave. In my observation, if we're not careful, with all this rushing we are in danger of crashing into the wall and shipwrecking our journey. Or, avoiding that, we'll bounce right off into a new church, a new job, a new style, a new house or city, a new marriage. We'll have to retrace steps, covering old ground, only to find ourselves at the Wall again.

The discipline of slowing helped me approach the wall at a human pace.

I remained intensely busy in my calendar. But spiritual direction, the Exercises, walking, journaling, and more, enabled me to slow my interior world enough to notice the questions that were propelling me, to attend to the desires that were drawing me. Standing at the Wall, I came face to

---

[39] *The Critical Journey*, Hagburg and Guelich, page 114

face with myself, face to face with God. I came to discover that the only way forward was surrender.

Standing before God, I surrendered to love. Surrendered to being loved.

<u>Answered Prayer</u>
"Show us your glory!"
The cry rings out.
Our hearts filled
With faith and fear
And love and doubt.

A pause.
Pregnant.
Waiting.

And what should appear?
No burning bush,
Or smoky cloud.
Not this time.
A person strides forth.
A man, with a name.
And a face.
Bearing the family likeness.
Kindly and kingly
His grace.

To gaze into his eyes,
Is to understand the response to our cries.
His glory our hearts refine
And cause to shine.
Jesus.

In surrendering to love I realized that I am enough.

Maybe it's better said that I'm able to surrender because I discovered I am enough. Full stop.

I stand before God in the vulnerability of my nakedness, of every type, and I am seen and known and loved, just as I am, without shame. In surrender I can live in the present because I discern that God is with me through every joy and trauma of my past.

Surrender means I can trust God with the outcome. I can trust and release the other person without having to make them conform to my agenda. I can let them work out their own life and be responsible for it.

Surrender means I can consent to what I would not choose.

Surrender is not defeat, nor is it inaction. It is an active responsiveness, like the hunter or the birdwatcher or the soldier in an outpost. It's an active delight, like a landscape painter or between two lovers. It's an active trust, like a trapeze artist or the relationship between parent and child.

I think of my experience drawing out my "9 Headed Hydra" Mind Map, the serendipitous discovery of what God was trying to tell me and my response of loving obedience to Jesus' invitation. This is my surrender. Slowing made it possible. It's a lifelong journey, of course, yet I can walk it out in the freedom that surrender brings. I now understand how important this exercise was. In Managing Transitions, Bridges proposes that a key part of ending well is acknowledging what we're losing in the transition. To make space to acknowledge the emotion of this, and even maybe take a piece of what you're losing with you. When I met with all the members of Renaissance Vineyard during my pastoral transition, this is what I was doing for them. Making space to honor what would be lost in the transition. To end well. My "Nine Headed Hydra" Mind Map was an exercise in giving this gift to myself.

In addition to this ending of what I had known, my transition involved an awkward, uncomfortable middle season characterized by hardship and suffering. It wasn't like these "Five S's" were precisely linear, happening one after another. Like any journey, though we travel from Point A to Point B, the route is often circuitous with plenty of back and forth. Though difficult, this suffering was essential in refining and maturing me.

Like many who've gone before me, I would discover that the majority of my suffering came at the hands of those close to me.

A few years before my transition, a friend of mine who pastored a very large Vineyard church recommended I apply for a vacant lead pastor post in a large church in another state. In one sense I was honored. He believed in me enough to recommend me for this role. In his words, this larger stage would provide the proper platform for my voice to be heard in the wider movement. But I also recognized that in this line of thinking, my voice mattered more if it was speaking to a large crowd. It wasn't the call of God or the gifts and assignment of God, it was all about the size of the room.

People have often wondered why we left the Vineyard. I had been a member of the Vineyard for 25 years, and 21 of them as a pastor.

By the time we stepped down from pastoring, I had been in translocal leadership, bringing influence beyond my local church, for more than 14 of those 21 years. I served on the national church planting and missions teams. I assessed, trained and coached church planters, and strategized church planting efforts nationally. I coordinated mission efforts from the US to Africa, the Mid East and Central Asia. I served as a member of the missions board and the Multiply Vineyard advisory team. I was entrusted with informal assistant area leadership and helped plan both regional and missions conferences. I was a contributor to the core values booklet used nationally in local churches.

I wasn't just a member. I was a champion.

I gave gladly. I sacrificially volunteered my strengths, skills, and passions with the time, energy and relationships I had available. I did this joyfully and willingly. I had no regrets. I harbored no bitterness: not then, not now.

We received from the Vineyard richly textured relationships as well as access to opportunities to serve in accordance with what God had deposited in me. I am forever grateful for these gifts.

If the Vineyard is like a tribe, then our clan became the missions community, and the one place where we most experienced a sense of family was on the missions leadership team. That was particularly so for my wife. This team of friends was the one place in our tribe where she felt truly known, where we both felt a sense of being home.

"It's a shame Jim and Meg left the Vineyard. I wonder why they did?"

"You know," Megan replies, "people say that we left the family. They wonder why we left the Vineyard. But it isn't so much that we left the Vineyard family, rather it feels like they took the family from us."

To be clear, we did leave. No one kicked us out. It remains my firm conviction that Jesus called us from the Vineyard organization, so that we would have freedom for the new work he was giving us to do. Freedom from, freedom for. This is a longstanding pattern in God's kingdom, that God calls us to be free from one thing, even though it might be good, so that we are free for what he wants to give us next.

Yet the experience that Meg described is equally true.

For a decade I observed subtle changes in ministry philosophy. Then, what began as a redistribution of funds during Covid, and a reallocation of priorities and power during a denominational reorganization, turned into a "rearrangement" of personnel and a tearing apart of the team. The organizational leadership unceremoniously broke our missions family apart, with little in the way of gratitude, and in the end shamed us for who we were and what we had done.

When I offered my input into the movement-shaping process underway, I didn't even get a simple "thank you" for taking the time to participate. One person in leadership over me and our church admitted it was too much work to try to really know and understand me. Another tried to isolate me and then questioned my loyalty. I witnessed ugly things, dishonorable things, choices that seemed to me to be either cowardly, incompetent or both. In the end I was deeply discouraged because I had believed in and thought better of these leaders, most of whom were my friends.

A friend once asked me what were my expectations for these leaders. It was a fair question. Expectations are like opinions: everyone has them and there's no guarantee they're reasonable, valid or appropriate. Honestly, I'm not sure what I expected, but I can articulate what I desired. It boils down to a few core things. I desired that in the network of relationships that was the Vineyard, both informally and formally, I would be seen and heard and understood. To be known. Also, in this same network of relationships, both informally and formally, I desired that I would be able to creatively contribute with my strengths.

These desires were inconsistently realized at best, sometimes painfully so, particularly in any formal setting beyond the Missions Leadership Team.

Genuine differences in expectations were involved. My own shortcomings played a part. That's why I'm deeply committed to my formation and maturity in God. Some of these disappointed desires stemmed from the shortcomings of the leaders around me that I worked with. As for the rest, I'm convinced they're the result of structural problems in the organization itself. It's also why I stepped outside the system to partner with God in pioneering (rediscovering?) another way, a different structure, that is more deeply rooted in relationship.

I've spoken with whom I need to speak, both in the moment and since, so I harbor no ill will. I pray for my friends and this Vineyard family, that they experience faithful fruitfulness and the fullness of God as they abide in Jesus.

I did have one significant relationship that didn't go so well during this season. I tried twice to initiate a conversation with my mentor Steve about my concerns. After a few remarks, things turned quickly to other matters. I could have been more direct in expressing my desire for a mentoring-type conversation, yet I was trying to respect what seemed to be his desires and needs. We had, over the years, become very close friends. He had served long and faithfully and I wanted to honor our relationship.

Yet it was important that we talk, so we set up the time to zoom. I named my frustrations and concerns and described how I was considering leaving the denomination we both loved. It didn't go well. He felt reactive. It seems he failed to see how I had tried to reach out. My sense is that he personalized it. Yet I also bear responsibility. As his longtime friend I could have—should have—been more attuned to how my remarks would land for him. In hindsight, I'm very aware of how what I was thinking about would be triggering for him. I wish I had seen it sooner. I regret not being more sensitive. I regret not being a more aware friend. In my own pain I caused pain, which grieves me.

When we spoke next, I apologized as I was able, received forgiveness as it was offered, and also named the hurt I continued to feel. I mentioned how it seemed to me that he was withdrawing from relationship. He acknowledged he was. In part because no one he knew who had left the Vineyard had ever tried to maintain a relationship with him. That made me very sad for him. But it was also, he said, because I had "left the family, and we were no longer doing the same thing." I thought the family that mattered was the family of God, which I most definitely had not left. This confused me deeply and cut like a knife. Here was the man who had officiated our wedding, laid hands on us in ordination, whom I had invited to my 10th reunion from West Point, who had become a close friend, and he was pulling back because I had changed organizations. It hurt. It still hurts now. We've stayed connected, thankfully, but it's not really the same. Or maybe it's always been a little like this and now I see it differently.

Though I've been told I left the family, here's what I know: Abram was no less a son though he left Haran's house, and though Joseph had no tribe he was a son of Israel nonetheless. And so it is that I have left the land of my fathers, and while my inheritance may be given over to others, I remain no less a true son of the Vineyard.

All of this produced sorrow. It brought a measure of suffering. I bear the sadness and disappointment of unrealized legitimate desires of how I might have creatively contributed to the common good with all the strengths, experiences, relationships and energy that God has entrusted to me to steward. Just as muscles are torn and broken down before they're built up, suffering is how we grow stronger.

I'm reminded of these three scriptures, each of which was significant for me during my transition and the years following.

"We boast in the hope of the glory of God. Not only so, but we also glory in our sufferings, because we know that suffering produces perseverance; perseverance, character; and character, hope. And hope does not put us to shame, because God's love has been poured out into our hearts through the Holy Spirit, who has been given to us."[40]

"Consider it pure joy, my brothers and sisters, whenever you face trials of many kinds, because you know that the testing of your faith produces perseverance. Let perseverance finish its work so that you may be mature and complete, not lacking anything."[41]

"In all this you greatly rejoice, though now for a little while you may have had to suffer grief in all kinds of trials. These have come so that the proven genuineness of your faith—of greater worth than gold, which perishes even though refined by fire—may result in praise, glory and honor when Jesus Christ is revealed. Though you have not seen him, you love him; and even though you do not see him now, you believe in him and are filled with an inexpressible and glorious joy, for you are receiving the end result of your faith, the salvation of your souls."[42]

What each of these scriptures highlights, from three different early leaders in the Way of Jesus, is the connection between suffering, maturity, perseverance, love and joy. Just as the Apostle Paul and his team experienced the sorrow of being blocked from Ephesus in Asia, he encountered the joy of the new and maturing disciples in the church community in Philippi. We can persevere through the wilderness of our transitions, and the suffering and hardship it brings, with love and joy, because it is working in us maturity.

As I reflect on that Mind Map, I think it not only demonstrates the priority of surrender, but also of simplicity. I'm discovering that simplicity isn't so much about being easy as it is about being

---

[40] Romans 5:2-5
[41] James 1:2-4
[42] 1 Peter 1:6-9

uncomplicated. Focused. Attentive to what's most important. As I've heard it described elsewhere, "keeping the main thing the main thing."

I surrendered and said "Yes" to what God wanted, eliminating everything I was doing. God gave back to me what he wanted me to do: mentor missional leaders and make disciples, catalyzing simple spiritual families on mission.

It wasn't that everything else I was doing was bad. But it did dilute my focus. More deeply, these other areas of vocational concern were laced with my tendencies to be overly responsible. Honestly, it's difficult for me to admit this, even now, yet I can see how this is so. Recently I was traveling alone internationally for a work trip. I noticed how easy it was for me to be hyper-vigilant of my surroundings, aware of how everyone around me was doing, ready at a pin-drop to help lift a piece of luggage into the overhead compartment. I'm discerning that so much of my vocational life, particularly in the denomination of which I was a part, was the functional equivalent of this. It's not that it was bad, just laced with my shame. Unable to let things simply be, without my involvement, I would try to help. Jesus is setting me free. I'm learning to be free to help, or not, and serve in what way is best.

There are lots of other ways Megan and I are embracing simplicity too. We've spelled many of them out in the previous chapter as we continue to discover a "new way." Yet the essence of this is the simplicity God is transforming in our interior world.

This led me to a new understanding of success. I came to realize it's all about relationships. Of course I would've said that before. And I was being honest. Our church was relational. As a pastor, I prioritized relationships. But now I had a deeper understanding of what that really meant. Not a relational program, with relationship as an adjective. But relationship as a noun, relationship as priority, relationship as the point. Purposeful relationship.

I've had the opportunity to travel a number of times since I've transitioned, both domestically and internationally. No longer is the focus on formal teaching sessions with groups or even visiting work that is happening. Some of that occurs, of course, but the focus is truly on the relationship. The bulk of my time has been spent being with the folks I'm visiting. Sharing meals, taking walks, lots of coffee. My goal is to be with my friends in the context of their lives. I try to ask lots of questions and listen long, avoiding the temptation to formulate my answer before they've finished talking or trying to figure out a way to solve their problem. In fact, I'm not really looking for problems at all. Mostly I'm looking to hear their heart, discern their desires, notice what is stirring in them, and helping them be attentive to this aspect of what God is already doing. Especially when I'm with a small team, I'm learning to ask thoughtful questions and listen well enough to digest what they're saying, so that I can help them hear themselves better.

On one recent visit to a newer friend in a new country for me, I literally spent five days doing life with my friend and his wife. He asked me what I wanted to do when I came. I said, "Be with you. Anything you're thinking that I might want to do because others who've come have done that, I don't want to do. Chances are good I've already done it before in other places and my ego doesn't need that to justify this trip. I'm coming to be with you and your wife. I don't want to make you do any extra work. Being in relationship with you is my purpose."

So that's what we did. We ate meals, ran errands, explored the wilderness, together. I shared a story here and there, but mostly I watched him do what he's already doing very well, and then we talked about it after. It was so light, so freeing, so fruitful. I kept wondering if this wasn't a glimpse of what it might have been like for Jesus and Paul and the other apostles. My friend mentioned to me that sometimes he gets criticized because the weekly breakfasts he has with the guys he's discipling just seems like dudes hanging out, not ministry. I affirmed what he was doing was just as significant as any program with a flyer and a website.

Other friends host a gathering they call "Pretend Church." This twice monthly gathering features good home-cooked meals, plenty of raucous real-life conversation, and heaping helpings of love. The members, all of them either recovering from church-based spiritual trauma, or with no Christian background at all, can't believe there is something this cool and real that you can't find anywhere on the Web.

A painting hangs in our living room that first graced my paternal grandfather's office. It's a nautical scene from the Detroit River, displaying a small tugboat coming alongside a line of fine sailing ships in full regalia. The painting is titled "Champion," after the name of the tugboat. The hero isn't always the one who adventures out at sea. Often it's the unsung companion who helps them get there. I've been drawn to this piece of art for decades and now I understand why. I'm learning the secret of contentment, to be a tugboat champion.

Everything we do is in the context of relationships: teaching, training, even correction. Relationships with a purpose, not programs trying to be relational. God is in the relationship business, if that's not too crass a way of saying it. The Christian understanding of God is that God exists in a relationship of loving, joyful communion. We are made for relationship, both as an overflow of this loving communion, and to enter into it and experience its richness.

Think of how it was for Adam and Eve. Genesis 1 tells the story of creation as a rhythm of forming and filling, in the language of epic poetry. In Genesis 2, we see God's hands getting dirty in the mire of the work. At the pinnacle of the story in Genesis 1, we read that God looked at all he had done, culminating in the creation of humanity as an overflow of Trinitarian delight, and pronounced it "very good." A few verses later in chapter 2, we find God giving mouth to mouth first to Adam, then to Eve. God breathed the breath of life into their nostrils and they came alive.

This is personal. This is God up close.

Imagine the scene from their perspective. Their first awareness as they come into consciousness is of God's face hovering intimately close, and God's face is bright with joyful, loving delight. The sparkle in God's eyes, the turn of God's mouth, all communicate, "You are very good. I love you and I'm so glad to be with you and have you with me." This is the origin story of our species. And that story is repeated in healthy family situations around the world. We are made for relationships. It is in relationships that we thrive. And for all the times that our family situations may be less than mature, it is also the case that we are healed and restored in relationships too. We're discovering just how powerful this is and trying to live as if it is true.

Another dimension of my new understanding of success is my own growth. I'll never forget the question a friend asked me during one of my transition conversations leading up to my departure from pastoring: "But, Jim, what are you going to do for church? Where are you going to go to get fed?" There are all kinds of interesting things about this question. We might note the orientation around event and location. But that wasn't the main thing for me. In the flash of an eye, the question forced upon me a realization that I had known for a long time was true but had never quite been able to say. Until that moment.

"Well, friend, I get fed by Jesus in my prayer. I haven't been fed by this church in years."

I was growing. But despite the occasional pastoral interaction that stretched my spiritual formation, the fact remained that I was growing in spite of being a member of the church and not because of it. For how many pastors and elders and church leaders this might be true? For how many churchgoers too?

I'm learning that my way of being in vocational ministry can be integrally related to my experiencing growth in my discipleship. I have more aha! moments with scripture around my dining room table during our simple church gathering than I did in a year's worth of sermons I preached or listened to. I'm stretched to be patient or forbearing or humble like rarely before. I grow more in making disciples, as Jesus commissioned me, by asking better questions more than giving good answers.

Perhaps nowhere have I experienced this more than when I sit down with someone for a coffee, a meal, or a drink. Remember the fundraising book I mentioned I read shortly after my transition? The author was adamant: never let them buy your lunch because then they'll feel like they've given to you and you won't get their ongoing support. Logically, I can understand his point. Yet the challenge is something Jesus says in a very similar passage: *"Stay there, eating and drinking whatever they put before you, for the worker deserves his wages*" (Luke 10:7). One of the biggest areas of growth for me has been learning how to receive. This involves humility, vulnerability. Even now, as I write this, I feel the urge to defend myself, to rise up, to describe how I'm not a mooch, how I seek to be generous. Those things are true of me. It is a deeply held desire of mine to be generous. God is happy with that. Now God is molding me to be humble, vulnerable, training me to learn how to receive.

Ruth Haley Barton is someone my wife and I both admire. Her insights on spiritual formation, team discernment and the soul of leadership are profound. She has said that "the best thing a leader can bring to their ministry is their own transformed self."[43] I'm discovering that there is a way of leading in ministry, of being the church, that facilitates my own spiritual transformation too.

The last discovery I'm making is about the risk of failure, loneliness, and the reality of suffering. This is something we've all got to face. Dietrich Bonhoeffer warned against the dangers of "cheap grace."[44] When the Apostles James and John (and their mom) approached Jesus about having places of authority in his coming kingdom, Jesus responded by asking them if they were willing to "drink the cup" that he would soon drink.[45] In fact, the cost of following Jesus was one of his repeated refrains. He didn't back away from it. Am I willing to face the cost of obeying Jesus?

Most entrepreneurial ventures don't succeed; 20% fail within the first two years and almost half within the first five years. What I'm doing may fail. There is a track record of success in overseas environments, but it has not yet been fully successfully demonstrated in a US cultural context. There will be many false starts and lots of stumbling. In the dedication of this book, I reference a biblical proverb to this effect. I will fall down. I will fail, hopefully forward, though not always. Yet this failure will make me stronger, if only I persevere.

---

[43] https://transformingcenter.org/2004/09/the-transforming-leader-giving-the-best-ive-got/
[44] *The Cost of Discipleship*, Dietrich Bonhoeffer, 1937
[45] Mark 10:38

I've put all my chips on what I'm doing and I have to face and embrace the risk of failure.

Yet I remember what Jesus told me 25 years ago when I stepped out to plant our first church, "Nothing ventured, nothing gained."

So it is well with my soul. I pray only that Jesus is exalted in my life, whatever the cost.

In addition to the risk of failure, I've had to embrace the risk of loneliness. In making this transition I've had to step away from close relationships. Groups who provided a sense of tribal identity. Rooms where everybody seemed to know my name. Friends who have been confused by my choices. Other friends have stopped returning my texts. Several friends have been frustrated and one told me they're "praying for me to rejoin the family." Despite the many relationships I have, many have changed and some have been lost. This is a sorrow for me. Yet, I'm learning, I'm not truly alone because I am with Jesus. And his promise to receive "a hundredfold" for every good thing left behind is true as I am discovering.

I have experienced some suffering for my choices. It's almost embarrassing to say so since I've not suffered to the point of bloodshed like others I know. I've known no lasting deprivation. Yet I've chosen a pay cut at a time of inflation. I've embraced uncertainty at a time of launching my children into adulthood. I've forsaken a well-worn road to embark on an unmarked path. My choices have elicited misunderstanding and brought about loss. There is the reality of hardship.

Yet, as weird as it may seem, all this brings peace. Not so much the absence of conflict variety, but rather of the presence of well-being type. Several months ago, we had a baptism celebration for a friend who had come to trust and follow Jesus after decades of seeking satisfaction in just about every other possible source. As the small group of loved ones standing riverside chatted after the ceremony and prayer, one of his friends shared a story. He described how in his childhood church, at the end of the service, people would greet one another with the benediction,

"God's peace." He never understood what they were getting at the time, he said. But now he did after seeing Patrick baptized and experiencing the peace he was radiating. "It's been a long time since I've been to church," he went on, "but you're experiencing what they were talking about. What they wished they'd all get. In fact, that's what we're all looking for, what we all need, to experience this peace, to be seen and known by God." I agree.

This peace is the peace that God experiences, the peace that God enjoys, a deep and lasting experience of well-being. And God is inviting us into it in ever deepening ways. And it comes as we receive being seen and known by God. There will be moments where we'll sense it and it will leave us breathless. There will be seasons in which we might struggle to remember it even exists at all. Yet we can come to experience in ever-increasing ways this well-being of God, God's joyous delight. *"And we all, who with unveiled faces contemplate the Lord's glory, are being transformed into his image with ever-increasing glory, which comes from the Lord, who is the Spirit."*[46] This is the ocean in which we swim. The atmosphere in which we live and move and have our being.[47]

In all of this there is a certain patient perseverance. I've hiked a lot of trails and one thing I've learned is that you never know when the beauty will come.

This has been especially true as I've hiked the mountain valleys of Grand Teton National Park. I know there will be vistas of beauty. I just never know around which bend the trail will turn and open up into a vision of glory. Those scenes are the moments you remember, the ones you post on social media and share with your friends.

These moments make the trip worthwhile.

Yet, in reality, they're only a small fraction of the trail. For much of the hike we can't quite see where we're going, shrouded as our way is by trees or bushes or clouds or rocks. We've got to trust the trail, trust the markers that those who've gone before us have placed. On life's journey, we practice patient perseverance.

---

[46] 2 Corinthians 3:18
[47] cf Acts 17:28, where Paul quotes the Cretan philosopher Epimenides

Slowing Down To Catch Up With God

Jesus' work is urgent. It matters.
Jesus' way is unhurried. Never worried.
I walk in Jesus' unforced rhythms of grace.

The only way I know how to do that is through multiplying myself, empowering and releasing others instead of being the center of attention.

All this is possible through what I call "the Love Loop."

If you've ever hung around a church or Christians, chances are you've heard the admonition to love God and let go of sin. Understandably so, it seems to me, since even Jesus identified loving God as the greatest commandment and loving our neighbors as we love ourselves as a parallel second.

Yet Jesus knew, in fact Jesus experienced, something that many Christians have forgotten: that we love God because God first loved us.[48] As we encounter and receive the love that God has for us, then we respond in love for God. We love because we are loved.

It is this experience of being loved, and of loving such a joyously good God in return, that enables us to express our love by laying aside those disordered attachments that are the result of our hurts and hangups in which we are seeking a surrogate love. As we release these false attachments and take hold of the good gifts God gives, we grow in our capacity to freely love God and others.

Yet there is a problem. Humanity in general, and Western society in particular, has lost track of a clear picture of who God is.[49] The image of God revealed in the face and character and actions of Jesus is marred by the debris of political machinations, money grubbing, moral hypocrisy, a lack of concern for the priorities and practices of Jesus. There is so much trauma in our society that it is hard to receive the love of God whom we cannot see. So it helps to experience being loved by our friends

---

[48] 1 John 4:19, among many other scriptures
[49] Consider Philip Yancey's classic, *The Jesus I Never Knew*

and neighbors, whom we can touch and see and feel, so that we can begin to believe that God might really love us too.

We receive this gift of love by others. As we grow, we in turn will be able to share this gift with others. And as we share we also receive. In loving others, we are loved. We continue our journey of transformation.

Be deeply loved by people → Experience being deeply loved by God → Grow in loving God deeply → Let go of those things that we might love more than God and take up those gifts that help us love God → Grow in deeply loving God and others → So that we and others can be deeply loved → …

I call this "the Love Loop."

It is the gift I received.

It is the gift I am learning to share.

All that work of slowing, surrendering and simplifying, refined in the crucible of suffering, happened as I learned to let go and receive from God another way as I grew in confidence of God's love for me and the love that my friends have for me too.

Postscript

One of my favorite books as a young adult was *Out of the Silent Planet* by C.S. Lewis. It's the first in his Space Trilogy, much less known than his more famous *Narnia Chronicles*. A memorable scene for me is when the main character, Ransom, is in space for the first time, on his way to Mars. Lewis' vision of the heavens, narrated through Ransom's experience, is not a "black, cold vacuity," an "utter deadness that was supposed to separate the worlds." He continues, "the very name 'Space' seemed a blasphemous libel for this empyrean ocean of radiance in which they swam. He could not call it 'dead;' he felt life pouring into him from it every moment. How indeed should it be otherwise, since out of this ocean the worlds and all their life had come? He had thought it barren: he saw now that it was the womb of worlds."[50]

The space beyond our world is a fullness. This mirrors my experience as I keep walking with Jesus. Particularly in the realm of prayer.

In her book describing her life, Teresa of Avila articulates a vision of prayer as four waters.[51] I've reimagined her basic concept as a series of four fountains, like those Meg and I found in the plaza mayors in small towns across Spain. The first fountain is filled with water. The water in that fountain is drawn by hand, bucket after bucket after bucket. It never gets very full. This signifies the way of prayer for beginners on the journey. It is hard work, filled with tempting distractions, including long pauses to step aside from the effort. I remember the time, as a brand new seminary student kneeling next to my bed with folded hands, that I felt

---

[50] *Out of the Silent Planet*, C.S. Lewis, pg. 32
[51] *The Book of My Life*, Teresa of Avila

my words pouring forth into what I thought was a void as my prayers seemed to echo off the ceiling. Then I began to grow in my friendship with God. Slowly I learned to encounter his love, weeping my way through gentle worship songs.

As this continued I discovered a second fountain. This one had an aqueduct bringing water from an outside source. As the life of prayer develops, we enjoy more water for less effort. Helping to fill our fountain is water resourced from community, from the ministries of the wider church, from nature, service and more. We experience frequent consolations as we savor the sensory experiences of our spiritual life. Like many, I sat with this second fountain for years. Decades, in fact. For six years, as I encountered Jesus ever more deeply month after month, I experienced in prayer, like Ransom in the heavens, a growing sense of the beauty of this "womb of worlds." There was an extended season, a full year, for which three hours of prayer, from 4-7am, was too little and I'd have to end with a sigh in order to take my kids to school and get to work. And then one day it stopped. Late August, 2023.

To better describe what happened, permit me to jump ahead and describe the fourth fountain. This fourth fountain is like an artesian well, fed by a fresh, life-giving, underground spring. In fact, this spring lies deep in hidden caverns below all the fountains. This fountain is God's own life, flowing to fill us to overflowing. This corresponds to the prophet's vision in Jeremiah 2:13, *"They have forsaken me, the spring of living water, and have dug their own cisterns, broken cisterns that cannot hold water."*

God is our spring of living water.

It relates also to one of my favorite narrative arcs in all of the Bible. In Genesis 2 we read of how the flowing rivers watered the Garden, giving it life. Then the prophet Ezekiel, in the 47th chapter of the book that bears his name, articulates a vision of a river flowing from the altar of God in the Temple, flowing throughout the Land and dumping into the Dead Sea so that even this barren lake now teems with life. All along the river grow trees which flower and fruit every month. Weaving these two themes together is the vision in Revelation 22, the last chapter in our Bibles. This river of life flows from the throne of God through the city of God, lined with trees whose fruit is for the healing of the nations. This is the hope that awaits us. How will this hope be fulfilled? Jesus stands and says that if anyone is thirsty, let them come to him and drink, and out from within will flow rivers of living water.[52]

Jesus, our Beloved, is the fulfillment of the promise. The artesian well of his Spirit overflowing from within, renewing us and empowering us to participate with him in the restoration of all things. This is the fourth fountain.

What about the third fountain? I'm learning that to pass from the sparkling splashing of the second fountain to the artesian well of the fourth, God knocks down the aqueduct and lets the water drain out so that he can dig. Delve deep to the caverns where the hidden spring lies. At the second fountain we pray with relish in conversational dialogue with God, meditate imaginatively on scripture, enjoy all the many resources God's creative people have developed to assist us in connecting with God. Then, slowly, God gives the gift of contemplation. A lingering look of loving awareness. Words are silenced. Tools become useless. Noises, even consolations, fade. The third fountain is characterized by quiet, by stillness, by dryness. The only respite being the occasional rain that God in the heavens provides, a sweet and tender brush of Love come close. This third fountain is, far as I can tell, the Night of Sense that John of the Cross describes. He was a close companion of Teresa of Avila and, along with Ignatius of Loyola, I've come to deeply admire these three

---

[52] John 7:37-38

16th century Spanish saints. This is not the better known "Dark Night of the Soul." That comes further on the journey, perhaps the other side of the fourth fountain.

Though diverse in experience, this "Night" has a specific meaning. More than the generic sense of a difficult time, it is a removal of sensory experiences of God, of consolatory encounters, so that we can learn to rely more deeply on the Giving God and not depend on the gifts. It aims at the transformation of the human person, particularly in reference to the qualities of faith, hope and love. Three scriptures have had significant resonance with me during this season. I've known each of them by heart for years, yet only in the past number of months have I come to understand them more profoundly in their depths.

"Faith is confidence in what we hope for and assurance of what we do not see."[53] Pardon the pun, but do you see it? The essence of faith is that we are certain of what we do not see. At the second fountain, I enjoyed frequent sensory communion with Jesus. This was a precious gift and I am so grateful for it. Now I am learning to have the same confidence in God, even though I do not see him, have no sensory engagement or consolatory encounter at all.

"But if we hope for what we do not yet have, we wait for it patiently."[54] You cannot hope for what you already have. Hope is patient waiting for what we do not yet have. I cannot tell you how many times in the past months I've sat still in silence, gently, sometimes falteringly, leaning into loving attentiveness, for long periods of time, patiently waiting for God to meet me. Only to return the next day, and the next, and the next, to sit in hopefulness again.

"I pray that you, being rooted and established in love, may have power, together with all the Lord's holy people, to grasp how wide and long and high and deep is the love of Christ, and to know this love that surpasses knowledge – that you may be filled to the measure of all the fullness of God."[55] This scripture has become so meaningful for me. Shortly before my Night descended, the Lord showed me a series of three

---

[53] Hebrews 11:1
[54] Romans 8:25
[55] Ephesians 3:17-19

images. The first was of a sink with a small collection of water always about to wash down the drain except for a thin trickle from the faucet. The second was a large clay cistern filled with water. The third was of a wide lake, shore lined with trees, sun rippling on the gentle waves. Seeing the first I felt anxious. With the second I felt happy. At the third I experienced peace. Then I sensed the Lord asking me, "Jim, which measure of fullness would you like?" To be filled with the measure of the fullness of God, we become increasingly aware of and know a love that surpasses knowing. This blows my mind. How can I know what is beyond knowledge? Yet this is what I'm experiencing. As I sit in stillness and silence, patiently waiting, I am moved to love my Beloved that is beyond my knowing—at least in part—by loving those whom I can see.

For these past many months I've journeyed through this Night, devoid of nearly every sense of God, yet growing closer every day. I follow a Person, my Beloved, so close as to be almost within me, as I step into the Radiant Night of Dark Light.

The Night of Sense
I miss the mountains.
Traversing turf riddled with roots and the soft glow of speckled light.
I miss the aroma of spice, coffee on plastic benches along dusty roads, the gentle cacophony of whispered prayers in unknown tongues.
I ache.
My soul is heavy with the weight of sorrow.
Carrying dying desires in my arms like a mourning mother,
Grieving the passing of long-familiar pleasures
I know Jesus is worth it, yet where is he?
He is not hidden in the shadows.
Jesus is the Dark Light.
So pure that I cannot see him, as he chooses to reveal himself, untranslated.
The baked crust encasing my heart a burden, cloying as it cracks and slowly chips away.
Lord, come.
Come and bury my desires. Burn me with the healing fire of thy holy love.
Whom have I but You?

I have always conceptualized my walk with Jesus as an outward journey. Going out, going up, to meet with God. No surprise, right? I've always felt alive walking rising trails in cathedrals of dappled light, roofed with green canopy, pillars of wood and earthen floor.

In fact, one of the last pictures God showed me before I entered this Night was of Jesus and I walking together along a steep mountain trail. It reminded me of the 24 hours my son and I spent hiking the Great Range Traverse in the Adirondacks. Jesus was in the lead and I was close enough behind to see the contours of the tread on the bottom of his sandal as he took a particularly large step up. And in that moment it dawned on me. For 35 years my discipleship had been mediated through a mentor. First Corey, next a mosaic of cadets and staff at West Point and in the Army, then Steve, and lastly Mark. Each was a helpful guide. Now Jesus was inviting me to follow him directly.

I feel the weight of this responsibility, yet I experience it as a light and easy burden because I am learning to live in tandem with Jesus.

These days, in place of an outward journey, my trail leads inward, to the depths. This is where I'm discovering it is most profound, most authentic. To meet with God in the inner cavern of my soul, the secret place in which he has placed the Spring of his living water.

Joy cloaked in faith's obedience.
Pupating.
Awaiting.
Glory and what it cannot name.

My sense is that in those six shining years with Jesus he was attuning me to him and developing earned secure attachment. Now it's like I'm learning to carry that with me (as an adult) even when I can't perceive him with me. It's a journey of patiently showing up. I have confident hope that my love will be requited as I see God face to face. It will, most certainly, not be like what it was before. It will be better, more intimate, in ways I cannot yet comprehend.

Epilogue

I often visit with my friend, Nick, in his upstairs flat in the wildly diverse neighborhood of Hamtramck. Sometimes he and I watch football together, while we weave in conversation about life and God. Among many other things, he's helped me learn to appreciate the world's favorite sport and I'm grateful for that.

Hanging in his living room is a banner from one of his favorite teams, Liverpool. Prominent on the flag is their motto: "You'll never walk alone." This motto comes from the song of the same name, an anthem born of tragedy for the club and its supporters, when 96 fans were killed and hundreds injured in a crowd crush among Liverpool faithful at the Hillsborough stadium in 1989.[56] Sixteen years later, Liverpool was down 0-3 against AC Milan in the UEFA Finals, when their faithful started singing *You'll Never Walk Alone* over and over again. It fortified the players, who went on to win the Cup in penalties. In that moment they helped their club know that they weren't alone in their hardship and struggle.

As I was in the early stages of writing this book, I had a conversation with my friend, William. In that brief chat he shared some powerful stuff. "You know, Jim," he said, "they say if you want to run fast, you'll run alone." That's true in my experience. Not everyone in your circle of relationships (whether office, church, school or neighborhood) will want or be able to keep up with you. Also, the fast-movers are so often in competition-mode and they don't know who they can trust. He went on,

---

[56] https://www.goal.com/en-us/news/ynwa-how-youll-never-walk-alone-became-a-liverpool-fc-anthem/selbcrlre9lz1n9dat1b1e60q

"I've sometimes found that if you want to run slow(er), you'll often run alone too." I've often found that to be true as well. "Fast" is the American Way. (As my African friends have repeatedly told me, "You Americans all have watches, but you have no time.") Slowing down defies the norm, cuts against the grain, and tht can be hard for some people to embrace.

Going slow can mean going alone. Yet I don't think it has to be that way. We don't have to be alone.

I've run three marathons. That's not meant to be a flex. In my experience, while there is great reward in finishing, the most demanding part of the marathon is the training. That's where the personal growth happens. I'm definitely not fast. Let me put it this way: in my first marathon, in the Twin Cities, it took me more than twenty miles to catch the runner in the full chicken costume, and another mile to catch the guy in the full mailman uniform, complete with mailbag and those 80s era black walking shoes. I'm not winning medals! While I may lack speed, I'm solid on the pacing.

Thinking about that first marathon, all throughout the first eighteen miles, the route was lined with crowds. People celebrating their loved ones, suburban homeowners offering their own water stations, sometimes augmented with orange juice and/or beer, people enjoying the spectacle. The nineteenth mile was run along the Mississippi River in an industrial zone and was eerily quiet and lonely after those first hours.

Then at the moment we turned right to cross the river and finish the race in St. Paul, my step-dad was there, leaning as far as he could over the barrier, cheering me on.

It was the first time I had seen him since the start line, and I didn't know if he'd make it to this point to see me in time. He did. He wouldn't have missed that moment for anything. It was one of those magical moments in my life.

It reminded me deeply of how God celebrates us.

On the other side of the bridge was Mile 20, when most marathoners hit their infamous "wall." This particular wall was accompanied by the longest, steepest hill of the entire course (whoever planned that should be checked for evil genius tendencies). As I started huffing and puffing my way up the ascent, before I had caught up to the Chicken and the Mailman, wondering what in the world had ever possessed me to do something as stupid as running a marathon ("Didn't the first guy who did this, a Greek soldier at the Battle of Marathon, *die* after he had made that run?!?"), a woman's voice called out to me from over my left shoulder, commenting on how steady my pace had been for many miles. As she came alongside, she thanked me for this, saying it was exactly the pace she had been wanting to run, then passed me and finished her race. We had been running together and I didn't even know it. I wasn't alone after all.

An African proverb says, "If you want to run fast, run alone. If you want to run far, run together." I'm discovering my African friends are right.

In writing this book, I'm inviting you into my story, an offer to share our journeys so that we can run farther together.

What's more, the act of writing this book has been an exercise in remembering and holding onto those shining moments of joy and love and gratitude, as well as an exercise in naming and walking through the shadowy seasons of pain and grief and disappointment. It's been a healing journey for me as I partner with God in his work of bringing beauty from ashes. I've been learning to find perseverance and peace and praise even in the big, difficult emotions and experiences.

Never is the hope for humanity and our own lives greater than when we gaze into the eyes of God and see reflected there ourselves, gazing with the same love which is shining from God's face, and in the resilience of that joy rise to sacrificially serve others.

My hope is that by entering into my story with me, you'll be able to remember your moments of joy and connection, find healing for your seasons of sorrow and trauma, and learn to tell your own story more truly, so that you can experience how God is working to bring the renewal of all things – in you, first, and also through you to our glorious, hurting world—so that together we can join with God in that creative, beautiful labor of love.

Leaders are Learners

Leaders are lifelong learners. Often this involves reading, though other formats are common as well. I enjoy reading and from time to time people have asked me for book recommendations. This isn't a bibliography. There is some overlap between the list below and the works referenced in the notes of this book. Those quoted there augment those listed here. Any of those listed below that aren't quoted previously are such that they've been read, digested, internalized and now it would be hard to identify where the thoughts of the original author end and mine begin. That's just what good books do, right? Next to the Bible, these are some of the books that I have enjoyed the most.

Biography
1. David McCullough, *John Adams* (New York: Simon & Schuster, 2001)
2. Doris Kearns Goodwin, *Team of Rivals* (New York: Simon & Schuster, 2005)
3. Jean Edward Smith, *Grant* (New York: Simon & Schuster, 2001)
4. Edmund Morris, *Theodore Roosevelt*, 3 vols (New York: Random House, 2010)
5. William Manchester, *The Last Lion: Winston Spencer Churchill*, 3 vols (New York: Bantam Books, 2013)

Fiction
1. J.R.R. Tolkien, *The Lord of the Rings* (UK: Allen & Unwin, 1954)
2. C.S. Lewis, *The Space Trilogy* (New York: Colliers, 1965)
3. C.S. Lewis, *The Voyage of the Dawn Treader* (UK: Geoffrey Bles, 1952)

4. Jules Verne, *Journey to the Centre of the Earth* (New York: Penguin, 1965)
5. Fyodor Dostoevsky, *The Brothers Karamazov* (Moscow: The Russian Messenger, 1880)

History
1. Thomas L. Friedman, *From Beirut to Jerusalem* (New York: Anchor Books, 1995)
2. Howard French, *A Continent for the Taking: The Tragedy and Hope of Africa* (New York: Alfred A. Knopf, 2004)
3. Peter Hopkirk, *The Great Game: On Secret Service in High Asia* (Oxford: Oxford University Press, 1990)
4. Jean Edward Smith, *Grant* (New York: Simon & Schuster, 2001)
5. Taylor Branch, *Parting the Waters: America in the King Years 1954-1963* (New York: Touchstone, 1988)

Leadership
1. J. Robert Clinton, *The Making of a Leader* (Colorado Springs: NavPress, 1988)
2. Ruth Haley Barton, *Strengthening the Soul of Your Leadership* (Downers Grove, IL: Intervarsity Press, 2018)
3. William Bridges, *Managing Transitions*, 4th ed. (New York: Hatchette Book Group , 2017)
4. Jim Wilder and Michel Hendricks, *The Other Half of Church: Christian Community, Brain Science and Overcoming Spiritual Stagnation* (Chicago: Moody, 2020)
5. Tri Robinson, *Revolutionary Leadership* (New York: Ampelon Publishing, 2005)

Spirituality
1. Dallas Willard, *The Divine Conspiracy: Rediscovering Our Hidden Life in God* (New York: HarperCollins, 1998
2. Brother Lawrence, *The Practice of the Presence of God* (Christian Classics Ethereal Library, 1692)
3. Jacques Philippe, *Interior Freedom* (New York: Scepter Publishers, 2002)
4. Saint John of the Cross, *Ascent of Mount Carmel* (Orleans, MA: Paraclete Press, 2010)
5. Janet O. Hagberg and Robert A. Guelich, *The Critical Journey: Stages in the Life of Faith* (Salem, Wisconsin: Sheffield Publishing, 2005)

About the Author

Jim Pool is the happy husband of one wife and father of four children. He loves to travel though he always finds the way home to his native Detroit. He's adventured on four continents and all 50 states, plus Puerto Rico and DC, though he's yet to spend the night in Mississippi. He loves Trappist ales and Imperial IPAs, Spanish Reds and Espresso Roast, and tends now to serve Sloppy Jim over spaghetti in place of buns.

A multi-season captain for his Pee Wee hockey team, and contributor on the 1994 Company F-4 Brigade Championship Rugby Team, Jim placed third in the 2003 Michigan State Fair Hog Calling Competition. He recited an original poem co-authored with Megan for an upcoming documentary on legendary baseballer Turkey Stearnes and also played the role of "Pastor at Riley's Church" in the 2021 film, *Trafficked: A Parent's Worst Nightmare*.

He's an advisory member on the Executive Committee for the West Point Class of 1994 ("With Courage We Soar") and a director on the board of the Mission Immanuel Network serving the city of St. Louis.

He's already begun work on his next book exploring the theme of "the kind of movement he would want to join." To continue the conversation, you can reach him at hello@bambooinitiative.com.

Made in United States
Cleveland, OH
08 May 2025